SURPRISE PARTY

A MEMOIR OF SURVIVAL

STANLEY N. ALPERT

HUTCHINSON
LONDON

First published by Hutchinson in 2007

1 3 5 7 9 10 8 6 4 2

Copyright © Stanley N. Alpert 2007

Stanley N. Alpert has asserted his right under the Copyright, Designs
and Patents Act, 1988 to be identified as the author of this work

Hutchinson
Random House, 20 Vauxhall Bridge Road,
London SW1V 2SA

www.randomhouse.co.uk

Addresses for companies within The Random House Group Limited can be found at:
www.randomhouse.co.uk/offices.htm

A CIP catalogue record for this book is available from the British Library

ISBN 9780091796198

The Random House Group Limited makes every effort to ensure
that the papers used in its books are made from trees that have
been legally sourced from well-managed and credibly certified
forests. Our paper procurement policy can be found at:
www.randomhouse.co.uk/paper.htm

Printed and bound in Great Britain by
Mackays of Chatham Plc, Chatham, Kent

This book is dedicated to my parents, Arlene and Ben,
who taught me that helping those less fortunate than us
was more important than amassing wealth, and
to my grandparents Leon and Flora, who gave me
comfort and strength when I needed it.

AUTHOR'S NOTE

This book is all true, nonfiction. The quotes during the kidnapping are re-created from what actually happened and are obviously not a perfect transcript, though every event described in those quotes and the rest of the book really happened just as I tell it. Where the quotes seem the most outrageous or funny they are closest to actual, direct quotes, according to my memory. Descriptions of events that occurred where I was not present and some of the dialogue in connection with those events are re-created based upon interviews with the people involved. The details of the investigation are based on police reports, interviews with NYPD detectives and FBI agents, interviews with witnesses, videotaped confessions, and court records. The records directly confirm a good deal of the kidnapping details that I relate from memory. Where opinions are expressed, that is what they are. Many of the names, particularly last names, have been changed to protect the innocent and the guilty. Street addresses have been changed, as well. The names of the detectives and agents are real.

I want to thank my agent, Ron Goldfarb, for seeing the value in this book and inspiring me to finish it. Thanks to the people at Putnam—Neil Nyren, Ivan Held, Susan Allison, and Michael Barson—for their decision to publish this book and the genuine human concern they exhibited about what I had experienced, and to Neil Nyren for his wonderful and incisive edits.

CONTENTS

PART ONE
MOUSE

PART TWO

CAT

MOUSE

ONE

BROOKLYN FED

In New York City, 1998, crime was down, but not out, as I was to learn the night before my thirty-eighth birthday. All the experts agreed that it should have gone the other way. My case should have been handled as a homicide.

Blindfolded, I could hear the leader of the gang pulling duct tape off a roll, the sound framed by a bitter night wind that filled the open trunk of the car where my body was headed. I sat in the backseat on the hump, a gangster's right leg pressed to my left, another gangster's leg pressed to my right, each jabbing a pistol at my chest. I had no idea why God had done this to me, and I felt definite I was about to meet him and find out.

Maybe it shouldn't have been a big surprise. I grew up in New York in the 1970s, and things had been a little unbalanced then: Vietnam, drugs, race riots, and crime, crime, crime. My grandparents and great-grandparents had sailed to America for streets rumored to be paved with gold, but for me, Brooklyn had had streets paved with land mines. Getting off the bus on my way home from a high school night out, I would have to steel my nerve and sharpen my senses, praying that no figures would emerge from an alley or behind a parked car, knives unsheathed, faces gripped with determination, those with less taking little from me. I can't tell you how many times I ran, fought, or gave up a few bills to buy the bastards off.

Giuliani had put an end to all that by 1998, or at least that's the way the publicity made it sound. Cops had been given freer rein to bust heads and reclaim the streets. Murders were down by two-thirds. Kids from the Midwest sporting goatees rode the L train home at night without a care in the world other than Corona versus Amstel. Tourists were flocking back to Times Square to catch *The Lion King* and drop a few bucks on a Midtown hotel. It was nothing short of a renaissance. Or so I thought.

I'd begun my career with a federal court clerkship in Miami, then come back to New York City to work at a fancy Park Avenue law firm, which for a kid who'd toughed it out on the streets of Brooklyn was a big deal. But my heart told me I needed to do something bigger with my life, and when the offer arrived in 1990 from Andy Maloney, U.S. Attorney for the Eastern District of New York, to become an Assistant U.S. Attorney, I knew I was going to take it, even if it meant going *back* to Brooklyn. Brooklyn was a place to grow up and get out of after all the excitement of the disco days. But this was progress. The office of the United States Attorney for the Eastern District of New York covered Brooklyn, Queens, Staten Island, and all of Long Island. Long Island: the home of Joey Buttafuoco, Texas-style high hair, and some of the finest white sand beaches anybody'd ever want to sift through their tired bare toes.

Maybe because I was a city boy whose skin touched asphalt as often as a snake's touched grass, I was all the more keen on the outdoors. In Maloney's office, I became an environmental prosecutor, to try to keep those beaches clean. Most of my defendants did not put guns to people's heads to make them turn over their money. My law enforcement career dealt with contamination of the air, water, and land, threatening the basic quality of human life. Industry in America needed to be properly regulated and violators relentlessly pursued by the federal, state, and local governments. Otherwise they gave you widgets plus some surprisingly nasty free gifts: asthma, genetic mutations, filthy air, and lakes and oceans where the fish gasped and the humans were required by local authorities to keep their butts out of the water. Black mothers in the Bronx wanted to know why their kids had so much more asthma than the separate but equal children in the Village of Scarsdale, and I wanted to help.

As a federal prosecutor, I got to hunt bad guys, those who killed people the slow way. My bad guys kept Sloan-Kettering in business. They wore thousand-dollar suits when they sent their loyal employees to inhale the sweet aroma of a benzene pool knowing that nobody would wear the respirators even if they knew where to find them. They poisoned the fish so that when a Latino casts his sorry rod in the Dyckman Street Hudson, what sits under the cilantro and next to the *plátanos* that evening will eventually kill a member of his family. My bad guys put profit over human health and safety, and it was my job to stop 'em cold in their tracks. If it was a typical violation, you'd pay me a heavy penalty and clean up your mess and have a court supervise you for the next ten years. If the violation was rotten to the core, you could go directly to jail do not pass go.

When I mentioned over a jack and ginger that I did environmental law in New York City, people would screw up their face muscles and say, "New York—what environment?" like there was nothing worth saving. They didn't understand that the Eastern District of New York was a great place for my job. There was lots of industry slopping lots of chemicals on the ground. A sole-source drinking water aquifer soaked up oil company gifts of MTBE so the pasta could smell like turpentine. The area was rumored to have the highest rates of breast cancer in the country. Sludge was dumped in the ocean, dredge in Long Island Sound, with lawsuits for and against the government. On the gorgeous white beaches, men and dogs killed endangered species such as the piping plover. Touch 'em, boys, and me and my fed pals will take you to see the friendly judges for life on Cadman Plaza. We had two of the country's major airports, through which flowed not only the illegal drug trade but the illegal wildlife trade, not to mention the ozone-depleting canisters of banned chlorofluorocarbons smuggled in by Russian mobsters. Other Serbs recently over from the former Yugoslav republic thought nothing of ripping out asbestos with no moon suits, spreading fibers that kill, in basement laundry rooms where unsuspecting tenants hauled their quarters to get some clean socks. I wanted them—or at least their bosses—in jail.

Federal law enforcement, to which I had devoted my career for some seven-odd years, had made a positive difference. In 1998, the New York City air was a lot more breathable than during the leisure suit days twenty years earlier when people doing the hustle were coughing and wheezing. Enforcement of the federal Clean Water Act saw to it that the Cuyahoga River in Ohio no longer would catch fire. And even though PCBs remained, a few people seeing a cleaner river were brave enough to start swimming in the Hudson again, as one could do when my father was a boy. The herons had even returned to nest on small islands in the Arthur Kill, a body of water in New York harbor once infested with the industrial desolation that had become the emblem of Staten Island and New Jersey, but which was now clean enough for the birds to struggle back to. A lot more work needed to be done.

Not that that meant a whole hell of a lot to me now, as I rode fetal-positioned in the backseat of a spanking new Lexus, my head in the lap of a stocky, angry African-American young man, holding a TEC-9 automatic machine gun against my skull.

IT HAD BEEN AN ORDINARY DAY. IN THE MORNING, I WENT down to the Second Circuit Court to join some of my colleagues in rooting on our friend Scott Daniels, a Jew who looked like an Irish ex-Marine and who in fact was in the Air Force Reserve, as he argued a case. Scott was the government's immigration lawyer. Today he was in court with what most people would consider a fairly simple proposition: If you sail past the Statue of Liberty into these United States and use your new home to commit vicious felonies such as murder, robbery, and rape, we'll send you packing and fast. No more hearings, no more delays—if you're convicted of a felony, when your sentence is over, we put you on the next plane out. Scott should have gotten battle pay, though, because as the government's immigration litigator, he lost a lot of cases. The Second Circuit Court of Appeals was well known for its liberal views, and in our hearts we all knew that this case would be lost, too. Still, we enjoyed watching him deftly spar with the three judges sitting on high, and afterward, some of us Assistant U.S. Attorneys and Scott's smiling brother Matt plowed across the frozen tundra to debrief in a hot oasis of Thai food. It was then that Matt made the anticrime argument come alive.

"You're not gonna believe what happened to me yesterday," he said. "I get on the number nine train at Seventy-ninth Street, you know, the usual day, spiffed up for work, suit, trench coat, my backpack on my back, my usual copy of the *New York Times* in hand. I just managed to slip onto the train as the doors were closing. The train was packed tight, so I was pressed up against the doors as they shut and the train pulled out of the station.

"I looked up and saw that there were seven Hispanic guys surrounding me, ya know, high school kids—but a couple of them were real big. They were pushing each other around, roughhousing, and they were real loud. I didn't want any part of it. I tried to avoid them by grabbing the pole to my right and twisting my body so that I only faced two of them, with the other five of them behind me."

Matt explained that he kept his gaze off them and on the stock page of the *New York Times*. He made his face impassive to hide his fear. He prayed that they would lay off him. But the biggest ones in the gang steadily closed in, cutting off escape like seasoned ranchers cornering cattle in a canyon.

As he told it, Matt's smile hardened a bit. "I heard this big guy, six-foot-two, talking in Spanish to another guy. It sounded like the big guy was egging him on, like 'You can do it, you can do it.' I don't speak Spanish, but every few words I could hear a good old English curse word, fuck this, pussy this, motherfucker that, so that plus his tone of voice and I knew I was in trouble. All of a sudden, the six-foot-two guy shoves the other one at me, and he crashes up against my chest, pushing me backwards so I almost fell over. I reached in my pocket for my keys, looking for anything I could use in self-defense, ya know?" Matt grew up in the City and he knew the tricks of the trade, just like me.

"Then the big one came at me, and raised his hand to punch me in the face, with the others moving in with him for the kill."

"Jesus," I exclaimed.

"All of a sudden, right before his fist flew, I hear coming from the side somebody bellowing at the top of his lungs, in a Spanish accent, 'What . . . the fuck . . . do you think . . . you're doing?' The subway was packed with people and I couldn't even see the guy who was yelling. So the seven guys around me leaned back and looked to the right where the voice came from. They weren't sure if it had anything to do with them. Then, as though the sea were parting, pushing through the crowd comes this huge, ferocious guy. Six-foot-three, two hundred twenty-five pounds, a big barrel-chested muscle dude, ya know, a tough-looking Hispanic guy, with a leather jacket and a grungy green sweatshirt, two-day-old stubble crawling down his face. You shoulda seen 'im. One of these guys who could be either a corrections officer or a wise guy himself.

"He pulled close and screamed again, but slow and deliberate, 'What . . . the fuck . . . are you thinking about? What . . . are you doing to that guy?' He also said some things to them in Spanish, I don't know what.

"Meanwhile, the six friends are circled around their tough guy buddy like they're ready for a fight. The guy helping me screams, 'Yo . . . you're gonna do something? You want a piece of me?' as he's shoving people aside like a bowling ball through pins, ya know?, coming down the aisle.

"The punk who was gonna hit me shouts back, 'You want a piece of *me*? . . . You want a piece of *us*?' He was talking big and braced for a fight, fists pumping in front of him, but even with his friends around him while he said it he was stepping back, sheepish, like he was worried and really didn't wanna fight. The big guy ripped off his leather jacket and showed this huge muscular chest. I thought that one of the seven kids would pull out a gun and start blasting. I mean it. But they just backed off instead. I got the hell off the train at the next stop, Seventy-second Street.

"From the platform I watched the guy who helped me talkin' to the kids. He puts his hand on the big guy's shoulder, and says, 'Yo . . . man, you can't be doin' this . . . man, you're gonna be givin' us a bad name.' Ya know, like they were all Hispanics. They turned around together, like a father with a son, and they walked a couple of steps together back up the aisle of the train. I called into the train, 'Thanks a lot.' He looks up and says, 'No problem.' The door closed and the train pulled out."

"Holy shit, are you lucky," I said.

Matt replied, "You're not kidding. I owe that guy big-time. I'd like to find him on the train and thank him properly."

"Who would expect getting attacked during the morning rush hour?"

"Look, Stan, you know the story. You know how it was growing up in New York. Once I was on the train in midday and saw a lady get her gold chain ripped right off her neck. Or—you know—in high school we had race riots. One day I've got two best friends who are black guys. The next day some Irish kid purposely steps on a black guy's foot in the cafeteria. The place erupts in a race riot, and your black friends won't even talk to you. Usually I feel like I can weave my way out of these situations, but here I was stuck."

"Why do you think those guys picked you?"

"I think they picked me because I was wearing my trench coat. You know, it looks expensive. I usually wear a beat-up parka instead. I'm still shook up from the whole thing."

I was dressed up that day and wearing my trench coat. "Wow, Matt, I am so sorry," I said. "Nothing like that has happened to *me* in New York in a really long time."

The table grew silent as we ate and digested the account. As Matt said, I knew the story. I remembered the time when I was twelve, hopping the subway to the Bronx Zoo with another kid from yeshiva. Three older Oliver Twist meets Boyz n the Hood street-hard urchins pounced on us in the gorilla house looking for cash. The only thing that saved us was a busload of black kids from a school in Brooklyn, who watched us getting assaulted and had the mercy to tell their teacher to let us join them. We then walked around the zoo with them, two white polka dots sticking out in an adoptive class of beautiful black kids. The teacher drove us home. It was a lesson in race relations never to be forgotten, too: Black kids mugged us, but black kids saved us.

Riding the subways then, you might get jumped at any time. If adults or cops were not around, there were packs of young hoodlums slithering through the rail cars seeking the chance to separate you from your money or whatever else you might be unfortunate enough to have on you. I will never forget the vision of a burly teenage boy on the subway, blaring his boom box at full volume in the face of an elderly woman sitting next to him, and everyone on the train was too frightened to get up and ask the kid to turn it down. It was the Wild West.

But this was 1998, and by now things seemed to have eased up. Now I was a grown-up, living in the relative safety of Manhattan, with the adventures of my Brooklyn teen years behind me. The mean-looking dudes I always saw on the subways and in the streets of my neighborhood seemed to have faded off the scene, which was why Matt's story was so startling. More startling still was the invasion of New York by firepower that put to shame the switchblade knives I faced as a boy. The most you could do was to hope that fate would keep you and the guns in different parts of the City.

TWO

BLIND SPOT

I suppose I should have refused all the blind dates I was constantly being offered. "Stanley, I met a woman at the senior citizens' center who has a lovely thirty-five-year-old daughter who lives at home with her," my mom would announce triumphantly.

"Have you seen her?" I would mix my ninety-nine percent permanent skepticism with one percent wishful thinking.

"No, but Zelda Kaplowitz says she's beautiful."

"Ma, everybody thinks their daughter is beautiful."

"Look, Stanley, it doesn't hurt to try. What's so terrible about spending one evening with the girl? Ya never know."

People who were better at math than I am can calculate the number of dates that one person can go on in a lifetime, making certain assumptions about life expectancy and stamina. One evening wasted could indeed be a terrible thing. Still, with age thirty-eight rolling into my life the very next day, I figured I needed to be scientific about ending my single state. Over the last few years I'd convinced myself it was time to stop fooling around, and if I had to read one more personals description of a woman who was "equally comfortable in jeans and a T-shirt as in a black cocktail dress," I would scream.

Two years earlier I'd thought I was on the right track when I met and fell in love with a live-wire thirty-four-year-old Ph.D. student, a woman whose lightning intellect was incongruously equaled by her exceptional physical beauty. She liked to show her long, skinny legs by wearing tight little miniskirts, and she would ribbon the package with a blackened camisole of thin lace, hidden in part by a loose-fitting but open overshirt, which focused the male attention on her worthy chest. I was never bored by her. Even at a sleepy Sunday-morning brunch after a night of love-making, I still relished listening to her wax eloquent on Russian literature or on some obscure classical musicians about whom I knew nothing. But her beauty and intellect were both equaled by an emotional explosiveness that made it impossible to maintain a relationship. She would attack me on the thinnest provocation with a ferocity befitting Russian literature but more than my own feisty disposition could suffer. Her own male friends admired my strength and ability to stay with her as long as I did, but eventually I, too, wearied of the game. Two years later, I was still mucking about trying to meet somebody else, although I was casually dating an old friend, Darcy, after sparks had ignited three weeks earlier when the crowd thinned out on New Year's Eve.

I picked up tonight's blind date at her apartment building on York and Eighty-ninth, and she appeared in the lobby, smiling but nervous, an attractive dolled-up brunette. Actually, she looked a little like my mother. We had been fixed up because I was Jewish and breathing and male; she was Jewish and breathing and female. What more did the yentas need to know? Predictably, I suppose, she turned out to be not really my type, nor I hers, so after an hour, we agreed to ditch the Merlot, and I headed home to try to salvage the evening.

I thought about plans for the next day. It was my thirty-eighth birthday, and rather than throwing a big birthday party, where friends and friends of friends would torture the downstairs neighbors with wild dancing and singing till three or four in the morning, I'd opted for a small group of us going to the Bottom Line to see one of my favorite guitarists, Freedy Johnston. Earlier that day I had pulled $200 from an ATM machine, bought seven tickets, and slid them into my leather wallet next to the cash.

I should have been home in half an hour, but just then my luck changed—for the better, I thought. Leaning on the subway door next to the sign DO NOT LEAN ON THE DOOR, I eavesdropped on a guy and a girl in the two-person love seat down and to my right. They had apparently been at a Jewish lecture together at the Ninety-second Street Y, and were chatting about the lecture and the girl's work for United Jewish Appeal. She was an attractive, slender brunette, with a huge head of curly hair perched atop her slender frame. And she seemed bored with the guy. As they spoke, the eyes under the carpet of hair darted about, even at times pointing in my direction. At Forty-second Street, the guy got off the train, and Ms. Head of Hair was left sitting not five feet from me, all alone. I honestly had never picked up a girl on the subway before. What the heck. I dove in.

"I heard you mention UJA. I'm going to the UJA conference in Washington in March. Are you?"

Of course she was. She went by the name of Lisa P. Marantz, and she programmed lecturers by day, and splashed huge abstract paintings by night. Until recently, she had lived on the Upper West Side along with masses of Jewish yuppies who thought they were still in sleepaway camp. Now, though, Lisa the cool artist chick had broken free and emigrated down to my neighborhood. She was on Tenth Street and Sixth Avenue, a mere five blocks away on a cold winter night or a warm summer morning.

She got off the train with me at Union Square, which was her stop, too. As we walked down Fourth Avenue in the direction of my house, I made small talk, and mentioned the new Entenmann's chocolate chip cookies that had recently come out, larger and with more chips. At the corner of Thirteenth Street and Fourth Avenue, I asked her, "Do you mind waiting a minute while I go into the deli to look for some?"

"No problem," she replied cheerily, a warm smile on her lips.

They only had the old ones and if I had just been satisfied with that, I could have been home in my apartment a few minutes later, happy and warm, eating chocolate chip cookies and sipping hot ginger tea.

But I didn't get to where I am in life by settling for second best. Lisa suggested, "There's a place on University, in the direction of my house."

It was already past ten-thirty, and on such a bitterly cold night, the streets were mostly deserted. At University, that place was closed, and she mentioned an A&P on Sixth Avenue, near where she lived. I said, "Well, I suppose I should be a gentleman and walk you all the way home."

She responded, "Sure, sure, all you want is those cookies."

Not quite true, but I really couldn't argue. At the A&P supermarket they had what I wanted, and I bought her a box of cookies, too (Chips Ahoy! for her). As we left the store, two loose items rested in my hands: the cookies, and a thick book on the Vietnam War called *A Bright Shining Lie* that I'd meant to read on the train.

I walked her a block to the corner of Sixth Avenue and Tenth Street, and outside her nineteenth-century three-story building, I asked, "Would you like to go out for a cup of tea?"

"I would love to," she said. "But it's close to eleven o'clock already. Better do it on another night." She glided her business card into my hand and I gave her mine. We said good night, and I watched her slim figure climb the building's stairs. Mission accomplished, I slid the body engine back into gear and started rolling up the street in the direction of home.

They may have followed behind me in the Lexus.

I moved down Tenth Street toward Fifth Avenue, and although the wind and the chill blew right through me, I was very happy. I had had a fine day observing my friend argue and getting ready for my birthday. The success with the girl from the IRT made me a fisherman headed back to port with a full load of fresh catch. The next day was my birthday, and seven of us were going to go see one of my favorite artists at the Bottom Line. There was a definite skip in my step.

I was so preoccupied with feeling good I didn't notice that because it was late and so very cold, there was not another soul on the street. The Village was usually packed with people, which lent an element of safety. This night, though, was dead, and I was oblivious. While in Brooklyn I had learned to crane my head every which way, prepared to run for my life at the sign of danger, in 1998 Manhattan I never even thought about turning around. Cold waves of shimmering darkness rose off the streets as a gray sidewalk reflected the streetlamps and a struggling moon.

As I approached Fifth Avenue on Tenth Street, less than a block from Lisa P. Marantz, without warning I felt a tug on my right elbow from behind. I teetered back to my right. He had come from out of nowhere, but now facing me was a short, stocky, black male, and out from under his long coat he pointed at me the thick round barrel of a large automatic machine gun. The hand did not let go of my elbow.

"Don't say a word. Just get in the fuckin' car, motherfucker."

THREE

DEFENDING YOUR LIFE

The shock and the grab from behind forced the book and the cookies out of my hand and they tumbled to the concrete, not to be seen again.

There was another shadowy figure behind me. I couldn't see if he had a gun. He pressed up behind and rammed against my back. "Move, move," cried the second assailant. He and the first gunman twisted me to the right and heaved me toward the gutter. They then shoved me through the roadway to a point about thirty feet back, where a brand-new black Lexus shining in the dim light of the streetlamps lay in wait, double-parked on the far side of the street. Thrilled with their hunt, breath expanding and contracting in rapid fire, the assailants hustled me to the left side of the car with demonic glee.

Stabs of fear shot through my heart as they swept me toward the car. It came in such a rush that I had no time to think or absorb. But I was no dummy. There had been many times, growing up in New York, when I had been threatened by thugs with every kind of weapon shy of a gun.

I knew what to do. Sometimes I stayed and fought. Other times I turned and ran. Other times I gave them what they wanted. I certainly knew how to let off a bloodcurdling scream if that made any sense. This time, though, they wanted not money, but me. This time, they had not knives, but guns. This time, screaming was pointless, as not only were the streets devoid of humans, but there was not even a single car racing by that I could hurl my body in front of and pray that it stopped in time. If I ripped my arm loose from the grasp of stocky pistolman the first, and sprinted down the asphalt, it was a fifty-fifty bet as to whether the gun would *rat-tat-tat* behind me and penetrate my spine in a wild splaying that would leave my life forever stunted on the corner of West Tenth Street and Fifth Avenue. Maybe they wouldn't have fired. Maybe if they fired, they wouldn't have hit the mark. Maybe I would have been home drinking ginger tea by eleven-fifteen waiting to see what the local news had to say about tomorrow's weather. Maybe, maybe, maybe, coulda, woulda, shoulda. Conventional wisdom holds that you should never get in the car with the robbers, because if you do you'll never be heard from again. Very nice in theory, but at that moment, with a fat, black-barreled automatic machine gun sticking out from under the coat and a second mugger who might be similarly armed, there was no real choice. I couldn't argue with that kind of firepower and I couldn't take the chance.

The second male to sneak up behind me ran slightly ahead of us and opened the rear left-side door.

"Get in the car," he cried. They pushed me in. Inside, a third black male, a massive, menacing presence, sat in the front passenger seat, waiting for the other two to bring in the prey. He turned to face me and pointed a large automatic pistol in my face. Someone slammed the door behind me and the second assailant took his place in the driver's seat, while the little gunman with the big machine gun eased in beside me on the right and clicked the door shut tight. The car began to roll.

I was trapped. A prisoner, five blocks from home. As the car eased slowly down Tenth Street to make a right turn on Fifth Avenue, I could see outside to the familiar streets of my Greenwich Village neighbor-hood, but they might as well have been a million miles away. In tight, cold space, the faint smell of new car leather wafting through my nostrils, two to three guns attached to male youths were poised to blow my head off. At the same time, just outside, mere inches away, were the familiar and ordinarily welcoming brownstones and prewars and pedestrian promenades of my hometown. The contrast was so absurd that at that moment I almost wanted to let out a huge laugh in the midst of the terror. I had left the appealing Lisa P. Marantz two minutes and two hundred yards away, but now the hope of budding romance had been abandoned on the concrete along with the cookies and the book on the Vietnam War.

The thug of thugs immediately bared his teeth. Twisting to face me from the front passenger seat was a tall, meaty presence who immediately emerged as the meanest of the three. Eyes and voice denuded of any sign of contrition, he demanded flatly yet viciously, "Give me your wallet." I glanced over and handed it to him naturally and without question, as though I were handing my passport to a customs agent at the border. He rifled through the personal effects in my wallet: cash, ATM card, credit cards. The Freedy Johnston tickets.

The man in the driver's seat now took control. "Sen," he asked softly, "you got his cash machine card?"

"Right here, Lucky," said thug of thugs—"Sen"—from the passenger seat.

"All right, give it here," Lucky said.

Lucky was obviously the leader of the gang. Taking the podium, he launched into a cool, businesslike presentation in a generic corporate-speak worthy of *In the Company of Men*. In a clear, clearly educated, businessman's tone, with a voice of knowledge and professionalism, and a bit of a whiny, perhaps Southern twang, he spoke:

"What's your name? Stanley? All right, Stanley, let me explain to you what is about to happen. You have an ATM card? All right, you do.

What's your PIN number?" I gave it to him. Surrender was my only option. I could hear the touch tones as he punched my number into the green iridescent face of his cellular phone, which rested comfortably in its automobile base, designed for ease, convenience, and style.

Lucky asked, "You know what kind of car this is?" I did. Even as I stared at the back of the car seat, in the periphery of my vision I could see the raised plastic letters on the dashboard. L-E-X-U-S. In my sadness, I saw no point in lying. "It's a Lexus," I said.

"By the way, do you have PIN numbers to get cash off of any of your credit cards?" Lucky asked.

I didn't. "No, I'm sorry, I've never gotten any." I never wanted them—especially not at 24.8 percent interest—but I realized that now my not having them could have painful implications. Thankfully, they did not react.

"All right, let me tell you what we're going to do. We are going to drive you to a cash machine and you are going to help us remove your money. Do you understand? Now, you are going to keep your mouth shut and not try anything stupid. My associates here will be very unhappy if you do anything stupid. Do you understand? They will kill you if you open your mouth or if you do anything stupid."

"Don't worry," I responded. "I'll do whatever you ask. I'm not going to do anything stupid." I kept my eyes down, on the back of the driver's seat in front of me. It was a bad idea to look at anyone—they would think I was challenging them or trying to recognize their faces so I could identify them. As for Lucky, I couldn't see anything but the back of his head from where I sat, anyway. A beige leather bucket seat, smooth and luxurious, with the top of Lucky's head sticking out above, was what I saw. Decorating it was a stylish haircut, razor-close at the neck and up but then left thicker at the second tier.

"Keep your eye on him, Ren," Lucky said.

The shorter, light-skinned black man who first grabbed me outside sat quietly to my right with his big-barreled automatic machine gun aimed at me. I had only glimpsed Ren's short, stocky frame for a fleeting moment when he pointed the firepower at me on the street. No way was I going to turn my head to the right and look at him and give him a reason to shoot.

But Sen, sitting diagonally across from me in the front passenger seat, spoke to me yet again after pointing the gun and then getting the wallet. He stated, without emotion, "I'll kill you if you do anything."

I glanced up at him when he spoke but quickly looked away at the back of Lucky's seat. Sen had a large face, with almond-shaped eyes and a prominent nose framed on top by a knit cap that came down almost to his eyes. He was a light-skinned black man, not more than twenty-five years old and probably younger.

Sen took center stage as he eyeballed my gold watch and my gold ring. The watch was a gift from my father when I graduated from law school. The back was inscribed *Love Dad 5-21-84*. The ring was from my grandmother, also for graduating from law school. It had my initials across the front and *5-21-84* scratched on the inside. These were the rare precious items that my middle-class family could afford to give me, and they were not replaceable.

The sad truth was that the watch and the ring actually were replacements. For my bar mitzvah years earlier, my dad and my grandma also got me a gold watch and a ring. These had been stolen around 1982 from my mother's three-room apartment by a cat burglar who had broken through the fire escape window and raided the paltry booty inside. The poor stealing from the lower middle class. Getting burglarized in New York City either by an unknown stranger or even by the always suspected superintendent or doorman was a common experience. Just ask anybody.

"Give me the watch," Sen barked.

I handed it over.

"Is this gold?"

"I don't know," I replied. "I got it from my father for graduating from law school." My gut told me to humanize myself. If they knew I had a father, they might feel less like murder.

"What about the ring?"

"I think it's gold. My grandmother got it for me."

I still avoided looking at any of them. In answering Sen, who was sitting in the front passenger seat facing me almost straight on as he spoke, I reflexively glanced up again in response to his questioning. Our eyes met.

He spat out a bloodcurdling growl. "Motherfucker, you got big eyes. I should kill you for those fuckin' big eyes."

I looked ahead and down as fear flooded my brain.

Finished appraising my watch, Sen apparently concluded that it was worthless to him and he handed it back to me. I put it back on my wrist. They left the ring alone.

The car made a right turn on Fifth Avenue, went down one block and then made a right onto Ninth Street, a beautiful block of stately old brownstones occupied by people who had a lot more money than I did. These robbers must have come looking for action on Manhattan's Fifth Avenue with the idea that Fifth Avenue meant money. They needed to be farther uptown, in the vicinity of my blind date, for the real bucks. Though not as rich as the Upper East Side or the West Village brownstone crowd, I suppose I did have enough money to interest these gangsters.

At Ninth Street and Sixth Avenue, we made a right turn onto the broad commercial boulevard. Below Fourteenth Street it consisted of little restaurants, specialty shops, cafés, ice cream joints. Above Fourteenth you could buy furniture or go to the weekend flea market or exercise your plastic at a series of new megastores—Bed Bath & Beyond, Old Navy, Today's Man, Barnes & Noble. No shopping for me tonight. I peered straight forward and down at the light-brown leather upholstery as the Lexus glided smoothly past these familiar locations. Without actually looking out the window, I could sense where we were by the glow of the familiar lights entering the periphery of my vision.

Suddenly we had pulled onto Twenty-third Street, and a U-turn brought us to a double-parked position. In my peripheral vision, I could feel the navy and burgundy colors and I knew we were at the Chase bank and cash machine vestibule at Twenty-third and Sixth.

"Stanley, what's that ATM number?" came Lucky's businessman twang.

He was checking to see if it matched the number I had given him minutes earlier that he had punched into the cell phone. I gave him the same number. It had been with me for years, as much a part of me as my phone number or date of birth or Social Security number.

"How much do you have in your checking?"

"I don't know. Maybe two thousand dollars."

"Do you have a savings account?"

"Yes."

"How much is in there?"

"About a hundred and ten thousand dollars."

My savings and checking accounts were chock-full, in part because I was one of the few people who by 1998 had not gotten hip to the stock market mutual funds that were making middle America rich as the price-to-earnings ratios rose into the stratosphere. America was high on stocks, and because I was unorganized in my finances, I was still keeping a huge chunk of my change from three years in private practice in a low-yield savings account. Another prosecutor and one of my best friends, Dan Moretsky, had repeatedly told me to get my act together and get into the market and make some money.

Lucky practically turned around in his seat and so did Sen. "What do you *do* for a living, Stanley?" Lucky asked with apparent admiration.

I answered in a sheepish tone, almost apologetic. "Well . . . uh . . . you really kinda picked up the wrong guy. I'm an Assistant U.S. Attorney."

The debate rages as to whether a prosecutor who is the victim of a crime is better off telling them what he does or not. For me, no debate was necessary. In my wallet, emblazoned with a gold seal proclaiming the

Latin *"Qui pro domina justitia sequitur"* (Who prosecutes on behalf of justice), was a stack of Department of Justice / Assistant United States Attorney business cards. Lisa P. Marantz had only gotten one of them. One lie could land me dead and the documents my persecutors needed in order to cross-examine me with a pistol had been turned over during involuntary discovery.

But they didn't quite get it. They probably hadn't looked at the cards. Sen, acting impressed, said, "Ohhh . . . you an attorney."

They had a big fish to fry, but it wasn't sinking in that I was law enforcement–connected. Lie I couldn't, for fear of getting whacked, but I sure as hell was not going to make greater efforts to hammer home my professional status since the fifty-fifty risk was that I would be murdered *because* I was a prosecutor. Images flooded my mind. Just a few months earlier, Jonathan Levin, the son of the wealthy Time Warner chairman Gerald Levin, had been the victim of a torture slaying. First, a former student and crack dealer had stabbed him in the neck repeatedly, probably to get his ATM PIN number, and then he'd been shot stone cold dead. I didn't need to enhance the risk. I kept my mouth shut.

Lucky twanged, "Stanley, what's your mother's maiden name?"

"Robins."

"Social Security number?"

I gave it up.

With a PIN, Social Security number, and someone's mother's maiden name, you can live their life and own their money. It's called convenience. They set it up so you can call them on the phone and do large and small transactions without showing your face at the bank. All you need is the magic passwords, and you can move your own, or somebody else's, life savings around to your heart's content.

This was becoming a pretty high-tech robbery. From the 1998 Lexus, Lucky picked up his cell phone and related beautifully to the Chase operator in corporate speak as me, Stanley Alpert.

"This is Mr. Alpert . . ." My Social Security number followed. "Robins . . . I want you to transfer fifty thousand dollars from savings to checking. . . . Right . . . Thank you very much . . . Right, have a good night."

"All right, we're all set. You all wait for me here. I'll be back soon."

Lucky went into the bank. We sat in the new black Lexus at the corner of Twenty-third Street and Sixth Avenue at eleven P.M. and waited. Where were the police in the greatest city on earth? Just one cop car pulling in alongside us and seeing a well-dressed white man sitting in the back of a Lexus with two young African-Americans wearing knit hats that helped shade their identities should look suspicious enough for the cop to ask them to roll down the window and see how everybody was doing. I sat there and prayed that would happen so I could go home. I also realized that if it did happen I could easily be shot in the crossfire, since the stakes were too high for these gangsters simply to stick out their hands and get cuffed. What would I have said when the window rolled down and the officer asked me if I was all right and Ren's big-barreled automatic under the coat was sitting literally inches from my circulatory system? Like some flirtatious Southern belle, blinking my eyelashes, would I have chimed, "Oh, yes, Officer, I'm being kidnapped—would you kindly arrest these boys?" And then what would have happened? Ren and Sen would have laid down their arms and faced their just punishment without shooting the lone cop and then me? Not a chance. It would have been an impossible spot. It didn't happen.

As I sat there with Ren and Sen and waited for Lucky, I felt royally screwed. It had taken me years of slave labor to earn that money. When I got out of law school, I was penniless. It was a huge thrill that law firms would pay obscene salaries to virgin lawyers with the right academic credentials, and I had them: I was University of Pennsylvania *cum laude,* law review, legal writing instructor. I worked my ass off in state college at Binghamton earning a bachelor of science in economics and I'd worked even harder in law school. I could pick my firm.

There was a Faustian side to the bargain, though. To get the big bucks, your body if not your soul was sold for all hours of the days, the nights, and the weekends. You belonged to them. One miserable partner comes to mind who would give people an unnecessary, total-waste-of-time assignment that was billed out by the hour. He'd hand you the assignment on the eve of a major holiday such as Thanksgiving, and he didn't give a damn if your seat at the family dinner table was empty and you ate a turkey on rye with Russian dressing in your windowless office at eleven P.M. on the same night that you missed the Macy's Thanksgiving Day parade. I earned that money with three and a half years of sweat and blood. I earned that money so I could have the cushion of a bank account, giving me the freedom to go to a government job and not fret about having nothing to fall back on if my mother got sick or my father had to go to a nursing home or something else happened. That money was my nest egg. Money is stored energy, and several years of the stored energy of my life was about to slip out of my hands.

It felt silly. How could these punks take away my paycheck for years of work? How could I have gotten so much comfort from numbers on a page in my bank statement every month? Why hadn't I invested in mutual funds like everybody else and my friend Dan had told me I was foolish not to? In a minute, it would all be gone. And I actually didn't care. I just plain didn't care. Take the money and keep it if I can get out of here in one piece and without a broken arm or a broken leg or a missing eye. Take the fucking money. My life is more important.

Lucky jumped back in the car. Businessman twang: "Stanley, do you have a limit on your cash card?"

"I really don't know."

"It seems to be limited to one thousand dollars, and I got eight hundred." He quietly conferred with Sen.

Lucky had a problem and his problem was my problem. I had already grabbed $200 that afternoon for the Freedy tickets, so although Lucky had transferred $50,000 from my savings to my checking, he could get to only $800 of it. He was stymied and we sat there while he thought over his dilemma. He made chitchat to find added ways to coerce and steal from me.

"Do you have any PIN numbers for your credit cards?" he asked again.

"No," I answered honestly.

"Do you have a car?"

"No."

They were shocked. "You mean to tell me that you got a hundred thousand dollars in the bank and you don't own a car? What is wrong with you?" Lucky chortled incredulously. The others laughed and shook their heads.

I tried to explain. "It's tough to have a car when you live in Manhattan." No matter; these criminals living in Brooklyn, little more than half my age, were cruising around in a brand-new Lexus. I was a successful attorney and I didn't even have a car. Worlds collide.

Lucky followed up. "Do you have a girlfriend?" With that information he could get more leverage in the situation by threatening to go after her.

"No." I was telling the truth, because while I was dating Darcy, it was nothing serious. Not that I would have fessed up and put somebody else in danger.

"How old are you?"

"Thirty-eight."

"Any kids?"

"No."

They all shook their heads in disbelief.

"Stanley, man, you mean you are thirty-eight years old and you don't have a car and you're not married and no kids . . . What the hell have you been doing?" asked Lucky with derisive incredulity.

He had asked a question to which I did not have a satisfactory answer myself. In his world, people had sex when they were still children and they had kids not much later. And fool that I may have been not to have started a family by thirty-eight, stuck in the frightening situation I was in, I might actually never get the chance.

"You should talk to my parents," I said. "They're wondering, too."

Self-effacing humor; let me respect them and soften them up, I thought. Maybe bringing in the fact that I have a family would humanize me in their eyes. All delivered on instinct to avert the evil decree. They actually chuckled, mid-kidnapping.

The Lexus eased forward across Sixth Avenue down Twenty-third Street toward the west side of Manhattan. Corporate-speak Lucky had a plan to announce. They had decided to keep me. "Stanley, let me tell you what we're gonna do. I'm not even from around here—I'm from out of state—so nobody will ever be able to track us. We're going to take you to a place we have to crash at and keep you there overnight. Tomorrow morning we will take you to a drive-through bank and you will withdraw fifty thousand from your account. Do you understand?"

My face filled with blood and my stomach sank low as I absorbed this sickening blow.

"Yes."

Sen: "Don't worry, man. It won't be too hard for you to make it back."

Sen thought, though, that the drive-through scheme was flawed: "Yo, Lucky, it gonna look a little strange takin' fifty thousand cash out in a drive-through." The car made a left turn onto the West Side Highway, heading downtown.

"All right, then, here's what we'll do," Lucky twanged. "Tomorrow morning we will take you to your bank and you will go in and take out the money. But we'll be nearby and watching you. Someone will go with you into the bank and will be on you with a gun. If you pull one false move, we will shoot you, Stanley. Understand?"

"Yes."

Sen stared back at me from the front passenger seat as Lucky schemed on their behalf. My mistake; our eyes met again.

He screamed again: "This motherfucker got big eyes! I should kill you for those fuckin' big eyes!" This time, as he said it, with a swift and seamless motion, Sen shoved his large automatic pistol straight in my face, inches away. I carefully studied its smooth, dark metallic barrel in frozen fear. Sen's face was filled with sadistic glee and the thrill of violence, the thrill of outburst.

I was petrified. There was no doubt in my mind that Sen could shoot me as easily as I might scratch an itch. I could be dead or dismembered in a matter of seconds or hours. It was painfully obvious to me that my thirty-eight years might crash to an ungodly end that very night. Still, my body did not tremble, and my heart did not have that swollen, thumping beat you get when you're being followed by a mugger but you still have a chance to get away. That's because there was nothing I could do. I was overtaken by a sickening calm. The man who faces the firing squad eats his last meal and stands against the wall smoking his last cigarette, waiting for the sharpshooters to load their weapons. Only by suppressing my fear did I retain the slightest hope of ever eating another cookie again, or talking to my mother on the phone, or stepping outside without a heavy coat on the first day of spring.

Lucky ordered backseat Ren to take my scarf and use it to blindfold me. The scarf was a piece of green-gray sweet-soft velour artwork I'd bought off some Israeli woman on the Upper West Side. She sold scarves and searched for a husband simultaneously and with equal measures of enthusiasm. Ren removed my eyeglasses and handed them to me, permitting me to slide them into my trench coat pocket alongside Lisa P. Marantz's business card. Ren slid the smooth scarf from under my trench coat and around my neck. He drew it across my face so it covered all the way from my forehead to the bridge of my nose. The velour was soft and warm as he knotted it at the back of my head. I descended into blackness. My ears took over. Ren shoved me down in the seat next to him, so that my blindfolded Caucasian head did not stick out as a lightning rod for Giuliani's police. It was intimate; my head lay against his leg and practically in his lap, my body curled next to him in a fetal position.

To my horror, my ears picked up another language besides Lucky's corporate speak. Ren and Sen had their own way of talking. It came out low, at the bass end of the vocal cords, in machine-gun spurts of some secret guttural singsong. Lucky didn't seem to speak it. I guessed that Ren and Sen were brothers and that they spoke some African language dialect. Maybe they were from Ghana or someplace like that. It sounded something like this:

Sen: "Duggamenabugga. Ikeaathugga disre inabuuga eyepagugga dugga uggaout bugga wentou agugga."

Ren: "Uggaeye wentou disopea einwugga boreanow worsaw agugga pornowen a blau bugga rentoray agugga."

It looks bizarre on the page, and you can only imagine what it was like hearing it.

Their actual and psychological grip on me had just tightened. How could I keep the lid on the situation if I couldn't even understand what they were saying to each other? With the sound of their strange language buzzing in my ears, I could hear and feel the car descend into a tunnel. I thought it might be the Holland Tunnel. Maybe Lucky's out-of-town crib was a crash pad in Jersey on the other side of the Hudson. From there they would take me to the bank in the morning. This was one night that I was not going home. No chocolate chip cookies or ginger tea or good night's sleep on this cold January night.

FOUR

COURTING DISASTER
BACK IN BROOKLYN

I was wrong about New Jersey. Had we crossed the state line, it would immediately have turned this kidnapping into a federal crime. Soon after we rolled out of the tunnel, I could feel us ascend a hill that gave off the familiar whirr of rubber on metal of the East River bridges. We had gone down past the World Trade Center, into the tunnel that curved around the bottom of Manhattan and brought you back up on the FDR Drive heading up the East Side. Now we were crossing either the Brooklyn Bridge or the Manhattan Bridge, the first ones you hit on the way back up the east side of the island.

We were heading back to Brooklyn, where I'd been brought up and where I now practiced law. My new companions decided to pick up supplies on the way home.

"We need to stop and buy some tape to tie him up," Lucky said.

"Ah-ight. I know a spot off the highway," replied his partner Sen.

A stab of fear shot through me and it felt as though a thin strong twine tightened slightly across my Adam's apple.

Lucky inquired, "Stanley. Have you ever been on the Brooklyn-Queens Expressway?"

Yes I had. It ran right past my downtown Brooklyn office. In my mind's eye, I could see us driving past the mammoth new brown Pierrepont Plaza building with the illuminated, green pointed top, housing the office where I had devoted so much energy over the years. We drove just spitting distance from the United States District Court for the Eastern District of New York, where the lawyers in my office practiced, and the scene for me of many legal battles. Not only did I litigate in that court, the summer before I had litigated *for* that court. Thanks in part to me, a new courthouse was soon to go up on that same spot.

Congress continually saw fit to expand the jurisdiction of the federal courts, seeking political benefit by federalizing many crimes that had traditionally been handled by the local criminal justice system. With more judges being added to deal with the increasing complexities of our modern and highly litigious society, the Eastern District judges needed space. Like kids who'd been promised a new toy, they were tickled that Congress had approved funding for a tall, sleek, well-appointed new courthouse, which would replace an unimpressive 1960s-construction old federal building that formed part of the existing complex.

Ironically, the same spirit of litigation that created the need to expand the court in the first place inspired the people who lived in Concord Village, a group of tall residential buildings towering over neighboring brownstones that was a stone's throw from where Lucky, Sen, Ren, and I were driving on the BQE. Concord Village didn't want another tall building going up near their tall buildings. Last one in, turn out the lights. So they used the court system to fight the court system. That past summer I had beaten back their challenge, and some powerful federal judges who considered me their lawyer were now my friends. I didn't think they would be too happy to find out that their lawyer had been kidnapped. Someday in two or three years, I had hoped to have the opportunity to stand up and plead my cases before them in the new courthouse that I helped to see through. Or, better, if the long odds went with me, maybe I'd get to see the Lucky-Sen-Ren gang standing in that courthouse, wearing shackles and upside-down smiles.

The old courthouse was the place where I had cut my eyeteeth as a young lawyer. Coming out of three and a half years at a large corporate law firm, even having been in their litigation department, I knew very little. The large firms almost never got you to court at all, and if you went, you were carrying the briefcase of a partner who did all the talking. If you wanted real experience, you had to get a government job. At the time it was one-third the pay but thirty times the experience. I put more trials under my belt in a couple of years than I could have even spending a lifetime at a big firm.

My first five trials for the U.S. Attorney had been to defend the government against personal injury cases. Somebody would slip and fall in front of a post office. Somebody else would get into a crash with an FBI sedan. I've always believed that plaintiffs injured in accidents or by defective products should be well compensated for the harm they suffered, but in defending these cases, I quickly learned that a large percentage of the cases involved plaintiffs lying about how the injury happened or about how hurt they were. And it was obvious that many of the lawyers encouraged it.

The same oratorical skills I honed defending fender benders could be put to better use, I thought, and soon enough they were: in bringing lawsuits for the people of the United States on behalf of the environment. As a city kid I'd spent most summers playing and getting in trouble on the hot steamy New York pavements. That scrappy upbringing made me want to get outside and gave me the passion to fight for what open space was left, and the air and the water and the land. The corporations who made it their business to pollute the environment in order to maximize the wealth of their executives and shareholders could lie as badly as personal injury plaintiffs when it suited them. Their representatives were more sophisticated, yes. Better dressed while they sat across from you in

the deposition room. But more honest, no. Criminals came in all styles and colors, and the U.S. Attorney's Office transformed me into a warrior bent on catching those suits in their web of deceptions and making them pay. Not long before, in that same old courthouse, I had brought Fortune 500 mining company Phelps Dodge to its corporate knees at a trial before the Honorable John Gleeson, and forced the company to pay a $21 million judgment for failing to clean the hazardous wastes it had dumped. And I was halfway toward giving a similar spanking to mammoth Mobil Oil.

This evening, in stark contrast, I was powerless. Lucky twanged in, invading my thoughts. "Stanley, I asked you whether you have ever been on the BQE?"

"Sure," I responded. "I grew up in Brooklyn." I really didn't know in which direction on the BQE we were headed, east or west, but my mind's eye saw us swinging around the south of Brooklyn and heading toward Kennedy Airport. I might not be going to court for a long time, if ever.

FIVE

THE GRIP TIGHTENS

Fifteen minutes later, the car stopped in what felt to me to be a gas station. Over the past years, the oil industry had made sure to include small convenience stores in most of their gas outlets. Their marketing studies showed this to be a good investment that would maximize profits. I litigated a trademark case at my old law firm in which two companies had duked it out over the trade name "Coastal" on gas stations, and I learned all about their marketing plans. It turned out this particular station was convenient not just for buying a quart of milk but also for picking up a roll of tape if you needed one for a kidnapping. Lucky stepped out and returned five minutes later with the professional supply he needed for tonight's business.

A few minutes later, the Lexus pulled to a halt on a quiet street and the motor turned silent. It felt totally isolated. I did not hear any humans and I did not hear cars. In my mind's eye I was on some out-of-the-way street in East New York, close to Starrett City and Kennedy Airport. With warlike determination, the boys hustled me out into the cold and across the street. Two, three sets of hands pushed my blinded body in the direction it needed to go. A slight rise brought me onto a sidewalk and five paces later put me in front of a building. Three steps up and a door swung open. Three steps more and a second door opened inward, as I moved though the entranceway, past the intercom and mailbox vestibule of a typical New York City turn-of-the-century tenement building. I had lived in one in the West Village. I had been in them a million times growing up in Brooklyn. My grandmother on my father's side had lived in one on the Lower East Side for $26 a month—rent-controlled—until she passed away in 1972. The ones in poor neighborhoods like my grandmother's, and like the one I was just entering, reeked powerfully: a musty smell-combination of age, dirt, dead cockroaches, and rich greasy ethnic cooking that unmistakably announced poverty. I was in the ghetto.

The blindfold had a design defect. With my eyes focused downward, I could see out the bottom. The floor of the building hallway was a faded white cross-patterned tile, with an elaborate border around the outside consisting of a repeated geometric diamond pattern in faded black and red tones. I studied the tile pattern carefully. I memorized it. They hustled me down the narrow hallway to the stairs. At this age, New York buildings were walk-ups. Two flights up and a quick turn and I was introduced to my new prison.

They shoved me down a narrow hallway all the way to the back of a railroad-flat apartment. As they guided me toward a room, I felt lumpiness under my feet. I was walking on clothing. Clothing was strewn on the floor and covered maybe half the place—I could see bits of it out of the bottom of my blindfold. And no one cared if I walked right on it. This was a crash pad. This place was unruled.

Besides clothing strewn everywhere, out of the bottom of the blindfold I could see a red plastic fire truck, the kind big enough for a kid to pedal around in. It was not just a crash pad, I saw: This actually seemed to be somebody's home. There were two large mattresses on the floor, one on either side of the room.

Sen commanded, "Take off the coat." I did it. He shoved me down onto the mattress, on the right side, far corner, sitting upright. Once prone on the mattress, the tiny window of vision out of the bottom of the blindfold was gone, and all I could see if I wanted to was my own chest. Not that I really wanted to keep violating the blindfold. Any slight reaction to something I saw, and they would suss out that I was being a bad boy. I could easily die for that. As insurance, under the cover of my own soft velour scarf turned blindfold, I shut my eyes tight, closed. I was alone in the darkness.

Ren, Sen, and Lucky were excited, and they ran around the apartment in an energetic frenzy. The wildcats had dragged a still-breathing Thomson's gazelle back to their lair. Ren and Sen jabbered in their unknown language. Lucky didn't seem to mind that he was left out. With the three exulting over the thrill of a successful hunt, it got even better. Several minutes after we arrived, calling in on the cell phone was a member of the opposite sex who came over the wire by the name of "D." She was out on the street working for a living, and judging from Sen's flirtatious banter, she was about to bring her professional equipment over for some home entertainment.

"Yo, D, what's happenin'," Sen exclaimed with obvious salacious glee. "Where you girls at? Downtown? You had a good night? Made much? When are you coming back over here? What? Pay your taxi to get over here? How much? About sixteen dollars? Sure, no problem. We'll cover you. Just get over here soon."

I was blindfolded and helpless and I was scared shit. But my prosecutor's instincts took over. Downtown meant either downtown Brooklyn, or downtown Manhattan just across the river. More likely Manhattan for prostitution, I thought, but I really didn't know. In case I ever made it out, the amount of the taxi fare corresponded to a distance from either downtown Brooklyn or downtown Manhattan, which would form the radius of a semicircle that could be plotted on a map, and these criminals might be found someplace on the circumference. Clue number one to our location. I registered the figure in my head and kept it there. The hunter had become the hunted, but inside the blindfolded cocoon that was my head I couldn't stop from doing a little hunting myself.

The likelihood of my ever making use of the information was not great. The boys began planning tomorrow morning's trip to the bank to rid me of my finances.

"We're going to take you to your bank in the morning, Stanley," Lucky twanged. In my mind's eye, I could see the Chase branch on Montague Street in Brooklyn Heights, just a short distance from the office of the United States Attorney. My personal branch. Surrounded by stately brownstones on one side and a genteel shopping promenade on the other, it had a grandiloquent lobby of marble floors and carved ceilings, and carried a proud message born of a different era, when decency was the official currency, carved in smooth gray marble thirty feet above the ground, over the exit sign:

SOCIETY IS BUILT UPON TRUST AND TRUST UPON
CONFIDENCE IN ONE ANOTHER'S INTEGRITY

"I know you're not going to try anything stupid, Stanley. Tomorrow morning you will go into the bank and tell them you want to withdraw fifty thousand dollars. We will be with you. One of us will be right outside the bank. No, one of us will be in the bank, just away from you at a short distance, but ready to blow your fucking head off if you pull anything stupid. Do you understand?" His voice rose to a demanding boom, still in professional businessman mode. The man meant business.

"I'll do whatever you say. Nothing stupid." I was cooperative, very cooperative. I was so cooperative that as time went by I noted that they did not feel the need to use the tape they had bought to tie me up. That was a godsend. Tape would have compounded the torment. I sat on the mattress unmoving and impassive.

Sen was not convinced of the wisdom of Lucky's logistics. "Man, Lux, that shit's stupid. What if he pulls somethin' at the bank, yo? This shit ain't gonna work."

Lucky pondered silently. "If he tries anything, we'll kill his father." There was a pregnant pause in the room, as the horror of Lucky's threat slammed into my solar plexus.

"We'll kill him and we'll kill his father. Stanley, if you fail to cooperate with us tomorrow morning, we will break every bone in your father's body." Lucky left the room and went somewhere else in the apartment.

I could hear his footsteps plodding outside the room, and this sonar mapped out in my mind a basic outline of the rest of the railroad flat apartment. Seemed to me to be one room to the left of the one we were in, and one to the right. I felt some other activity in the other rooms. Maybe someone else was there, but it was sketchy, all a mystery to me.

Little Ren, the main gunman but the least active in the scheming, sat down on the mattress next to me and trained his weapon on me. I could hear him cocking the weapon on and off, telling me with no words needed that the hammer was set and he was prepared to fire instantly. Sen plunked down across from me and to my right. With Lucky out of the room, Lieutenant Sen took command.

"Where does your father live?" Sen asked.

"In Brooklyn."

"What's his address?"

Fuck. In my brown leather wallet, along with a driver's license, ATM card, credit cards, membership cards for Channel 13 public TV and the Sierra Club, and other assorted junk, was my father's business card. It listed his home address.

My dad was a cantor. That's the guy who sings the prayers in the synagogue. For most of his life, he had poured out his heart and soul singing the Jewish liturgies week after week. This was the Jewish people's soulful-sounding minor-key way of trying to talk to God, and my dad was the spokesman because he liked to sing. After he was discharged from America's army at the end of World War II, there was a mad rush back home of people getting married. The press of the war had delayed people's plans. Individual and collective near-death experiences made people hurry to the altar to build their lives, now that the Nazi threat was crushed. The imperative for Jews was powerful, too, since although so many of our people had been cremated, Hitler's plan to wipe out the world's Jews failed as far as the shores of America. On weekends in the years after the war, my father went from wedding to wedding to wedding, and he could join as many as four or five or even six Jewish couples in holy matrimony in one productive weekend. *Mazel tov,* they cried, as the groom crushed under his right foot the glass that represented the loss of the holy temple two millennia earlier. In every celebration, or *simchah,* in Jewish life, we were enjoined never to forget our sorrow, and even at the pinnacle of joy, which was a marriage, the tragedy of the loss of our temple and exile from Israel could not be forgotten. Our joy was our sorrow unmasked. The weddings were a joy for my father, as they were very lucrative and very heady for him, the well-paid center of attention at these ceremonies. He also enjoyed free feasting on the smorgasbords of sweet stuffed cabbage, spicy pepper steak, kosher Chinese chow mein, gefilte fish, and chopped liver that inevitably marked each affair.

Now he was retired, but he maintained a business card with his home address and phone number on it, just in case somebody might need him at the last minute to officiate at a wedding. Some people he had married forty years earlier would hunt him down so he could marry their children or grandchildren. I proudly carried his card in my wallet, a superstitious voice in my head telling me that by carrying it on me I affirmed his life and put a spiritual protective shield around him. What I had paved with good intentions, however, was now a road leading to hell. If I lied about my father's address, they would kill me. The business card, after all, was sitting right there in my wallet. One false move, one deception, and the atmosphere would turn grim. On the other hand, if I told the truth, the probability of them actually succeeding in going to 772 Ocean Parkway and killing him was much lower than the probability of them killing me. In a bitter calculus, I chose the truth.

"Seven seventy-two Ocean Parkway," I answered Sen.

My calculus seemed off. Sen reacted. "I think one of my homeboys should be in that area. I'm gonna send him over to check it out. You hear that, motherfucker?" he screamed at me. "We'll break every bone in his fuckin' body."

My heart sank through my shoes. This was getting a lot worse. Hurt me, okay, kill me, okay, I thought. I'll take it and it will be over. But don't go for my father. Fear and loathing welled up in me and my face swelled with blood as tears of desperation filled my eyes under their velour cover.

Sen dialed his cellular phone. "Yo, B, whussup? We need you to do somethin'. Where you at? Oh, good, you're pretty near to where we need you to go. The guy's name is Benjamin Alpert. He's at Seven seventy-two Ocean Parkway. I want you to go there and check out this motherfucker. See if he's there. Then wait there overnight and don't let him leave in the morning. We got a job to do. What? Oh, right . . . Yo, Stanley, what apartment is your father in?" Sen inquired.

That was more than I could take. My father had Parkinson's disease. Parkinson's had forced him into retirement early. He was also seventy-seven years old and had slowed with age. The thought of some thug going to my weakened father's apartment and threatening to kill him was too painful for me to bear.

"Four-N," I lied. He really lived in apartment 3N. I couldn't give them the real apartment number and let them near my father. I lied, knowing that things would turn ominous for me if the lie was revealed. I prayed that their henchman would not actually go into the building and ring the bell. My father's building had a doorman. In the vestibule as you walked into the building, there were intercom buzzers in a gold frame, but I was pretty sure that only the apartment numbers were listed, not names. At times no doorman was on duty, so it was possible that

Sen's man could go in and ring the bell, but maybe the person in 4N would just not answer. Or, with luck the doorman would be there and the guy would keep a safe distance away. It was also possible that my father was not home; he often stayed at his seventy-nine-year-old "girl-friend's" apartment.

I purposely crafted my lie to be off by only one number—4N instead of 3N—so that if they did discover it, I could claim that I had made an honest mistake.

"It's four-N," Sen told his homey. "Go over there. Check out the situation and call me back." Sen hung up.

"Yo, Stanley, you're not gonna fuck with us, are you? Don't make us waste your father."

"I'll do whatever you say." The room became silent as we all waited for their associate to call back. My state of surprise and shock was ascending as I contemplated the unthinkable—the possibility that I could be the instrument that would lead these viruses to a place in time in which they could hurt or kill my father. I descended further into a personal hell of fear, remorse, and self-pity.

The silence was punctuated occasionally, though. To constantly remind me of the threat, I could hear the sound of steel against steel, as Sen, sitting on the mattress across from me, cocked and uncocked his gun. You could feel in the air the sheer pleasure it gave him to flex his metal muscle. Ren did the same, cocking and uncocking his gun every so often, sitting right next to me on the mattress I rested on.

"You ever try one of these, Stanley?" Sen inquired. "All you got to do is give it a little squeeze and it puts out ten bullets in a second. Bam! Bam! There's nothin' left of you except pickin' up the pieces. I hope you don't fuck with us so you don't have to find out. It wouldn't be nothin' for me to let this bad boy loose on your ass. You understand." I think he had gotten up and was pointing the gun at me at point-blank range. I thought I felt the breeze.

A wall was behind me, a wall to my right, and before me and beside me to my left were ready guns. Sure, a false move on my part and I would be dead, but just as easily one of those guns could be fired accidentally at close range and then I would be just as dead. I remained perfectly still. Sen didn't need an answer to his threat.

Just a few minutes later, Sen was back on the phone with his man. "Are you there? Good. Did you check him out? Yes? You rang the bell? Is he there? Okay, good. Just stay there. Don't let the guy leave. We'll call you in the morning."

After Sen hung up, he said, "All right, Stanley, we got your father covered. I know you're gonna be smart tomorrow morning when we go to the bank. I'd hate to see anything happen to your pops."

"You won't get any problems from me."

It seemed to me that the calls to their man to send him to stalk my dad were probably a ruse. They spoke a second time to their man too soon for it to be credible. And even if he had gone to my dad's building, the doorman is usually on duty, so the thug would probably not have risked going near the intercom. Plus, I had given the wrong apartment number. It was possible that the guy did ring the wrong bell and that the person in that apartment answered over the intercom, and Sen's man thought it was my father up in his apartment. Sen's man could be waiting downstairs at 772 Ocean Parkway, ready to prevent my father from walking out the door in the morning. But that didn't seem all that likely. The problem was that although it seemed to be a dirty trick, I couldn't be sure. I was now at risk this night of losing my father and losing myself. I was solidly submerged under their power.

SIX

GETTING TO KNOW YOU

After about a half hour of quiet, the intercom buzzer suddenly rang from downstairs. A great hubbub erupted around me. Sen and Ren jumped up, cold steel audibly in hand, and moved to guard the apartment door. They were nervous about someone new entering the scene. Sen ordered Ren: "Make sure it's them and not them motherfuckers from upstairs. We can't take no chances and they might be packin'."

"Ah-ight," Ren replied. Apparently, a rival bad-boy crew had its hideout in the building, too. A shoot-out over my $800 was not out of the question. This thieving business was fiercely competitive.

A moment later, the girls entered the room. The overhead light went on, creating a warmer radiance that seeped through the bottom of my velour blindfold.

"Hi, D. Whussup, Mystic." Sen greeted his friends with an air of lusty good humor.

Before they noticed me, one of the girls said, "It was sixteen dollars and forty cents. You gonna pay?"

Apparently, these chicks were lousy tippers. "Yeah," Sen said. I logged the clue.

"What the hell have you dragged in here?" exclaimed one of the girls in apparent disbelief, upon spotting the suit perched on the mattress.

"We found him on the street, D. We just got a little business to do with him."

"Y'all are askin' for trouble. Draggin' some businessman back here like it was nuthin'. Ain't you all had enough trouble already?"

"Don't worry, baby. We got everything under control," Sen responded, trying to stay on her good side for obvious reasons.

"I didn't say I was worried. I just wanna know what you think you doin'," D replied.

"How was the night out?" asked Ren, not wanting to be left out.

"Business was slow tonight," responded the voice of the other girl.

"Don't worry, Mystic. We got some money tonight," said Ren.

"I can see that."

"Y'all?"

"We did owah job. That ain't yo bizniss anyway, since we ansah to Lucky, not you." I couldn't tell whether Lucky was in the room, but the answer seemed negative.

"Don't ever forget that Ren and me is your protection," countered Sen.

My little lawyer brain processed the facts like a Cuisinart. The girls had been out turning tricks "downtown." Lucky was their pimp, and Ren and Sen were friends, lovers, business associates, and muscle in a loosely knit clique of criminal associates. The girls brought in bread and butter with their whoring, while the guys had gone out fishing tonight for a bigger catch. Me.

The girls were hungry. So were the boys. Mystic and D volunteered to run out for McDonald's. The boys approved and Lucky agreed to drive. My mistake—he in fact had never left the room. Sen and Ren placed matching orders for Big Macs, fries, and Cokes.

D spoke out with compassion. "I feel sorry for this guy. Do you want something to eat?"

"Stanley, man, we gettin' McDonald's," said Sen. "You want something?"

Lucky: "Yeah. You boys better make sure to take good care of our guest."

I was worried that the food might be drugged. I needed to keep my wits. I wasn't feeling too hungry, either. It was only three and a half hours earlier that I had sipped Merlot and eaten kosher shish kebab on the Upper East Side. "No, thanks," I replied. "I'm not too hungry at the moment."

"How about something to drink?" D persevered.

I responded cheerily and not without appreciation. "No, thank you."

The girls left with Lucky. With the others gone, Sen and Ren had a private conversation in their African-sounding language. The words just buzzed in my head as they spat back and forth in a low-pitched, ominous tone:

Sen: "Eyepagagugga wentou rangabuuga disrenightoeugga ablau abugga."

Ren: "Bunterminfugga op reagugga aye oprebugga asrouninugga apoleyneeabugga."

It went on like that in low conspiring voices, the secret language throbbing in my ears. Minutes later, the front door opened. Footsteps sounded down the hall and drew nearer. The rustle of white paper McDonald's bags signaled food, but without a normal Pavlovian reaction from me. Eating was the furthest thing from my mind. More rustling of paper-covered burgers and large Cokes slipping out of white bags. Soon the acrid-sweet smell of grease-covered french fries flooded the air. I was surrounded by stereo sounds of chewing and swallowing.

"What's his name?" asked one of the girls.

"Steven," said Ren.

"My name is Stanley," I insisted gently. My identity was my life.

"Oh shit, I mean *Stanley.*"

"I feel sorry for him," she said. "Stanley?"

"Yes."

"I brought you somethin' to drink. It's a Snapple. Do you like Snapple?"

Many days I would have a Snapple for lunch, peach-flavored iced tea, lemon-flavored iced tea, pink lemonade. Tuna on rye washed down by a high-fructose-corn-syrup Snapple. Tasty but bad for the waistline, as even my skinny one was getting a little plumper with age. "I'm not thirsty, but I do like Snapples. Thank you *very much*," I emphasized.

Propped on the edge of the mattress low to the floor, I was still dressed in lawyerly elegance. My trench coat was off, but it was chilly enough in the place for me to keep my suit jacket on. Shiny black shoes hung over the edge, planted firmly on the floor. Between them a set of hands placed a bottle.

"Here," she said. I reached out and felt the plastic of a thirty-two-ounce bottle of Snapple. The glass bottles were sixteen ounces, but I knew the plastic to be thirty-two. I was reluctant to drink, on the off chance that they might try to drug me. I was actually thirsty, though, and to be impolite was to risk the ire of my gracious hosts. Grabbing the plastic top, I twisted counterclockwise and was relieved to hear and feel the clicking plastic of an unopened bottle. I let the cool sweet peach iced tea flow down my parched throat, relieved to get some sustenance from the sugar and the liquid. It was probably two and a half hours since I'd been nabbed on West Tenth Street. I kept the bottle tightly covered and at my feet when not drinking so as to prevent tampering.

"Those are some nice shoes you got there, Stanley," Lucky said admiringly. "Real shiny. Must of cost you some money."

My goal was to minimize the distance between us. "I just got these. They were actually pretty cheap." The shoes were brand-new Florsheims, hard shiny leather that hurt my feet. They were cheap, as dress shoes go. I had bought two pairs at once—an expensive pair of Johnston & Murphys with a molded comfort foot massage system, and this pair of shiny, uncomfortable Florsheims, a nod to frugality that made me feel more comfortable buying the other expensive pair.

"How much were those?" Lucky queried.

"I think about sixty-nine dollars." I purposely underestimated a little.

"Oh shit," Lucky exclaimed. The entire room burst into uproarious laughter. Ren had a distinctive snicker that sounded like he kept his jaw shut while he laughed. Lucky, chortling: "My sneakers cost twice as much as those."

With everyone laughing at me, I didn't feel bad. Some things in life bother you and some things don't. My interest in material goods had always been limited. I didn't have too much growing up; my father had lived through the Depression, so whatever money he did have did not get spent easily. I certainly never had access to much money. After about age sixteen, I worked three days a week and Saturday nights in my friend Jeffrey's family candy and stationery store. I also came from a slightly left-leaning Eastern European Jewish philosophy that cared more about the environment and the fate of the poor than accumulating expensive objects. Insulting my cheap shoes was just not a way to bother me.

But these kids who grew up even poorer than me had different needs. Their self-worth was defined by a pair of $130 Air Jordans. It would bother them if you made fun of their shoes. You'd probably get popped for doing it. Young Lucky was leading a 1998 Lexus, $130 sneaker lifestyle that could be maintained only by stealing. I couldn't care less about $70 Florsheims.

"Why don't you take off your shoes?" Lucky asked. "Make yourself comfortable."

Taking them off would have made me feel too vulnerable. Shoes on my feet also preserved some hope that the opportunity might arise for me to walk out the door. I was keeping them on. "No thanks. I'm fine," I said, cheery, deflecting as though he had made a kind offer.

"All right, Stanley," he responded. "I'm getting out of here. Goin' to see my fiancée. I'll be back a little later to check up on things." Lucky exited stage left and a moment later the outer door slammed. A fiancée! How lovely! I could only hope to be invited to the wedding.

With Lucky gone, the room grew quiet. Ren, Sen, Mystic, and D relaxed after their meal.

D pierced the silence. "I got to be in court tomorrow."

"What for?" asked Ren, sitting next to me.

"I got picked up bein' out on the street. I got to be there at nine-thirty and pay a hundred-and-ninety-nine-dollar fine. If I don't pay it I got to go to jail for thirty days."

"You gonna go to court?" asked Ren.

"I don't know," she replied. "I need seven dollars to get there. One of y'all gonna give me seven dollars?"

"No problem, Mercedes," answered Sen.

I now had some more clues. I had D's first name. In 1998 New York City, the subway cost $1.50 each way. I already knew a cab to either downtown Brooklyn or Manhattan was $16.40. Seven dollars could only correspond to a round-trip on the Command bus, which cost $3.50 each way. The Command buses were a privately operated system of express buses from Manhattan to various locations in Brooklyn, some of which were not easily accessed by subway. One could follow the Command bus routes out from Manhattan and narrow down the possible places in Brooklyn to find the home base of these perpetrators. Also, if I made it out, how hard would it be to find Mercedes? I thought. All the investigators needed to do was to go to criminal court in downtown Manhattan, possibly Brooklyn, look at the docket, and see who was due to appear that morning on a prostitution charge calling for either a $199 fine or thirty days in prison. "Mercedes" may have been a street name or she may have just lied about her name, but the details of the prostitution charge would be specific enough to lead directly to D's file. I logged the information.

"Now let's get down to business," Sen declared in a conspiratorial whisper. Somebody shut off the overhead light, extinguishing the soft glow penetrating the bottom and the top of the scarf wrapped around my face. The sound of a match head striking flint was followed by the sickly sweet smell of marijuana and the sound of inhaling as it was drawn into Sen's lungs. He passed it to Ren sitting next to me. And to the girls. Dope makes you happy, and I could feel the tension in the room dissipate a bit.

Ren felt friendly. "How 'bout some weed, Stanley?"

Sen liked the idea. "Yeah, how 'bout some smoke with us, Stanley?"

That's all I needed. I didn't even smoke pot when I wasn't being kidnapped. After years of passing it up, Mr. Uncool was not going to experiment with drugs when his mind had to be clear.

"Thank you very much, but I'll pass."

Nobody seemed to care if I didn't share their weed. They handed it around some more. Everybody seemed nice and relaxed, lying around on the mattresses, Ren next to me, Sen and D on the mattress across from me, Mystic's voice coming from the floor to my right in front of the other mattress and right next to Sen.

Sen was a natural-born romantic. "Why don't you bring some of that sweet stuff over here, Mercedes?" he commanded.

"We need condoms," said Mystic.

"Right. We ain't givin' no blow jobs or nothin' else without no condoms," Mercedes agreed. Planned Parenthood would have been proud.

Mystic volunteered, "I'll go out and get some." She walked out of the room and then I heard the apartment door slam. The room went quiet.

Sen broke the silence. "I wonder where Ramos is."

"I ain't seen him tonight," responded Ren.

"He won't mind if we use his stereo." I took note: a "Ramos" lived here. A minute later, the sound of Hot 97 filled the air. The pounding beat of rap music filled the room. Minutes later, Mystic returned with the condoms. On the mattress next to me, a foot or two away, I could hear that another body came over and was lying on top of Ren. Rhythmic swishing sounds came from beside me. Across from me, on the other mattress, more gurgling told me that Sen was busily occupied. The blind-fold was turning into a blessing in disguise. No moaning came from the tough guys, but subdued noises went on for several minutes and then all grew quiet in the room. Somebody was satisfied. The room stayed quiet for quite some time.

I was left with my own thoughts. It was really late, maybe three A.M., and I wished that I could sleep. I was thinking that I should have been home in bed so I would be well rested for tomorrow morning's meeting. I am a person who loves to get a good night's sleep. In law school I never pulled the all-nighters that classmates did. I liked my eight hours. Tonight it was out of the question; I couldn't do much, but at least if I stayed awake there was some chance that I could react and influence my fate. After all, this was the big one. The final exam. If I couldn't stay awake for this one, there wouldn't be another. I lay in the heavy silence and listened, intently.

Ren and Sen broke the silence with their secret language. I couldn't discern a word.

"What time is it?" asked one of the girls.

"It's three-ten," Sen replied. "Lucky should be back soon."

People got up and started walking around. Hot 97 kept on playing with the raw beat of the raw city. It shook my body and soul to the core. Sen played with his gun and I could hear the cold steel as he checked it, cocking it to fire, then uncocking it.

"Have you prayed yet, Stanley?" Sen wanted to know.

Say your prayers was an option I hadn't even thought of yet. "No," I responded. I hadn't had time to think of it, since I'd been trying to stay alert and focused on what was going on around me. A Jew in trouble typically says the *Sh'ma Yisrael*, the core prayer that declares the oneness of God. "Hear, oh Israel, the Lord is our God, the Lord is One." Genera-tions of martyrs had gasped that prayer as one tyrant after the other slaughtered Jews just because they insisted on being Jews and refused to convert to one form or another of Christianity. You were also enjoined to say the *Sh'ma* when you woke up every morning, since sleep was akin to death and the *Sh'ma* was said to proclaim the greatness of God for having brought you back to life one more time.

"You believe in God?" asked Ren.

"Yes, I do," I replied. I was a bit on the agnostic side but pretty close to believing that some divine presence was responsible for all of this. On the other hand, what strange God had brought us the Holocaust? What strange God had created kidnappers? What evils had I committed to deserve this fate?

"You Jewish, Stanley?" asked Sen.

Now I was in big trouble. The relationship between Jews and blacks was a complicated and troubled one, as I was painfully aware. Dr. Martin Luther King, Jr., recognized the natural commonality between Jews and blacks, both slaves at different times. Both communities had faced a wall of prejudice in this country. Jews had marched with blacks in the civil rights demonstrations down South and suffered Police Chief Bull Connor's dogs and water cannons. And this Jew personally had fought for civil rights in the *United States v. Island Park* case as an Assistant U.S. Attorney, when we had done battle against Al D'Amato's home village for keeping blacks out of federal housing.

But in 1998 the average black man on the street was not sitting around giving thanks for Jewish efforts on his behalf. One night in 1991 the unfortunate death of a sweet and beautiful young black child, Gavin Cato, led the racists among the blacks to cry for the scalp of a Jew, any Jew, and a sweet and beautiful Talmudic scholar visiting from Australia, Yankel Rosenbaum, who had nothing to do with the conflict, paid the ultimate price in blood. The Klan was in New York. The Nation of Islam churned out race baiters who slithered up to the podium and exhorted the black man to kill the whites, the Catholics, the faggots, and the lesbians, but reserving special status for the Jews, who one psycho said were the bloodsuckers of the black nation, having "crawled around on all fours in the caves and hills of Europe, eating juniper roots and eating each other and having slept with [their] dead for 2,000 years, smelling the stench coming up from the decomposing body."

I knew painfully well the way that the propaganda had trickled down into the consciousness of the black man on the street. There was now a generalized hatred of Jews among a lot of blacks. With Sen asking me straight on if I was Jewish, it seemed to me I was in big trouble. This conversation was about to spiral downward in a nasty way.

There was no point in denying the obvious, however, so with the dread rising in my heart as it thumped ever louder, I replied, "Yes, I am Jewish."

There was a brief silence. Mystic, lying on the floor to my right, inquired a moment later as would a cute little schoolgirl: "Do Jews believe in God?"

"Yes, they do," I replied, professorially.

I waited for Sen's violent outburst. The seconds dragged like hours.

Finally, he surprised me. "That's cool," Sen said. "I like Jews. Jews and blacks is the same. You shoulda told us you was Jewish. If we'da known you was Jewish, we wouldn'ta grabbed your ass on the street. Oh, well."

Who woulda thunk? Sen liked Jews. I breathed a sigh of relief. He wouldn't have kidnapped me if he had known I was Jewish! I couldn't make this stuff up.

Ren jumped in. "Steven, where were you going when we picked you up?"

"My name isn't Steven. It's Stanley. I was on my way home."

"Oh, shit . . . *Stanley*," Ren said with emphasis. "I'm sorry. Steven is the guy we did this to last night."

"What would you be doin' right now if we didn't get you?" Sen asked, changing the subject.

"I guess I'd be home sleeping."

"What about later on today?"

"Well, I would be at work today. I have a meeting first thing in the morning that people expect me at." I thought I should let them know that in several hours people would start looking for me. "Also, today is my birthday. Those tickets in my wallet are to take some friends to a concert at seven tomorrow night. I guess people will be calling me today to wish me a happy birthday."

"It's your birthday?" Sen responded. "Oh, shit. We grabbed the mother-fucker on his birthday!" Everybody in the room burst into uproarious laughter. Ren's tight-jaw snicker echoed to my left. Sen: "Sorry about that, man. If all goes well at the bank, you may still get to see your concert. Just don't fuck with it tomorrow."

"Happy birthday, Stanley," Ren said with cheer.

"Thank you very much," I responded politely.

"Happy birthday, Steven," D said.

"It's Stanley."

"I'm sorry," D responded. "Happy birthday, Stanley."

"Thanks."

"Happy birthday," added Mystic.

"Thank you," I replied.

"Happy birthday, Stanley," Sen said. "Man, it's your birthday. You need a present. How 'bout a blow job for your birthday, man?" Sen generously offered the services of his colleagues.

Somehow the offer just didn't seem all that attractive to me. But I had a problem that I could see right away. If I said no, they might think that I didn't like or respect their women. That the white lawyer didn't like black girls. They might kill me.

With all the cheer I could muster, I answered Sen, "Thank you so much, but I'd rather not."

"C'mon, Stanley. It's your birthday. You deserve somethin' nice for your birthday."

Ren merrily joined in the fun. "Yeah, Stanley. How 'bout a blow job to celebrate your birthday?"

In addition to not wanting to insult their women, I knew that if I crossed the line in the direction they were pushing me, the whole thing would spin out of control. I had enough problems keeping it together with what I had faced so far. I was still fairly cool, letting my adrenaline and the fight to survive keep me on track. I was responding nimbly to their inquiries, a trial lawyer and street-tough kid giving the best performance of his life. A blow job in this macabre comedy of a room would violate me, tearing down my inner shield and the ability to defend myself. Besides the private psychological impact it would have on me, it would also have a practical impact in the room. As long as I sat there dressed, with my shoes on, even though I was totally within their control, I retained some element of dignity to which I could cling. They still respected me. A blow job would bring me down to a base level. I would be just another fucking john. That would make it a lot easier for them to feel good about putting a bullet or several through my head. I needed desperately to win this little tug-of-war, but I also could not afford to piss them off.

I politely declined again. "No, thank you," I said with subdued cheer. They didn't push the issue any further, for the moment. I quickly said to myself the *Sh'ma Yisrael,* now that Sen had reminded me that it might be a good idea to pray.

SEVEN

THINKING IT OVER

He spit it out, in words that sit roughly in my memory like this.

"You afraid of us.

"This ain't no game to us. You strange to us, that's why we dangerous.

"This is serious. You should have plenty fear of us."

Yelling: " 'Cause we is dangerous, so dangerous, our whole group is dangerous."

Fucking right, I thought. The fact that Sen had his fill of McDonald's, his fill of sex, and that he liked Jews didn't shut his violent ass down. He was one mean dude. He lay on the mattress across from me. Suddenly, from out of the blue, he had erupted with a vicious stream of verbal abuse. He ranted and raved at a pitch that was so scary, and so underscored the precariousness of my situation, that again I felt the urge to plain laugh out loud at the absurdity of my pitiful condition. Sen continued, just screaming at me:

"Nigger shit; you shot to death. Only the strong survive. I hold my heat under my seat. I'll cut you up, I'll fuck you up my black hole, I'll suck you up. A nigga used to be assed out, but now he's holding several money market accounts. You strange to us, that's why we dangerous." He yelled at me like he was ready to kill.

Ugh. This Sen was one sick gangster kid. With one big thick hand on my bank accounts, he could feel the power and it felt good. I was scared out of my mind. This motherfucker would snuff out my life with a gun or a knife, put a bullet through my heart and just for a start. I remained frozen in sheer terror, silent and unflinching, hoping he would not act.

But a bizarre realization slowly crept up on me. He wasn't yelling at me at all. Sen was singing. Sen was singing along with the music on Hot 97 droning out of Ramos's stereo. Busta Rhymes's gangsta rap from one of New York's top commercial radio stations was the perfect accompaniment for a true-to-life kidnapping. Suddenly it was as though we were in a musical—*The Sound of Music,* or, better, *West Side Story*—and someone had written a nice little ditty for Sen, to fill in the time between when he asked his victim whether he had prayed and when he finished the job.

Gilbert & Sullivan this was not. The background music to my life was the Beatles, the Rolling Stones, Elvis Costello, Motown, Jimi Hendrix, as well as show music, Cole Porter, Mozart, whatever. Men and women who sang of love and lost love and fear and desire; that's the music I would have on in the background while I sat around my apartment paying bills or chatting on the phone. Recalling early romantic frustrations, I could hum along with "Teenager in Love"; if I broke up with a girlfriend, I could find solace in Paul Simon's "Fifty Ways to Leave Your Lover" telling me to "make a new plan, Stan"; if I was driving fast on the highway, I could think about "Radar Love"; and if I was feeling good about New York, Sinatra would support me. These songs were my culture and helped to form my very personality.

The background music to Sen's life was death, rape, pillage, kill, destroy. When you see a young man like Sen sitting next to you on the subway on your way home from work, cut off from the rest of us by the headphones of his Walkman or iPod, blaring in his ears is a message urg-

ing him to kill a cop or to abuse a woman or to beat the shit out of somebody. Fuck 'em up with your pea shooter. These words filled his soul,
forming Sen's very personality. And now he was facing me with a song in
his heart.

Suddenly, a set of footsteps appeared on my aural-only screen. Somebody else had entered the room. The person plodded determinedly, obviously someone who belonged there and who scurried to and fro in a
way that said they were looking for something.

"How you doin,' Honey?" Mystic asked, soft and friendly.

"Yo, Honey, whussup," Ren chimed in, Sen not far behind.

"Where are my damn panties?" Honey demanded to know. "I left
them on the towel rack in the bathroom. Who the hell touched them?"

Mercedes covered herself quickly, defending lest the tirade sweep her
in. "I didn't touch your panties."

"I ain't seen 'em," added Mystic.

The boys were too amused at her predicament and had too much gun
power to care to mount similar preemptive defenses. "How'd you lose
your panties?" asked Sen, without sympathy.

Honey didn't answer Sen, but plodded out of the room with the same
fierce determination with which she had entered. She returned a moment later, livid.

"Who the hell threw my clean panties on the floor? I better not find
out who threw my fuckin' panties on the floor. This is my fuckin' house.
Whatever goddamn motherfucker threw my damn panties on the floor
had better watch they ass 'cause I'ma fuck 'em up good." She stormed
about the room, in no particular direction.

Honey was a real charmer. She had taken the trouble to hand-wash
her underwear and hang the pair fastidiously upon the bathroom towel
rack. Somehow, though, the clean pair of underwear had ended up on
the floor in the bathroom, along with the rest of the mess of clothes that
covered the floor of the apartment. Self-pride was hard to come by in this
place. In the lumpy apartment world these young souls had created, you

walked on your own and other people's clothing. Having washed those panties and meticulously separated them from the rest of the underlying mess in this hovel, Honey would suffer no incursions on that one small zone of pride. Nobody had better go near those panties if they knew what was good for them.

"I didn't touch 'em," defended Mystic.

"I didn't touch your panties," echoed D, emphasis on "panties." The boys didn't care to get involved any further.

Honey continued on and off for the better part of an hour in a frenzy of cursing and threats to fuck up whoever had had the nerve to drop her freshly washed panties on the floor.

Sen changed the subject. "Stanley, you got your checkbook on you?"

"No."

Following a pregnant pause, Sen continued. "Maybe we should go to this guy's apartment and get his checks."

Visions of Sen and Ren slipping past my doorman and into my pad brought the bile of fear and revulsion to the top of my throat, but it also gave me an inkling of hope. Maybe they'd get caught.

Ren did not respond. Sen fell silent in apparent contemplation. Then he opined, "I guess you don't got to worry about none of this, Stanley."

"What do you mean?"

"I mean we takin' your money and all. You can make it back, no prob- lem. You got your fine education, your good job. It don't matter to you if I get your money. You'll just make it again. You had every privilege given to you. In the street, you was wearing that trench coat, looking all fancy; that's why we grabbed you 'stead of somebody else.

"I got nuthin'. I deserve to get somethin'. I can take that money and do a lot with it. Go places maybe. My share of the money can give me a real start. Maybe get me the hell out of here. Rich white guy like you ain't got to worry about none of what I got to worry about. You know what them cops do to you out here? Bam! Every day they be fuckin' with nig- gers for nuthin'. A black man can't walk the street without some motherfucker cop bustin' his head. You don't know what it's like. My moms was a crack addict. You got everything handed to you."

Like hell I did. He didn't know or care what I had to go through to get that bank account. Education had given me that opportunity, but still, the money was accumulated the hard way. At the law firm, I would grab a few hours' sleep on the floor of my tiny windowless office as I slaved the nights away preparing a sixty-page memorandum on the law of real estate brokers' commissions. *I* was not spending *my* nights smoking weed and surrounded by a harem of women.

But more important, while my beginnings were not as humble as Sen's, my childhood had been pretty rough. My parents divorced when I was twelve years old. The two-bedroom apartment on the fourth floor on Albemarle Road was a boiling pot of yelling and hurt feelings. With my father out of the house, my mother was short of cash just to live on. I had next to no money to buy comics or candy or ice cream or to ride the old wooden roller coasters in Coney Island, and I was too young to get a job. My older brother Josh took mercy on me and slipped me a few bucks he earned as a delivery and stock boy at Church Pharmacy. I also learned at an early age that I could supplement my buying power by sliding stacks of comic books under my dungaree jacket when the shopkeeper wasn't looking or stealing balloons from Lamston's variety store with a deft hand and a careful eye and a steely heart. I permanently abandoned stealing when I was finally old enough to get a job, any job, first delivering dry cleaning and then at the candy store.

I was even arrested, though not for stealing. One day I was writing graffiti on the subway with a couple of other little white boys. As we pulled into the Beverley Road station one of my dumb friends stuck his head out the window to check for cops. Cops patrolling subway platforms look for people sticking their heads out of the subway cars to check for cops. One burly Irishman picked the three of us munchkins up. If our moms hadn't come to pick us up right away, three soft white boys would have spent the night in Spofford House, a juvenile detention home in the Bronx, where we would have been beat up, raped, or worse. Luckily, I was spared that particular ordeal.

Now, granted, my small difficulties weren't nearly as bad as having a crack addict mother and no father, like Sen. After the arrest, I knew that if I got in any more trouble, my career chances were shot, especially if I chose law. Still, I wanted this guy to separate me from the sea of whiteness and understand that I hadn't gotten everything handed to me on a silver platter. If he knew I'd had hardship, I thought he would have less appetite for my blood.

I tried to convince him. "My life has not been so easy. My parents were divorced and things got pretty rough. I've had lots of problems."

Sen wasn't buying it. "You'll make it back. You got your fancy education. I ain't got nuthin'. No opportunities. I got to do this to survive. My share of the fifty thousand is gonna go a long way."

How they decided to take fifty thousand dollars and not the whole lot was never clear to me. But I could see from Sen's response that there was no advantage in arguing the point. My problems were nothing compared to this guy's, and he would not be listening to my honky blathering. To Sen, I was not a person of complexity; I was a person of complexion.

Lying back on the mattress, playing with his gun, Sen mused, "I wonder what I would get for this if we was caught?"

Ren had no answer to offer. I was certainly not about to interject my own legal speculation. Of course it depended on how far they took it. A prosecutor grabbed for several hours and then set free would be worth one sentence. A prosecutor found belly-up in the Gowanus Canal would be a different matter.

"I don't care," Sen continued musing. He was philosophical. "Prison ain't so bad. The way I look at it, life is about living. You alive, you living, that's it. It don't matter much whether you're out here or inside, either way you are alive. Prison ain't shit."

I had heard no clearer testimony in favor of the death penalty than Sen's on-the-scene philosophical musings. All the bushy-eyebrowed academics would sit around and debate whether the threat of death made people less likely to kill. I had always felt that the death penalty was right in principle. The thug who once held a knife to my father's thoat in an elevator certainly would have deserved to die if he'd ended up killing him. The robber assumed the risk by putting the lives of others on the line, so it made sense to me that the robber's life ought to hang in the balance as well. That was how I felt in the abstract.

In practice, though, I knew that the court system was not perfect and that injustice could and did occur. If you were black in America and accused of killing someone, you were far more likely to face lethal injection than if you were white. Whatever color you were, if you killed a black man in America you were far less likely to be electrocuted than if you killed a white man. Sadly, black blood was worth less than white blood. And the almighty dollar trumped even the race card. One African-American known to everybody committed murder in cold blood and is walking around, free. A dream team of lawyers were able to buy it for him. It was very high-priced, that freedom, but he could afford it. These sorts of rank injustices made me question the death penalty in practice although the principle made good sense to me.

But Sen had added a new wrinkle. Killing me with no death penalty could only mean going to prison, but this guy didn't care one bit if he was sent to prison—he would still be living, inside or outside, and that was good enough for him. It was clear to me at that moment that the only thing that might make Sen think twice before loosing a TEC-9 submachine gun or a .45 automatic pistol on me was the chance that he might have his own life taken away as retribution for the loss of my life. As much as I never wanted to see an innocent put to death, at that moment I needed the death penalty, badly.

"I better not find out who knocked my fuckin' panties on that dirty floor," Honey interjected predictably.

"I wonder what I would get, but like I said it doesn't matter much." Sen continued discussing with himself.

"And who's seen my tampons?" said Honey. "I can't find my tampons."

"Not me," D said.

"Not me," said Mystic.

Honey continued, "Where are my tampons? I might as well have my damn period, anyway. I ain't gonna get me no dick." The boys had had their fun with the other girls before she got there and she got left out. She was a nasty little creature.

"I better get me some money out of this deal," she added. Seeing as how it was her apartment, she wanted her rightful cut of the take.

I sensed another person wandering the hallway outside the room. I heard footsteps and a couple of slamming doors.

"Looks like Ramos is home," said Ren. Ren went out in the hall and I could hear him speaking to someone in a muted voice. He came back in and sat on the bed next to me.

"Yo, Stanley," Ren started.

"Yes?"

"Didn't I knock something out of your hand when I grabbed you in the street?"

"Yes."

"What was it?"

"I was carrying a box of cookies and a book about the Vietnam War."

"Oh shit," Ren chortled, with that same muted giggle that sounded like he forgot to open his mouth when he laughed. His laugh made him sound like some species of tropical reptile. "Chh . . . Chh . . . Chh . . . ," gurgled his laugh.

Sen thought this was extremely funny also. "I guess you won't be eatin' those cookies," he gleefully exclaimed. "I wonder who got those cookies lyin' there on the street? Maybe they still lyin' there right now or maybe somebody eatin' them in the street, right now. Oh, shit."

East Tenth Street seemed a million miles away. While these characters were raving about everything under the sun, I had to exercise supreme self-control not to react, or when called for, to react in a friendly, nonconfrontational way. I commenced very deep breathing. I had taken a few yoga classes. They teach you to take long, deep breaths in, filling your lungs, feeling your abdomen and lower back expanding with it, down into the buttocks, and then to release the breath very slowly. This technique provides extra oxygen to all the organs, actually exercising you internally, and has a calming effect that reduces anxiety. Silently, I took one deep yoga breath after another and released it slowly into the room. Without the deep breathing, I'm not sure I could have made it through the madness around me. I had to stay calm to have any hope of staying alive. I had unfinished business to attend to back on Tenth Street—fighting for the environment, looking after my parents, and then building my own family, starting with a little romance with a cute girl with lots of brown curly hair whom I had just met on the subway a few hours ago.

"If we wasn't in Brooklyn, maybe we could go back and get those cookies for you," Ren said with a laugh, thinking he was Henny Youngman.

Confirmation of location. I thought we were in Brooklyn because Lucky had asked me in the car if I had ever been on the BQE, but we also could have crossed over into Queens. I took note.

Sen lowered his voice and turned Ren's joking 180 degrees into solemnity. All the deep thoughts were starting to give him cold feet. "I'm not sure this is such a good idea, mah man." He spoke quietly to Ren.

"What you talkin' about?" Ren asked.

"We plannin' to take Stanley here to the bank in the morning so he can take out fifty thousand. I'm not sure it's such a good idea."

"Why not?"

"Three African-Americans is gonna drive up to a bank with a Caucasian," Sen explained. "We wait outside in the car while he goes in and asks for fifty thousand in cash. It don't look right."

"I thought one of us was gonna go in the bank and watch him," Ren added.

"Sure," said Sen. "That's even worse. It just don't look right. You can't just walk into a bank and walk out the door five minutes later with fifty thousand dollars in cold cash. They gonna start askin' questions. They gonna wanna know what Stanley here is doin' with us. That shit ain't gonna work."

"Lucky ain't gonna be happy hearin' you talkin' like this. Ehabuuga ill-wugga eba ealrugga uckinabuuga adoumat usugga."

Sen followed Ren's lead into the language. "Dontababugga ouyugga inktugaa wehava ooklugga ou fotouselverugga. Ikeaathugga disre damina-buuga atwugga hetinksugga. Ownugga atugga mahsaynugga ro."

"But Sen." Ren reverted to English. "He's not gonna be happy."

"I just don't think three African-Americans can just walk up to a bank with a Caucasian and withdraw fifty thousand dollars. It don't look right. We better talk to Lucky when he gets back here at four o'clock."

I decided to take the plunge. "Actually, you're right. The last time I went to the bank and tried to take out a lot of cash, they made me see the manager. It took me close to an hour before I was able to walk out of there."

That was true. Most of the time I elected to keep still, speaking only when spoken to. Any self-started statements, comments, or inquiries on my part might have sparked their plugs, so I was keeping my yapper shut. Here, though, I saw a chance to convince them to let me go. In my mind's eye, I could envision things spinning out of control at the bank in the morning and me smack in the line of the cross fire. I was also desperate to get my father out of harm's way. If the bank plan was canceled, they didn't need him anymore. Plus, I was able to enter the fray with the timeworn negotiator's technique of opening with a line of agreement with my adversary.

It didn't backfire. "See," Sen said to Ren with added assurance. "This shit ain't gonna work. The bank ain't just gonna let us walk right in there and walk right out with Stanley and fifty thousand. I ain't doin' it. I'ma tell that to Lucky when he get here. You with me?"

"Aright, aright, Sen." Ren sought to calm him. "Let's talk to Lucky when he get back from his fiancée."

"Yoosenabugga irenugga doabonowabugga wentou iskre wugga," Sen replied.

"Maybe this guy needs to go to the bathroom," Mercedes commented. "Steven, you need the bathroom?"

"My name is Stanley." I felt that certain boundaries ought to remain firm, including my correct name.

"Sorry."

I actually had needed to pee for quite some time but was afraid to ask. "I could use the bathroom."

"All right, D, you take him and I'll follow right behind," Sen instructed.

Mercedes stood and grabbed my hand, urging me up off the mattress. As she did so, I could hear Sen across from me jump up on military red alert, pounding the floor with his big feet and cocking his automatic weapon at me. Ren fluttered up off the mattress from his perch next to me, too, and I could hear the metal of his machine gun as he, too, prepared it to fire. My Spidey sense alerted me to grave danger as they feared that I would try to pull a fast one on the trip to the toilet. The atmosphere was too hot for me to stand up. They could shoot me by accident.

I resisted the tug, not moving. "Whoa, whoa, whoa." I raised my voice. "Just hang on a second. I am just going to the bathroom," I declared. "I am not going to do anything stupid."

The tension dissipated a bit like air from a balloon. Sen was still on hyperalert but he responded reasonably. "Fine. I'll follow behind you and I've got my gun pointed right at your back. Don't do nuthin' stupid. D, you lead him in."

I allowed Mercedes to pull me up, and I creaked to a blindfolded stand. She led my hand toward the threshold of the room, my body following slavishly while Ren's and Sen's hands prodded against my back in the same direction. I walked like a blind man, each step a test of the water, a feeler, a sapper in a minefield. The floor under my shoes was lumpy with the scattered clothes. The forward direction and the acoustic reac-

tion of the sounds of our steps and their voices told me we were in a narrow hallway leading toward the front door where I'd been brought in.
Sen and Ren followed behind Mercedes and me, guns keeping things
clear inches from my back. We walked a long way down the narrow cor-
ridor, and we must have been very close to the apartment entrance when
Mercedes pulled me to the left into the bathroom.

"All right now," she said. "I'm gonna stand out here. You just go
straight ahead and the toilet is straight ahead."

Without a guide, I was more blind. With the most hesitating and
stunted of steps, I lurched forward atop clumps of clothing layering the
bathroom floor, and inched my way toward the rear of the room. D
could see that I would not know how many baby steps to take before hit-
ting the toilet, so she walked behind me and piloted me in verbally.

"You almost there. Keep goin'."

"We right behind you," added Sen, to keep me on my toes.

My right shin hit the hard white bowl. I found that I could "see" a lot
with my other senses even though my eyesight was removed, and I could
see the toilet in my mind's eye from the touch with my shin. I stood in
front of it and did my business. A huge sigh of relief came over me as I
finally released the physical pressure I had been feeling for hours but had
intentionally not addressed. Two or three sets of eyes were on me from
behind as I performed this most private of acts. I zipped up and reached
over to where the flusher should be, pulling it and hearing the loud
swoosh that would take the liquid through the pipe and to the Newtown
Creek sewage-treatment plant. Then, with the same level of military
alert, my captors led me back over the lumpy floor, where I was returned
to the seated position on the mattress. Once I was back safe with no incident attempted, the gang calmed down and slipped back to their positions on the mattresses or the floor.

It was quiet for several minutes. Maybe people were taking in the
bathroom trip and the fact that I did not try to run for it when I got near

the apartment door. Finally, Sen mused further. "Man, Ren, when you woke up this morning, could you have imagined that this is what we would be doing tonight?"

"Nah, Sen," Ren responded.

Now I had conflicting information. First they told me they had done this to a guy named Steven the night before. Now Sen was acting like kidnapping someone was something fresh. It seemed that Sen was trying to throw me off the track.

"I mean, who woulda thought when you woke up this morning that we would pick this guy up and bring him back here to Queens?"

Sen was definitely dissembling. First they said Brooklyn. Now it was Queens. I figured we were on the border, but now it could have been either.

The front door creaked open and then slammed. The leader of the pack was back.

"What *time* is it?" asked Sen, indicating that he intended to compare it with the time Lucky had said he would return.

Ren answered. "Four o'clock."

The leader was punctual in his business affairs—due at four, he arrived at four. "What's up?" he greeted all.

"Yo, Lux, we gotta talk," said Sen.

Ren and Sen rose and exited the room with Lucky to conference away from me and the girls. I could hear them sparring excitedly in the hallway but I had a hard time making out the details. It sounded like Sen was making his pitch to give up the $50K and the trip to the bank in the morning. Suddenly, Lucky appeared at the doorway to the room and directed a query in my direction:

"What did you say you *do* for a living again, Stanley?" he asked.

"I'm an Assistant U.S. Attorney."

This time he got it. He turned back toward his companions in the hallway and exclaimed, "Oh, no, the FBI will be after us."

Sen had already told me how much he hated New York City cops.

But despite their perceived toughness, the threat of getting caught by the New York police did not feel so real to these boys. They wanted nothing to do with the FBI.

Lucky, Sen, and Ren talked in the hallway for another minute or two in muted tones. I then heard the pounding of feet on the floor, with Sen returning to his place across from me, Ren back on the mattress beside me, and Lucky following behind. Lucky stood over his flock and announced their new plan.

"Stanley, I got good news for you," he said with his characteristic businessman twang. "I'm gonna come back here in a few hours, at seven A.M., and we will drive you back to your neighborhood and drop you off."

"Thank you," I responded.

In the presence of Lucky's command, Ren and Sen let him do the talking. "I'll see you all later," Lucky said, and left the apartment again, presumably to go back to his fiancée's. I breathed a sigh of relief, tasting freedom if he kept his promise.

EIGHT

NEW YORK STORIES

With Lucky gone and a promise that the kidnapping would end soon, the room around me turned quiet, punctuated by the rhythmic breath of sleep. Of course I couldn't tell if everyone was asleep, and I was pretty sure that if Ren and Sen were sleeping, it was with one eye open, like a couple of mean cowpokes in a dime Western who had just rustled up some cattle and were guarding them as the embers on the campfire still glowed a faint orange. Around six in the morning, my fatigued body took control and I must have dozed off for about twenty minutes, but for most of the time I succeeded in staying alert.

As I lay awake, I decided that if I made it out of there alive, I was getting the hell out of New York. This had gone too far. How could a normal person live here? In New York City, when two cars collided in even a minor accident, both drivers would jump out and start cursing, fuck this, fuck that, fuck you, fuck your mother, no matter whose fault it was. Either driver might throw the first punch or pull a baseball bat out of his trunk and start swinging.

Incidents were common, such as one that happened to my brother Josh. Josh was five years older than me, bigger and stronger. One Saturday night he was riding home on the D train at three-thirty in the morning from a night out at the bars in Greenwich Village. In Manhattan it wasn't bad, but once you crossed over into Brooklyn late at night, there was evil lurking. My brother saw them coming out of the corner of his eye. Three Hispanic men were mugging people at the other end of the car, slowly making their way toward him. As they moved, they selected only the white passengers for mugging, passing over the blacks and Hispanics as surely as the Lord passed over the houses of the Israelites when he slayed only the Egyptian firstborn. The doors between subway cars were locked to keep passengers safe, so there was nowhere for Josh to run.

When they reached him, the mouthpiece of the group said, "Give me your money."

Josh hesitated; they weren't flashing weapons. He looked at them, waiting for them to make a move or move on.

"Don't fuckin' look at me," snarled the mouthpiece. No positive IDs, please. One of Mouthpiece's partners was tall and silent, with a distinctive gimp walk. Gimpy pulled the switchblade out, not even bothering to open it. Seeing his life spilling on the floor, Josh knew it was time to pull the wallet and lose the money. We had an ex-con in my building, nice guy, who had told Josh that you can ask for your papers back when you're getting mugged, and they'll usually do it, so Josh asked. Mouthpiece pulled the cash out and accommodated by throwing the wallet on the floor at Josh's feet.

Now Mouthpiece noticed the gold Florentine-finish *chai* pendant my brother had chained around his neck. *Chai* means "life" in Hebrew, and it is a Jewish good-luck piece.

"Gimme the chain," barked Mouthpiece.

Josh was on the ropes. The chain was a bar mitzvah gift from our mom. "Look, this really means a lot to me . . . ," Josh hedged, his voice imploring Mouthpiece to let it go.

"It means more to me," responded Mouthpiece, as he slipped his fingers between the chain and Josh's neck and tore it off with a quick jerk.

The three hopped off and ran to the DeKalb Avenue station. Josh reported the incident to the cops. The next morning, Josh was still sleeping it off when the detective called. "We think we've got your guys. The MO sounded a lot like a guy we knew. Will you pick him out of a lineup and press charges?"

"Yes," Josh responded, adamantly.

Mouthpiece was easy to pick out. With Gimpy, Josh picked his mug shot, but then when he saw the lineup he told the cops he wasn't so sure. "All right," said the detective, disappointed, "we'll have to let 'im go." As the lineup was released, Josh kept staring through the peephole, and now that he saw him walk in that distinctive hip-hop, Josh knew a hundred percent it was Gimpy.

"That's him!" Josh exclaimed. "I can tell now for sure from the walk."

"Oh, shit," said the detective. "It's too late—you already said you couldn't pick him."

So Gimpy walked, but Mouthpiece, actually known as Angel Pabone, got to see Josh again in a court of law. They held a hearing during which a parade of crime victims appeared to tell the judge what this Angel had done to them. When Josh was waiting to testify, with nobody looking for an instant, Pabone shook his fist at Josh, mouthed "Fuck you," and then ran his index finger across his throat to show Josh what would happen to him if Pabone ever found him. Josh testified anyway, after getting permission to keep his home address out of the court record in the hope that Angel wouldn't pay us a visit someday. Pabone got three years, with a minimum of six months before he'd be out on the street doing it again.

My thoughts were interrupted as Honey came into the room, muttering under her breath, "I better not find out who messed with my damn panties."

"Why don't you put somethin' on instead of walkin' around with no pants and no panties?" Ren, stirring, advised derisively. A bottomless

Honey. Thank God for blindfolds. She gave no answer to Ren, and her plodding steps grew fainter as she exited the room. I assumed that she went back to her own room. I returned to my private thoughts.

The muggers of my youth would address their prey with one of a few predictable mantras, seemingly learned at the same school of mugging. The predominant pitch was, "Yo, lend me a dime." By casting it as a loan, they could claim to the police that this was not a mugging at all. Just a routine financial transaction. But we knew it meant "Yo, lend me a dime, or I'll punch your face in."

My main response to this sort of hustling was to pretend not to have any money. My friends and I devised a series of stash spots in which to store cash, in our socks or sometimes in the breast pocket of a dungaree jacket, where money was less likely to be found. I would respond, "Sorry, I don't have any money." To which I would then be faced with the next predictable line: "All I find I keep?" To avoid getting beat up or stabbed, you'd then let the guy go through your pants pockets and find nothing because the little money you did have was stashed away.

At one time when I was around fourteen, my friends and I got sick of this nonsense. John Maynard was a friend of mine from up East Nineteenth Street in Brooklyn; he's one of the guys I got arrested with on the subway for writing graffiti. He lived with his mom and two brothers after a rough divorce transported his pops to other locales. John was a good guy, but a little confused and angry, as he became the father to his two little brothers when he needed a father himself.

One night John and I were out at the Boys Club on Bedford Avenue, where we were the only two white boys swimming in the pool or smacking a Ping-Pong ball. On the way back home, one lone wolf kid, no bigger than us, approached and we let him go through our pockets, even though we were two against one. There was a new gang in the neighborhood that we had reason to fear, living in a building on Ocean Avenue, but John and I were still embarrassed that we had allowed one guy to do that to two of us. So the boys on my block had a powwow in Chucky Donoghue's bedroom, and we decided that the next time it happened we were going to stand and fight.

It didn't take long to get the chance. A few weeks later, Chucky and I were on our way home on Albemarle Road when a single kid about my size approached the two of us. Chucky was tiny but wiry strong from athletics at Catholic school. The kid asked, "You got any money?"

I responded, "Sorry."

"All I find I keep?"

I glanced over at Chucky with a raised eyebrow that said I wanted us to honor our pact and jump him. Why the hell should he get to go through my pants pockets? Chucky was feeling cautious, though. "Don't do it, Stan," he said. "He may be in a gang."

I buried my pride and indignation and allowed the budding young criminal to go through Chucky's, then my pants pockets. Then the mope reached for my jacket's breast pocket, where I had stashed a couple of dollars. I couldn't let him have it. Furious, I jumped on him, pushing, punching, grabbing, then wrestling. I got on top of the guy and tried to keep him down. From there I cried out to Chucky, "Don't jump in unless I'm losing." That way, if the kid was in the new neighborhood gang, and I won, at least I could say we had a fair fight. And if I lost, well, who wants to get beat up?

My assailant rose up and bucked me off him like a bronco. I grabbed him from the side and scissored him into my trademark headlock, shoving him and his head up against the steel shell of the nearest parked car. He couldn't move, though his legs were kicking away. We stood there in stalemate, till he started yelling, half crying, "Let me go, motherfucker, let me go." I was not about to let this punk loose so he could start punching me or pull a blade. Meanwhile, some nice middle-class folks who lived in the neighborhood came by. As adults, they didn't yet understand the new waves crashing over the neighborhood. In time, they would and they would leave. For now, they demanded to know why I was holding this poor kid in a headlock up against a car. I said, "Fine, you hold him while I walk away and I'll let him go."

They did just that. Two adults kept him in tow while Chucky and I walked home by a circuitous route so the guy wouldn't realize where we lived.

Two weeks later, I had to pay for my indiscretion. Sure enough, he was part of the new crew that had moved in on Ocean Avenue and they were starting to beat up and mug kids in the neighborhood. This time I was out with John when we were approached on Albemarle near Flatbush by the mugger I had held down, named Skip, and two of his friends and gang members. They bore down on us.

Skip shoved his body up against mine. "Yo, man," he intoned. I could feel his hot breath on my face. He had a nasty scar under his right eye. He looked like he hadn't had a bath in recent memory. "I should get you for what you did. Why you say to your friend that he should jump in if you was losin'?"

I guess I had a career as a lawyer written in the stars. I put on a real sincere look and started explaining. "Look, man," I said in my white-sounding voice. "I just didn't want anything to happen. I didn't want anybody to get hurt, you know, 'cause if somebody got hurt, the cops would be down on us all." I stared at him with sincerity and a "You must understand" look.

My bullshit had the guy confused. He seemed to buy it. "All right, but it better not happen again," he warned hesitatingly.

"Fine, no problem." John and I slipped away as quickly as we could.

Sitting on the mattress now, I heard the wail of a police siren, as a police car drove by maybe a block or two away. So close but yet so far. "I'm in here!" I thought. "Come get me," I screamed, telepathically. If only they knew what was happening, that a kidnap victim was on just the other side of a closed door, they could bust it and yank Jonah from the jaws of the whale. My hopes were vain ones. The siren roared by and then disappeared into the early-morning quiet.

I wondered exactly what Brooklyn neighborhood I was sitting in right now. In the silence of the room, I strained my ears to pick up noises from outside. Hot 97 was off. A new day was dawning over the City of New York, and I could feel daybreak penetrating my scarf blindfold. I was glad that they said they were going to take me home soon, but I definitely would not believe it until it was all over. I sat peacefully, listening to see if the street noise would yield any clues to where we were. I could hear the occasional roar of a New York City bus. We were on a major thoroughfare.

Every so often I also heard the sound of planes overhead. Not the deep, distant roar of a transatlantic or national jet, but the lighter buzz of a small commuter or private plane. Maybe even a propeller sound. To me our presence in the flight path seemed to say we were near Kennedy Airport, consistent with Lucky having asked me if I'd ever been on the BQE, which flowed into the Belt Parkway. Maybe we were in one of the old prewar buildings that still stood in the vicinity of Starrett City, a huge mixed-income housing complex that went up near Kennedy Airport in the 1970s.

I could also hear seagulls, faint, distant, but present. That would put us near the water and also was consistent with us being near Kennedy Airport, located on the shore of Jamaica Bay and its wildlife refuge, which I and my office worked to protect.

Growing up, my parents had suffered from the crime problem, just as Josh and I did. Our neighborhood had "changed," the white euphemism for saying that blacks and Hispanics had moved in. My mother had nothing against anybody moving in, but she ignored the changing landscape at her peril. I was twenty-one and just transitioning from college to law school. Mom had the night out in Manhattan where my brother was choreographing the lighting for a dance performance. Alighting from the

D, one of the new residents of the East Nineteenth Street where I had played stickball and punchball and spud and ring-a-levio slipped up behind Mom and grabbed her purse. She held on tight. The kid pulled back and she was shoved to the ground with a sickly crack and a fractured foot. It was a black kid who made off with her purse. Other blacks on the street helped her and pointed out which building the kid had escaped to, so she could tell the cops. Even after this incident, she wanted to stay, as she felt, rightly, that this was her home and no one should be allowed to push her out. Josh and I pleaded, cajoled, and threatened for several weeks before she finally agreed to get out of there.

I had a dream not so long ago in which I was back in that apartment looking out on the street. It seems very unfair to me that my family was robbed of its home because of the lawlessness of its new residents.

As I sat on the mattress, I racked my brain to think of where the decent places might still be in America. If I made it away from this one alive, I was going to find some safe place to live and raise a family.

I began to devise a plan. If they dropped me off near my place in the Village, in order to return to the apartment in Brooklyn or Queens, probably somewhere near Kennedy Airport, they would drive back over one of the East River bridges, the same Brooklyn or Manhattan Bridge they had transported me on the night before. As soon as they let me go, I would call the NYPD and explain quickly who I am and what had happened. I would ask them to float helicopters over the East River bridges, fast, and look for a brand-new black Lexus returning to Brooklyn and headed out on the BQE. It shouldn't be too difficult and they ought to be able to follow the car until patrol cars could corral the Lexus.

Then I realized there was no way a police operator was going to listen to some oddball claiming to be an Assistant U.S. Attorney who had been kidnapped and was now asking the cops to float helicopters over the East River bridges. It would not happen. I thought I would use a little political pull instead. As soon as they let me go, I would call the head of our office's Criminal Division, Valerie Carpacci. She surely had connections with the NYPD at the highest levels. I would ask her to place an emergency telephone call to her top-level NYPD connections, and get them to order the helicopters to float over the East River bridges and interrupt Lucky, Ren, and Sen before they even made it home to sleep off the night's pleasures.

I thought it was a good thing that the plan was for Lucky to come back at seven A.M. to take me home. I needed to be at my office by nine-thirty. Another Assistant U.S. Attorney who worked with me, Michael Greenberg, had scheduled a meeting with lawyers representing community groups suing to stop the reconstruction of the Gowanus Expressway, an ugly segment of the BQE that sliced through communities and cut the depressed Red Hook off from the rest of the borough. After calling the cops, I would shower and go to work. I couldn't leave Michael hanging.

"Stanley?" Sen broke into my thoughts.

"Yes?"

"Lucky'll be back soon. We gonna take you home. You gonna go in the trunk and we'll drive you back to where you live."

It felt like a flat heavy iron had been smashed against my head. In the trunk?! That was way too risky. Bodies go in trunks, not people. If a live one was in a trunk, he was cargo, and could be dropped off at the nearest dump or river, probably with a little extra lead inside to weigh him down. Plus, even if their intentions were at this point benign, I might suffocate in the trunk. I was really frightened.

"I don't know. That makes me a little nervous."

"What makes you nervous?"

"Driving back in the trunk. I might not be able to breathe back there."

"Don't you worry, Stanley, man. We got a special compartment between us and the trunk that we use to keep our guns on you while we're drivin'. You'll get some air through there."

"It still makes me nervous. What if it's not enough? I could also die from carbon monoxide poisoning."

"Don't worry, man, we'll get you back," Sen reassured. I didn't like this plan one bit. It was near to seven A.M. and a few minutes later Lucky came barging in.

"You ready to go?" Sen demanded.

"Whussup?" added Ren.

"No, we can't take Stanley back right now," Lucky twanged. "I left the car outside my fiancée's. Somebody broke in, smashed the window, and stole my radio. I need to go to the car place and get them to fix the glass before we can bring him back."

"He's worried about goin' in the trunk," Sen noted with a touch of sadism. "He thinks he'll suffocate."

"Aw, you don't need to worry about that," Lucky soothed authoritatively. "I'll be back in a couple of hours, as soon as I can get the glass fixed. Should be by around nine o'clock. Then we'll take you back."

"Thank you," I replied. Now I was really getting the hell out of New York and moving someplace safe like Seattle or Burlington, Vermont. This place was so sick that even the robbers got robbed.

NINE

THE VIEW FROM THE OUTSIDE

By nine A.M. Lucky had broken his promise and failed to reappear at the Ramos estate. A greater frequency of buses outside said that the world was stirring from its sleep as a new day dawned. With a few flaps of their wings and some favorable gusts, the seagulls, still flying intermittently overhead, could make it to the East River shore at the Brooklyn Heights promenade, for gorgeous views of Manhattan and a taste of polluted fish. Only blocks from the promenade, around nine A.M., a few miles but a world away from me, Michael Greenberg rolled into the U.S. Attorney's Office for the Eastern District of New York, a short subway ride from his Park Slope family home. It was a sunny and clear but cold winter's day.

About a week and a half before, I had come to Greenberg and offered him the opportunity to litigate the Gowanus Expressway case. I explained to him that it was an environmental land use case that had been brought by various community groups that fell roughly in the path of the highway, and that it challenged the decision of the federal and state transportation authorities to reconstruct a portion of the highway and add a High Occupancy Vehicle (HOV) lane from Brooklyn Heights out to Bay Ridge.

I had my own approach to environmental lawsuits that were filed by citizens' groups against the government. In the Gowanus case, we had a legal defense that could have gotten us out of it on a straightforward motion to dismiss. That would have been easy, but I took our Department of Justice mantra seriously. We were supposed not just to win cases, but in doing so always to seek justice. *"Tzedek, tzedek, tirdof"*—Justice, justice (meaning justice pursued in a just manner) you shall always pursue— taught my ancient religion. The words peered down at me from my office wall in the painting Scott had bought for me in Israel. I wanted the client U.S. Department of Transportation to meet with the community groups who had sued us and to make some fair concessions to settle the case. This was good for the government's relations with the public; it was potentially good for the project, as the debate might yield positive changes in elements of the reconstruction; and it would avoid knock-down, drag-out litigation, which was always a risk and a definite time waster. I personally wanted to see them add a bike path under the highway as part of the settlement. It was a big mistake for New York not to have a comprehensive bicycle path system, as they do in Amsterdam and other European cities. And I'd be one of the first happy kids spinning his wheels on that path. But don't get me wrong; if the case could not be settled fairly, I would litigate for my clients like a bat out of hell and make sure that ugly injustice did not flow in our direction, either. Many a plaintiff learned their lesson with me as they rejected fair compromise only to find themselves holding a bag with nothing in it.

Greenberg's wife nearly took his head off when she learned he was considering my offer. Ever since he had read *The Power Broker,* Greenberg liked to pontificate around his house on the excesses of Robert Moses. Greenberg lectured his wife: "Sure, the guy was brilliant, and he did a fantastic job of building the main infrastructure and a lot of the wonderful cultural resources in New York." But, Greenberg thundered further from the armchair: "The guy was absolutely ruthless, and he abused a lot of people and a lot of neighborhoods along the way." Two of Greenberg's examples from *The Power Broker* were the Cross Bronx Expressway, which is so famous as a hellhole that nothing more needed to be said, and the Gowanus, whose construction cut off Red Hook and destroyed commerce along Third Avenue, formerly home to the Third Avenue El, a subway line that brought customers to the avenue rather than keeping them away. Since he had interrupted bagel bites for quite some time around their kitchen table to bemoan Moses's excesses, Greenberg's wife found it quite ironic that he would now take on a case that defended the existence of the Gowanus Expressway. But you couldn't roll the clock back fifty years, no matter how much the community groups wanted it. The multitudes of migrants that poured from Bensonhurst and Bay Ridge into Staten Island when the spout of the Verrazano Bridge opened were not about to quit using their internal combustion engines to get to the city. If they weren't driving on the Gowanus, they would be jammed up honking and spewing monoxide down on the streets where the people who were suing us lived. So Greenberg ultimately agreed with me to seek the best solution for the environment consistent with practical reality. A couple of days after I offered, Greenberg accepted, with strict instructions to try to get a bike path under the highway.

But where was Stan this fine morning? I had scheduled the meeting and then roped in Greenberg to litigate the case, since it was now his. It was his first environmental case, and since he was new to the alphabet soup of acronyms that made up environmental law, I had agreed to appear at the meeting and back him up. He was a little bit nervous and I promised to meet with him early, at nine A.M., to ventilate the issues before the others arrived. We expected ten to fifteen officials and attorneys from the state and federal departments of transportation, as well as the state Attorney General's Office, an imposing collection. Greenberg sat in his office, looking over some papers, fiddling with a paper clip, admiring the photo of his beautiful kids on the desk, and watching the clock tick by, 9:10, 9:15, 9:20, and no sign of Stan.

"Damn, why isn't Stan here?" Greenberg thought. Then he realized that in the days prior to the meeting I kept mistakenly referring to the meeting as being scheduled for Friday, but it was actually on Thursday. Greenberg had repeatedly corrected me, but for some reason I couldn't seem to get it straight. So he thought that maybe I messed up and had the day wrong.

But as 9:30 turned into 10:00, and the conference room filled with attorneys and transportation officials, and I had still not arrived for work, Greenberg grew more concerned. He did not feel prepared to handle the meeting alone, and it wasn't like me not to show up. Still, he sat in the conference room, first with the federal highway people, then the state people as they arrived, and did the lawyer's pre-business preening banter, trusting that I would pop in with a delayed-subway story or some other reason that the dog had eaten my homework. Finally, frustrated that Stan Alpert, the guy who'd called the meeting and who was supposed to run it, had still not shown up, Greenberg went out and asked my secretary to call me. She got nothing but an answering machine. Greenberg then sauntered down the hall to the next most likely source of information, the paper-strewn office of my best friend in the Civil Division, Scott Daniels.

Scott could see that Greenberg was worried. Scott was not concerned himself. Plus he decided to cover me in case I was playing hooky. He told Greenberg, "Stan probably took his birthday off."

Greenberg knew that something was wrong with the picture. Fine, take your birthday off, but not this day, when you have agreed to be at a big meeting. Yet between my having repeatedly been mistaken about the day and Scott telling him that I probably took my birthday off, Greenberg decided not to set off the alarm. Maybe I got drunk the night before and was home nursing a hangover. Maybe I was sick. Greenberg decided not to approach the chief of our division, because if I was AWOL he didn't want to dime me out. Back in the conference room, Greenberg sheepishly announced that the meeting would proceed without me. "He could never get the date of this meeting straight, anyway," Greenberg informed them, "and he's probably not in the office today at all because it's his birthday. Let's just start."

"Well, Stan kept asking us to change the date because he told me he didn't want to go to a meeting on his birthday," said Ken Dumont, an attorney with the federal highway office. "I guess he decided not to come." Then he added with a chuckle, "He's probably either drunk or right now he's with some lucky lady at her apartment."

Though I drink socially, I hadn't been really smashed since college. And just across town I was with Lucky and some ladies, not exactly what Ken was thinking.

Poor Greenberg now had to wangle a skeptical group of federal and state officials into believing that he knew what he was doing, whether he did or not. Greenberg, while out of his league on the environmental stuff, was no shrinking violet. "Meetings I do well," he said to himself, and he rolled up his sleeves and spent the next several hours trying to move the government mountain toward the community Mohammed.

It was a long meeting, as environmental meetings tend to be. There were periodic jokes about my sleeping off a drunk or spending the day with some chick I'd managed to pick up in a bar.

TEN

PALPITATIONS

Unintentionally, the jokes were very cruel. As morning became afternoon on my thirty-eighth birthday, I was tortured, not physically but psychologically. Lucky had contended that he would liberate me around nine A.M., but he failed to reappear and no one seemed to know why. About two or two and a half hours after Lucky left, around ten or ten-thirty, Ren and Sen decided not to be captive themselves.

"Ramos," Sen yelled to Ramos, who was in another room.

A moment later, Ramos appeared in the doorway. "What's up?" he asked sleepily.

"Me and Ren got to go. We want you to watch Stanley here for us. You hold my gun."

"Where's Lucky?"

"We don't know. He said he was goin' to get his window fixed and he'd be back soon. He ain't showed up. We can't wait for him, so you stay here and watch Stanley for us till Lux gets back."

To my left and across from me came the sound of feet slipping into shoes and laces rubbing as they were tied. Where were they headed? They could be young enough to be in high school. Were they going to school? I doubted if they had jobs, but it was possible. The two trudged out of the room. The apartment door slammed behind them. The girls still lay around me, in various states of sleep or wakefulness, but now there was a new sentry at the watch.

Ramos asked, "Do you want something to eat?"

"I feel sorry for him," Mystic interjected. "Can we get you something to eat?"

"Nobody asked you. I asked him," Ramos said.

No longer just worried about drugs in the food, I began to feel ill. An emaciated gurgle originated in my solar plexus and dissipated silently in the vicinity of my coccyx. "No, thank you. I'll wait till I get home and then I'll get something to eat."

Even as the words came out, I realized it was wishful thinking. Where the hell was Lucky? At this point, I was definitely missing the meeting with Greenberg and the transportation wonks. But was Lucky serious about taking me back at all? Why hadn't he returned? As early morning stretched to the hour of first coffee breaks, it became more and more inconceivable that I might be reintroduced to my Village habitat. After all, once the business day got going, if they really did try to bring me home, the average man on the street would think it a little weird that three nonchalant twenty-something desperadoes were strolling about town with a live suit on a leash. Lucky's broken promise to come back by nine A.M. and return me began to resonate as a cruel joke.

"You sure?" Ramos asked.

"Yeah. Thanks a lot, but I'll just wait till I get home." It is a timeworn negotiator's technique to lock in concessions that have already been made, incorporating their validity into your jargon.

Without food or sleep, I weakened. One thirty-two-ounce Snapple the night before was not sustenance. Ramos grew silent. For a short while, I could only occasionally hear him playing with the gun, but soon even that grew quiet. Lucky remained absent, and the clock slowly ticked. It did not appear that Sen and Ren were planning to return any-time soon. The girls breathed heavy, asleep, and Ramos lay still, though probably awake. I was very, very tired. My brain buzzed a little faint. The weakness in my flesh assaulted my conscious decision to stay awake for clues. Finally, around eleven A.M., I succumbed to bodily need and slipped mercifully into sleep.

My tired and drained body did not awaken for two hours. Did I dream? And, if so, what did I dream of? I really don't recall; all I recall is nothingness. A deep black sleep.

I was resuscitated by the not unpleasant voice of a little girl, Mystic, as she arose from her own, less troubled slumber.

"What time is it?" she opened.

Ramos, wide awake, answered: "It's five after one."

"One P.M.!" I exclaimed inside. Was I ever getting out of there? What happened to Lucky's promise to take me back? Where was he, damn it? I was in trouble.

"I'm hungry," said D, with the raspiness of reawakening in her speech. By now I recognized each one by voice.

"Let's get somethin' to eat," agreed Mystic.

"Where the hell is Lucky?" asked D.

"I don't know," Ramos responded. "I can't wait for his ass forever. I got to be at work."

"Who's hungry?" asked Mystic.

Ramos turned to me. "Yo, Stanley. You hungry?"

I could resist the food no longer. As a twelve-year-old boy I fainted in the synagogue on the holy day of Yom Kippur, when Jews neither eat food nor take water for twenty-six hours. I'd played ball in the street the whole day before and then I didn't eat well before the fast. That same blackout-from-hunger feeling, with the little dots before my shuttered eyes, was on the way. If I wanted to be strong enough to make it out of here, I needed to refuel.

"Yes, I am."

Mystic was enthusiastic. She exuded, "All right, Stanley, we gonna get you a ham and cheese sandwich. I'll go down and get it."

"I'll go with you," D said. "Luis . . ." she sang as "Loo-iss," "what you want?"

My computer registered the information. I now had his full name.

"I'll have ham and cheese on hero with mayo," said Mr. Luis Ramos.

I'm a Jew. I don't eat ham and cheese. Ham is not kosher. With cheese, mixing milk and meat, makes it worse. It would have nauseated me. "If it's no trouble, I'd prefer a turkey sandwich," I interjected.

"No problem," Mystic said. "How you like it?"

"With a little mayo, please." Lettuce and tomato would have cost extra, so I dared not ask for it.

"What you wanna drink?"

"Anything is fine. Iced tea, Coke, whatever. Thank you very much."

"You're welcome," Mystic responded pleasantly.

Ramos: "Where you goin' for the sandwiches?"

"We goin' to the Salaam Shop," D answered.

I locked it in. A small deli in a neighborhood in Brooklyn near the Queens border, or in Queens near the Brooklyn border, called the Salaam Shop. I recognized that there was a chance that they were using "salaam shop" as a generic description of an Arab-owned store, but I thought it more likely that "Salaam Shop" was the proper name of the deli. That shouldn't be too hard to find.

"Here's twenty dollars out of my own money for the sandwiches. I better get paid back," Ramos said.

"See you in a few minutes, Stanley," Mystic said.

"Okay," I responded with all the enthusiasm I could muster.

The two girls walked out the door.

Luis Ramos and I were now alone. I think Honey must have been sleeping it off in her own room.

"Stanley?"

"Yes?"

"I'm not part of this whole thing, you know."

"What do you mean?"

"I mean, I just live here. I wasn't part of no plan to take you here or nothin'. I'm only doin' this 'cause I got to. They told me to watch you. If I didn't do it, they would think I was gonna snitch on 'em. I can't mess with it, you know what I'm sayin'?"

"I understand." I could have asked follow-up questions. I could have led the conversation somewhere, maybe convincing Ramos to let me go. But it was far too risky. He might have flown into a rage, and if he reported it to the others, I could end up beaten or dead.

I fantasized. What if I just told Ramos, "Ramos, I'm gonna get up and walk out that door. If you want to stop me, you can kill me, because you're holding their gun. Right now you didn't do anything yet, just sitting here, but if you kill me, you'll be in big trouble. Killing a federal prosecutor is going to cause way too much heat and you might get the death penalty. You better not try to stop me." It was pure fantasy. Instead of getting killed, I might have just gotten whacked on the head with the gun. Ramos was a jailer just as sure as the others were, whatever his purported motivations, and I was willing to bet he was getting cut in on some of my money for his trouble. The thought of myself bloodied or blacked out, and the situation unraveling toward my death, was enough to deter me.

"Where'd you grow up, Stanley?" he asked.

"Brooklyn."

"I don't know nothin' about you. Things ain't been so easy for me, man. My fuckin' father is Dominican and he is one mean fuck, man, that motherfucker never treated me right. He wasn't good to my mother. He wasn't good to me. He used to fuckin' hit me for nuthin'. He hit my mother, too. I hate that motherfucker."

Ramos's voice boomed in anger. "Man, if he was here, I would beat his ass so bad he would wish his ass wasn't born. Mother . . . fucker."

Good thing I didn't try to work on him. He was not stable. Lucky was scheming and evil; Sen was vicious and genuinely frightening; Ren did not seem so bad, even if he did hold the gun on me in the street; but Ramos was disturbed. I needed to step gingerly here.

"But my stepfather—he Puerto Rican—he's a good man. I love him. He bought me that stereo in the hall. He's good to my moms. He brings me things when he comes back from bein' away."

My mental computer logged the info. Luis Ramos had a Dominican father and a Puerto Rican stepfather. More clues, in case I got to use them.

"I think I hear something." Ramos's footsteps left the room. I was alone. He did not return immediately and I could not hear any activity.

I had been keeping my eyes tightly shut under the scarf blindfold. But if I leaned back a little on the mattress, I could tilt my head slightly upward so that the angle looking out from the bottom of my scarf would face across the room. I risked it. I pulled back in my seated position, very slowly. I tilted my head slightly upward. My eyes creaked open, like old rusty dungeon doors.

The room was filled with bright sunlight. There was a wall across from me and the mattress Sen had spent the night on, which Ramos had been occupying a moment before, a blanket heaped unmade on top. Across was a small brown dresser, and I attempted to discern the items on top, but from my angle I couldn't make out much. Suddenly, Ramos's footsteps sounded from the hall and I snapped my neck back and shut my eyes tight.

I heard the outer door slam.

"The girls are back with food," Ramos informed me.

Footsteps drew nearer down the hall. "Hi, Stanley. We got you somethin' to eat," sang a cheery Mystic. "You like Welch's grape?"

"Sure," I responded. I always did like Welch's grape juice. Flintstone juice.

"Here's your sandwich," Mercedes said.

I heard the rustle of sandwich paper at my feet. A clinking sound put

89

a glass bottle of Welch's grape in front of me, too. I sat up, in a semi-cross-legged position, the food between my legs, reaching. I felt a smooth, paper-covered, slightly squishy cylinder, a hero sandwich. I tore the tape holding it shut and spread the paper open before me. Reaching further, I felt a glass bottle, sixteen-ounce shape, and I tore the plastic outer lid layer off, shook it, and with relief heard the cap's safety seal whoosh open. I drew a long sip and cool grapeness soothed my parched throat. I bit into a hero roll and felt the texture of the meat and some lettuce on my tongue as the smell and taste of turkey confirmed the right sandwich.

We all sat there eating, me my turkey, they their ham and cheese. "Is it all right?" Mystic inquired.

"Yes, it's good." Objectively it was a fine turkey sandwich, normally a tasty pleasure. But I chewed disconsolately, mechanically inserting raw material into the machine. I finished just half the hero, slurped down big glugs of grape juice on top of it, and had had enough. I gently folded the sandwich paper wreckage over the top of the remaining half and junked it at my feet.

Mystic and Ramos began conversing in Spanish. Her speech mannerisms bespoke an African-American, but now she had shifted to Spanish. Perhaps she was a black Hispanic.

"No me importa," Mystic said.

"Sí, pero podríamos disfrutarlo sin otra . . ." They spoke fast Spanish, hard to follow, hard to understand for a gringo still taking Spanish classes. A few words here, a few words there I could pick up. They had no inkling that the white establishment man might be eavesdropping on their chatter. It was too fast for me, but my Spanish was good enough to know that they were not saying anything of particular relevance to me. I continued to concentrate on their speech, in case I could learn anything.

". . . pero no tenemos ningún idea donde el está . . ." Ramos continued. I perked up.

"Where the hell is he?" Mystic said in English.

Now back in her language, Mercedes also wanted to know. "What I'm sayin' . . . where the hell is Lucky? He was comin' back by nine."

"What time is it?" Mystic asked.

"One-thirty."

"I ain't waitin' here forever. Stanley is theirs."

"Right?" D said with a rising lilt. "He better get back here soon."

"I'm sick of this shit," Ramos added. "I hope Lucky gets back here soon 'cause I wanna get the hell out. I got to take pictures and I got to go to work." I wondered what he needed pictures for.

"Why don't you go call him?" he added.

"All right," Mystic said. "I'll go downstairs and call him." That told me there was no phone in the apartment and that she would go to a pay phone outside.

Mystic continued, "What's his number again? Nine-one-seven-six-nine . . ." Her voice trailed off. "Oh, shit, he's here." She reminded herself that I might be listening. I was.

In law enforcement, telephone numbers can be a crucial tool. Every time a person calls on the phone, there is a record of the number of the outgoing call on that line, and there is a record on the receiving end of a call coming in from that number. Even though you only get the telephone numbers, and not the substance of the conversations, the fact that telephone calls were made can be put to good use before the jury.

I had done it myself not so long before, prosecuting an environmental crime. A Hasidic Jew, Isaac Itzkowitz, set up an illegal asbestos "rip and tear" job, failing miserably to honor the mantle of piety that he purported to wear with his religious garb. Asbestos is harmless if contained and doesn't get into the air. But if it becomes airborne, a single fiber may lodge in a person's lung and cause cancer and diseases by such unpleasant names as asbestosis and mesothelioma, and can kill you ten or twenty years later. For this reason, the law requires that the asbestos removal work area be cordoned off with plastic, with wetting to prevent dust, with negative air machines keeping the air pressure in so if dust is created none escapes, and full-length moon suits with gas-mask respirators to keep the particles off the workers. Studies from asbestos manufacturing plants showed that wives who did laundry would also be killed from the dust that rode home from work on their husbands' jeans.

Itzkowitz sent two low-wage off-the-books workers, one black and one Hispanic, into a residential building to tear out asbestos pipe wrapping dry and dusty, with no wetting equipment and no protection. He walked himself off the job site when the dust started to fly. He didn't give a damn about the possible death sentence he was imposing.

The landlord who saved a few thousand bucks by paying Itzkowitz to send in the two suckers instead of hiring a legal contractor was a partnership, of a Hasidic family named Landau, which owns many buildings in New York City. The Landau partnership pled guilty to the illegal job, but Itzkowitz, their contractor, hung tough and decided to leave his fate to a jury. One of Itzkowitz's defenses was that the illegal asbestos job was actually his worker "Slim's" personal side job and that he, Itzkowitz, had no connection to it.

Enter the phone records. The New York City environmental cops busted the job at around four P.M. on a Wednesday. They called the Landaus to find out why the hell they had tenants walking around the basement laundry room with washing machines and dryers covered with asbestos dust. Well, at the moment of truth, with the environmental cops breathing down the Landaus' neck and possible felony charges looming, who should one of the Landau boys be calling several times over the next hour or so, as demonstrated by the phone records? None other than our defendant, Ike Itzkowitz. How do you like that? Itzkowitz said he had nothing to do with it? So why were he and the Landaus running up the phone bill just at the moment that the job got busted? The jury agreed with us, based on Slim's testimony as corroborated by the phone records, that it was Itzkowitz's conspiracy, and the Honorable John Gleeson sentenced Itzkowitz to twenty-one months in a federal prison.

Unfortunately, however, 9-1-7-6-9 was not enough to locate the perpetrators of my conspiracy. 917 would be Lucky's cell phone area code. So all I had of his seven-digit cell phone number was 6-9. The numbers alone would not lead the police to these defendants. I locked it in anyway. The number would corroborate my story. Once Ramos's crash pad was discovered, the subpoenaed records of Lucky's cell phone would show a telephone call coming from a pay phone in the neighborhood of this apartment, at right around the time that I would testify the phone call happened.

Realizing she had started Lucky's cell phone number inadvertently in my presence, Mystic got a little nervous.

"I think he can see out of that blindfold," she stated suspiciously. My blood pressure took a jump. I could hear the gentle patter of stocking feet, barely perceptible, coming toward me. A light breeze indicated that her hand was waving back and forth in front of my face to determine if I could see anything. I sat completely still, completely expressionless. Though senses other than sight perceived her, I would not let on to that perception, or it would confirm for her that I could in fact "see" out of my blindfold.

She backed up. She groused, "I don't know. I think he can see out that blindfold. I don't trust this shit."

"I can't see." The simple declarative with no obsequious effort at explanation was the most highly credible.

She hesitated a few feet from me. Defeated, she shifted focus, "All right, I'm goin' to find out when the hell Lucky is comin' back to take care of you. It's not my problem." Her feet trekked out and the front door slammed.

Five minutes later, she was back. "He ain't answerin'. I don't know where the hell he is, but he better get back here soon."

"You're telling me?" said Ramos. "I'm not watchin' this guy all day. Yo, Stanley, I wanna get out of here."

"I understand," I said gently.

"This motherfucker is probably gonna go to the cops. You gonna go to the cops, Stanley?"

"Look, nothing much has happened so far. Lucky should be taking me back soon." I spoke calmly. I carefully implied an offer not to go to the police, conditioned upon my prompt release. Ramos did not respond.

Even though I was in law enforcement, perhaps I might have considered not going to the cops, if they let me go unharmed and if it was just about me. But I knew full well that if these loose cannons didn't kill me, in short order they'd whack somebody else. Some frat boy who thought he was a tough guy would let them know how much trouble they'd be in if they harmed one hair on his head or would tell Ramos that he and Ramos ought to be duking it out one-on-one, mano a mano, fair fight, no guns. Or some nerd would have started crying or begging them not to hurt him. Either one of those behaviors would be an engraved invitation to whomp him upside his head. For the sake of the next guy, I had no moral choice other than to pursue. Not to mention the death threat against my father. Not going to the cops, if they didn't kill me, was out of the question.

I managed to speak soothingly to Ramos, but I was starting to lose it. There's a limit to how far you can push even a scrappy litigator. I felt physically weak. I was emotionally spent. The longer they kept me, the more their power grew and the cheaper my life became. If you get away uncaught for all this time, you know you can do with the motherfucker whatever you want, and neither Giuliani's guys nor the FBI will ever figure out who dumped the body.

My stomach was already jumping, and now the rest of my body got into the act. The nerves took control, and my heart rate increased alarmingly. Sometimes it pounded and then skipped a beat. Sweat spontaneously blanketed my face and the back of my neck. My nostrils detected the sick-sweet smell of unwashed and unanointed underarms, growing stickier. Breathing became uneasy, shallow and too quick. My head buzzed with faintness, even with the turkey in me.

However, feeling sick could be an opportunity. Too much time had passed since Lucky's broken promise, and Ramos, D, and Mystic were caught up in confused speculation as to the next element of the war plan. I decided to up the ante.

"I'm not feeling too well," I started.

Ramos: "What's wrong?"

"My heart is bothering me. My heart is skipping and I'm sweating. I hope I'm not having a heart attack."

The move was strictly calculated. I felt lousy, but that was beside the point. There was an off chance that if the current cast—particularly Ramos, who was arguing for a minimal role in the conspiracy—thought I was going to die right there, they might lose their nerve and let me walk. Ramos had not thought through how to handle a dead body.

"Oh, shit," Ramos blurted with alarm. "I hope he's not gonna mess us up. What's the matter with your fuckin' heart?"

"He don't look so good," said Mystic, sympathetically.

"He better not be fuckin' with us," Ramos thundered. "What if he's lyin'? What's Lucky gonna say? Shit! I hope he ain't makin' this up. Yo, Stanley, if you know what's good for you, you better not be makin' this shit up."

I was walking on a tightrope. Instead of motivating these mopes to release me, the prospect of me dying on my own was destabilizing. Ramos was a pressurized, somewhat paranoid kid, and the thought of trouble with Lucky or the law from my premature expiration was more than he could handle. The gun in his hands could erupt out of frustration or even by accident. I wasn't too sure I could afford to leave this genie out of the bottle for long.

I backtracked, still seeking credibility, my best currency. "Well, my heart doesn't feel so good. But this happened to me before. I had some problems before—I had to wear a heart monitor for twenty-four hours to see whether I had an irregular heartbeat." That was true; it happened during one especially stressful period at work. "But it was nothing—the test came out okay. I'm sure it'll be okay."

"Well, all right then," Ramos responded.

"I'll be okay," I reassured them.

Ramos reiterated, "I don't want no problems here."

"No problem."

Then I added, "By the way, would you mind if I used the bathroom again?" This time it was more relaxed, since D knew the drill. She grabbed my hand, guided me up, and led me to the bathroom, with Ramos trailing behind. I urinated for the audience and then they returned me to my spot on the mattress.

The room stayed mostly quiet as the afternoon hours wasted away. Hot 97 still offered its background mix of gangsta rap instructing these kids to fuck somebody up. Honey came by wanting to know where the hell Lucky was, but nobody could help her. Mercifully, she seemed to have abandoned the panties routine. She plopped down right next to me on the mattress.

"I better get somethin' out of this."

"What?" asked Mystic.

"I mean, this is my damn place. I want some money out of this," she said, turning her head and voice toward me.

"You right," said D. "They better cut us in for all this trouble."

Ramos: "Look, why don't you all shut up. It's my place, too. I want to get the hell out of here and go to work."

"You think you so bad," Honey responded, with characteristic nastiness in her voice. That conversation died.

My heart as a tactic was over, but as the palpitations and stomach unease and sweaty neck, face, and underarms persisted for another hour, I feared that I might pass out or vomit.

As the hours ticked, though, I slowly regained my composure for the next round. The human body is capable of many miracles. Maybe it was the turkey sandwich, and maybe it was just some quiet time while I did deep yoga breathing, but gradually my heart calmed, the sweats left, and I was able to sit calmly and revitalized. Over the past few years, I had had some lower back problems from too much time in a desk chair. Sitting erect on a mattress for all these hours, under extreme stress, I would have expected discomfort or even pain. Somehow, though, perhaps it was adrenaline or some other self-protective mechanism, my back actually felt fine. Wait till I told my chiropractor that being kidnapped was good for your back.

I sat and pondered my fate as the glow of afternoon behind my blindfold dimmed, and a second night with my captors loomed.

Only one more item of note transpired during that long dog day afternoon. At approximately five P.M., the intercom buzzer rang from downstairs. Ramos jumped up to get it.

"Yes?" I could hear him saying from down the hall.

The response was a woman's voice, though from where I sat I couldn't make out what she was saying. Ramos reentered the room. "What's Stanley's Social Security number?" he demanded. "It's Lucky's fiancée, and she wants it."

D answered, "I got it." She walked across the room and I could hear her handing a crinkling piece of paper to Ramos. They must have copied it off a Social Security card I carried in my wallet.

"Thanks," he said. He walked back out in the hall and announced my Social Security number to Lucky's fiancée on the other end of the intercom.

Now at least I understood something. They were using the extra time to commit additional crimes against me. Maybe the Social Security number would help Lucky commit credit card fraud. Or maybe he needed to speak to my bank again and manipulate funds between accounts. The news was not helpful. There was now a rational reason for them holding me all day, so that they could use my cards without me canceling them the minute I walked. My role as a continuing cash cow ran smack up against any plans for release. I had good reason to cry, and I was nervous, but I was so worn out by now that it was hard to even feel the news.

Eventually, the front door opened and in walked Sen and Ren, returning home upon the evening like two regular working stiffs. They entered with an air of exuberance, upbeat, flush with the day's experiences.

"Yo, Ramos. Whussup, mah man?" intoned Sen, cheery.

"Whussup, Ramos?" Ren greeted him.

"Whussup? I been stuck here with this guy all day. Where you been and what the hell is goin' on?"

"Aw, don't worry, man," Sen said. "We just had a little change of plans here for our man Stanley. Yo, Stanley, how you doin'?"

"I'm okay, thanks."

"What change of plans?" Ramos asked.

"We gonna keep him till midnight so we can get one last thousand dollars off of his ATM card. Where's my gun, Ramos?" They got me before midnight Wednesday for one hit, only $800, since I had taken out $200 that afternoon for the Freedy Johnston tickets. After midnight, they would have gotten the next hit for $1,000. By keeping me till midnight again, they could do it one more time.

Sen's words soothed and stung at the same time. At least they were still planning to release me. Thank you, God. I promised that if I ever got out, I would always try to be a good person and do many acts of charity. But the thought that I was stuck for another six hours felt like iodine on an open wound. I had had it. But what could I do? Hang tough, Stanley, I told myself. This is the big one. Just stick with it a little while longer, boy.

ELEVEN

WHERE'S STANLEY?

Meanwhile, back at the U.S. Attorney's Office, just an hour or so earlier, the Gowanus meeting finally broke up. As people rose to depart, Greenberg chirped to the others, "I guess I'll discuss these things with Stan if I can ever find him."

"Yeah," somebody quipped sarcastically. "Make sure you wish Stan a happy birthday when you see him."

Dumont, the federal highway attorney, also kibitzed to Greenberg on the way out, "Tell Stan we missed him, but the meeting went well. Maybe we didn't need him anyway."

It was baffling to Greenberg that I hadn't showed up or called in. He went back to Daniels's office. By now, Daniels seemed a little concerned but not overly so. "It's not like Stan not to call in," he pondered with Greenberg. "On the other hand, he probably takes his birthday off, so maybe that's what it is."

Daniels was wrong. I have always worked on my birthday because I am always too busy not to. My father, Benjamin Alpert, sitting in his rental apartment on Ocean Parkway in Brooklyn, knew that. He couldn't fathom why his son had not returned birthday calls all day. He had called the office a few times and left me voice mails. He tried me at home and left a message on my home machine. He called the office yet again, finally getting through to a secretary who informed him that I had not been seen there all day. As day turned into evening, he wondered what in God's name had happened to his son.

Just like my father, Dan Moretsky started out annoyed but grew seriously concerned by the time day faded into the early winter's night. From the Organized Crime Unit five floors up from mine, Moretsky called me two or three times and left voice mails with no response. It wasn't like me. Normally the phone calls to Stan were a welcome break from the hectic pace of figuring out how best to smash the tentacles of La Cosa Nostra. Dan tried more mafia cases than anybody else the office had ever seen, and I think he'd lost only once. To break up the tense job, he and I would deliver jokes, laughing hysterically as we performed endless imitations of people, some imaginary, some famous, and some famous only to us. We would chatter on like two teenage girls about women we were dating or trying to date, Dan still thrilling when he met somebody cute who was nice to him in this hard-ass city. Dan knew he could normally count on getting a quick call back from me, unless I was in court or out deposing somebody or interviewing a witness. Particularly today, when his voice mail messages asked me to remind him exactly what the plans were for that night, as to when to meet who where, he had a hard time fathoming my newfound distance. Dan also tried me at home, and the long beep on my answering machine told him I had a lot of messages that had not been retrieved.

Finally, he boarded the elevator and rode downstairs. My office was empty, but it contained a riddle. My computer was on, making it look like I *had* been in that day. On the other hand, the voice mail light on my phone glowed a steady red, revealing that I had not retrieved my messages. Dan walked four doors down the hall to Scott Daniels's office, and found Scott with a worried look on his face. Scott related how I had failed to appear at an important meeting and had not been seen all day.

"It doesn't look good, Scott," said Moretsky, a bit grim. "This is not like him at all—not to show up and not to call. And not to pick up his voice mail from the outside. He knows we're expecting to meet him tonight."

Dan was grim because he knew the evil this city was capable of from lots of firsthand experience. The West Seventieth Street building in which he grew up had been framed by a whorehouse on one end of the block and a welfare hotel on another. Dan's mother had been mugged in the elevator of his building by a man who held a lead pipe over her head. His family apartment had been burglarized. A former model smoking heroin on the fourth floor of his building had fallen asleep on the mattress and set the place on fire. A lady who kept a zoo of pigeons, cats, dogs, and other creatures down on the third floor checked out on pills with her Cuban husband in an apparent suicide pact, after she was diagnosed with some terminal illness. From above, one could hear the doctor in the penthouse apartment being whipped at night by his gay lovers while strung out on drugs, and he eventually bought it one night at the hand of one of his lovers or possibly one of his dealers. Then there were the three twenty-something young women from the Midwest who moved in downstairs. Three Hispanic men with knives forced their way into the apartment and raped them all night long. The girls left the city shortly thereafter, not to be heard from again.

Daniels was a city boy, too, but in Rockaway things were a little more peaceful and Scott was always the hardheaded optimist. Between football at Cornell and volunteer service in the Air Force reserve, his orientation was always the go-getter, never-say-die, storm-the-beaches approach. "You're right, it doesn't look right, Dan," he said. "But there may be some explanation. Maybe he took the day off for his birthday and ran off someplace. Let's not get too worried. We're due at the Bottom Line at seven o'clock, so let's just go there and hopefully everything will be fine."

"Okay, Scott." He didn't want to argue the point, but in the pit of his stomach Moretsky had little doubt that something was mightily amiss. The two prosecutors walked out the door for the subway.

At the same moment, a hot evening breeze was blowing past my grandmother's modest condominium apartment in West Palm Beach, Florida, fifteen hundred safe miles away from Brooklyn.

My grandma Flora moved to West Palm Beach, Florida, in about 1973, with dear old Grandpa Leo, who died on the eve of his ninety-second birthday in 1995. Flora and Leo had scrimped and saved their pennies, she managing a toy store for the rich on Lexington Avenue, he a children's shoe salesman at New York retail outlets, and they'd saved enough to enjoy their retirement in a diminutive two-and-a-half-room condominium in the sun. The Jewish Riviera. Each winter my mom would migrate to Florida for about a month, and at this very moment she was visiting with Flora and my uncle Herbie, who lived there, too.

Earlier that day, as was their custom on my birthday, Arlene Alpert, my mother, and Flora Robins, my ninety-one-year-old grandmother, had gathered on two extensions of the telephone line, one in the bedroom, one in the shoebox kitchen. My mother counted aloud, "One . . . two . . . three," the cue to sing in unison, "Happy birthday to you, Happy birthday to you, Happy birthday, dear Stanley, Happy birthday to you."

My mother, joyous on the occasion, couldn't help but add, in a minor key, "and many mo-o-o-re."

But now, it was past dinnertime, and I had still not bothered to respond to their sweet message. "I wonder where he is," Arlene said to Flora.

TWELVE

WHY CAN'T WE BE FRIENDS?

Good thing they didn't know. Sen and Ren were back to play with their new toy.

"Whussup, Stanley? How was your day?" Ren asked, in a friendly way.

"It was fine."

"Did you get any food? Ramos, did you feed him?"

"Yeah, man. What, you think I'm stupid?"

"What'd you get 'im?"

"He had a sandwich, nigger."

Ren confirmed with me. "You had a sandwich, Stanley? How was it?"

"Fine."

D wanted in. "How you doin', Sen?" she said flirtatiously. "Hi, Ren," she added.

"How you girls doin'?" asked Sen.

"Whussup, girls," added Ren.

"We fine. Where the hell you been all day?" asked D.

Mystic concurred. "Yeah, what's goin' on?"

Honey must have walked out of the room, as I did not hear her greet the boys.

"Aw, we just had some business to attend to," Sen answered. "Let's just hang out and relax till Lucky gets back."

I knew what he meant by "relax," having seen it with my ears the night before. Hopefully love would soothe the savage beasts.

Ren plopped down in his usual spot next to me on the mattress. "How you doin', Stanley?" he greeted, as though I were an old friend.

"I'm okay, thanks."

"Gimme my gun, Ramos," said Sen. A minute later, I could hear him back on the mattress across from me, checking it, cocking it and un-cocking it. Ramos moved to the edge of Sen's mattress, a little to my left and closer to me.

"I'm glad you made it back here finally. I gotta get to work, soon," said Ramos.

Ren was a little defensive. "You can go to work anytime you want."

Ramos: "This morning y'all said Lucky would be back in an hour to take this guy back. I was stuck here all day."

"Yo, Stanley, you scared?" Sen asked, ignoring Ramos.

"I'm okay. I guess I was wondering what was happening all day."

"We had some business to take care of. We're gonna keep you till mid-night and then take you back to your neighborhood."

Ren and Sen and Ramos and D and Mystic sat quietly for a few min-utes. The breathing to the left and across from me slowed, as Ren and Sen relaxed at home after a long day out of the house.

Sen had been thinking. "Stanley, can I ask you something?"
"Sure."
"You a lawyer, right?"
"Yes."
"What kind of lawyer you?"
This, I felt, was an opportunity to make Sen think I was a good guy. I

was, after all, out there fighting for the environment. "I'm an environmental lawyer," I started. I kept off the prosecutor part.

No reaction.

"For example, I've got a big lawsuit against Mobil Oil company." I thought the fight against Goliath might impress the downtrodden Sen.

Mobil Oil, before it joined forces with the people who brought you *Exxon Valdez,* owned a huge petroleum distribution facility on Staten Island known as Port Mobil. They moved the oil out on barges, and they ran an industrial barge-cleaning operation that generated hundreds of thousands of gallons of benzene-contaminated water. Benzene is proven to give cancer to humans. Mobil routed the benzene dump loads into two huge artificial ponds on the property, let the benzene waft into the air and mixed it up with rainwater before dumping it over the side into the Arthur Kill. When the federal Environmental Protection Agency and the State Department of Environmental Conservation investigated, the lying started. Mobil's spin doctors claimed that the wastes could not possibly be hazardous given all the dilution in the open-air ponds. Better still, they reported to EPA that they sampled the wastes, and by some miracle, Mobil's samples showed that the wastes were below toxic levels. Crooks came in all styles, some sitting on mattresses and others in boardrooms.

Sen queried, "What they do?"

"They have an oil facility in Staten Island. They handled contaminated wastes with benzene in it—benzene causes cancer—illegally, for a couple of years."

"So what you gonna do, put Mobil Oil company in jail?" Sen asked with sarcasm.

"No, it's a civil case. If we win, they have to pay a large amount of money." When we first brought the case, we didn't know just how outrageous the behavior really was.

"How much?"

"In this case, it could be millions of dollars."

"Who gets the money?"

"The federal government."

Sen lashed out. "That shit is stupid, man. The poor man is down here in the ghetto, suffering, and your ass is gonna take millions of dollars and just take it for the government? That money belongs here, in this neighborhood, helping us, not in some big-ass government."

Boy, was I stupid to have brought it up. *My* sensibility was pro-environment. Take it away from the polluter and give it back to the people, to punish Mobil and put a little extra cash in the U.S. Treasury. Sen was not my ally on this one. He had far more immediate problems. The long-term risk of cancer from so many parts per million of benzene meant nothing to a man with no foreseeable long-term. Bullets or blades were far more toxic. In a perverse way he was making perfect sense. Rather than belabor my weak point and seek to convince him of the wisdom of my far more esoteric goals, I wisely shut up.

Sen saved me, anyway. "But let's get to the point, man. Can I ask you a question?"

"Sure."

"All right. It's like this. I got arrested in D.C., right? That shit was false, man, I didn't do it. So I got me a lawyer in D.C. to sue the cops for false arrest. My question is, all right . . . so the problem is when they arrested me I gave them a fake name. Can I still sue the police?"

Now I saw why he was asking what kind of lawyer I was. He was checking my credentials. Too bad I didn't bring a résumé. "Why did you give a fake name?" I asked. A lawyer needs to know all the facts. I treated Sen with the same seriousness that I would treat any client.

"Look, these motherfucker cops pick me up for somethin' I didn't do. I was scared. Why they have to pick me up for nuthin'?"

"And you say you have a lawyer in Washington?"

"Yeah, man, I talked to a lawyer in D.C. I just don't know if I got a case since I lied about my name when they false arrested me."

I couldn't tell whether Sen had actually retained someone in D.C. "What does your lawyer in D.C. think?"

"I don't know, man. I got to talk to him." Maybe Sen didn't want to come clean on the fake name because he was afraid his lawyer would drop the case. "What do *you* think?" he demanded.

Creating arguments for clients with warts was something I would see from lawyers all the time. "Well, I suppose you could argue that the reason you gave the fake name was because you were falsely arrested in the first place. That you believed the police officers who arrested you falsely were capable of doing anything to you and that you were afraid to give them your real name because they would have used it against you. So it was them arresting you falsely that caused you to keep your real name to yourself."

This was not one of my proudest moments. A federal prosecutor certainly should not be advising a thug like Sen how he can best argue that it was the policemen's fault that he gave a false name. But given my extenuating circumstances and the necessity that I satisfy Sen, I hope it can be forgiven.

"Hmm . . ." Sen pondered my words. "So you think I could sue."

"It might work."

"Thanks a lot, man."

These guys must have thought I was Jacoby & Meyers. Ramos couldn't wait to get into the act. Not only was I a cash cow with ATM and credit cards, I was a free, convenient well of legal advice, too.

Ramos: "Yo, Stanley. Can I ask you something, too?"

"Sure."

"All right, so I was in a car accident. I got hit by a taxicab. Can you tell me how much I can get?"

"Well, tell me what happened. Were you in a car or were you a pedestrian?"

"I wasn't in a car. I was walkin' in the street and this taxi hit me comin' around a corner."

As I said, my first five trials for the U.S. Attorney had been to defend the government against personal injury cases. The field was a big camel bazaar: The lawyers would bargain over the value of bodily parts (so many dollars for a fractured tibula, so many for a ruptured spleen, etc.), number of days spent in the hospital, number of weeks out of work, and allegations of long-term pain. Some of the cases were legitimate, but others involved plaintiffs lying, and it was obvious that many of the lawyers encouraged it.

An example: A gentleman who came to this country from India thought the streets of New York were paved with gold when he was fortunate enough to get into a minor fender bender with a postal jeep. The plaintiff had driven illegally in a safety zone in the middle of the road, and veered out of it suddenly to collide with the jeep. Not only was the accident actually his fault, he falsely claimed that his back hurt so much that he had to stay in bed most of the day and was only able to go on short drives of less than an hour. The challenge in these cases was to be able to prove to the court how badly these people were lying. It turns out that Mr. Fender Bender Who Couldn't Get Out of Bed was collecting unemployment insurance by telling the State of New York that he was ready and able to work and that he was out looking for a job. It also turned out that the man who said he couldn't sit up in a car for more than an hour had actually journeyed home for some of his mother's *chapati* the summer before, a seventeen-hour flight to India, sitting up.

When he got to his schlocko lawyers' office, they flipped the Rolodex to one of an industry of doctors, who wrote a medical report that put all his back problems on the accident. I tracked down his old medical records, and they showed repeated medical visits and X-rays for serious back problems *before* he ran into the government car.

His four-foot-tall and very innocent-looking wife got into the act, too. In the car with him at the time of the gentle impact, the wife claimed that she'd been sitting in the front seat, with her seat belt on, but that the force of the impact had smashed her head against the dashboard, causing permanent injury. One little problem for her: The Postal Service investigators on the scene of the accident photographed her sitting in the backseat of the car, nowhere near the dashboard. The judge was tempted to sanction the clients and the lawyer for wasting her time on such a fraudulent case, but sadly the judges almost never had the guts to take sleazy lawyers to task for the junk they put out. She was very quick, however, to toss the plaintiffs out on their ear with no money. They did not appeal.

I brought my experience to bear. "Did you go to the hospital?" I queried Ramos.

"Yeah."

"How long were you in?"

"Oh, they let me out the same day." No overnight in the hospital? Couldn't be too serious. No worse than Mr. Fender Bender.

"What injuries did you have?"

"It hurt my back. I can't remember exactly what it was called. A lumbar something."

"Have you received medical attention since the hospital?"

"Yeah, I go to a chiropractor every two weeks." Cases involving just chiropractors for back adjustments were not worth much. Even Mr. Fender Bender saw an M.D.

"And do you have any continuing pain or other problems from the accident?"

"Not too much. My back hurts a lot sometimes, like when I sit in one place for too long. Sometimes I got to take Advil. Sometimes I got to lie down for a while. What do you think I can get?"

"Do you have a lawyer?"

"Yeah."

"What does he say?"

"I dunno. I keep askin' him how much I get and he don't tell me."

"Well, it's hard to tell without actually seeing the medical records. But . . . some back problems, outpatient hospital visit, once every two weeks at the chiropractor . . . Hard to say, but I think you can get something between five and twenty thousand. Maybe like ten thousand." I really thought it was worth a little less.

"That's all right, man. I just dunno when I'm gonna get that money. I got to call my lawyer. Thanks, Stanley."

"You're welcome."

"Yeah, thanks a lot, Stanley, man," said Sen.

"You're welcome," I responded professionally. So glad to help.

"Yo, Stanley, you should join our gang," Sen gushed. "You could recommend friends that we could kidnap." Then he realized that I probably wouldn't want to recommend *friends* for kidnapping. "Naw, I mean you could recommend your *enemies* for us to kidnap. If you join with us, we could make you a lot more money than you makin' as a lawyer."

Sen laughed at his own suggestion. Ren gave his characteristic reptilian snicker beside me. How was I to respond? I was glad that they liked me enough to want to see me again, but it wouldn't be credible for me to agree to join a criminal gang. On the other hand, I certainly didn't want to defy Sen by saying no. Just the off chance that he was serious gave him incentive not to kill me. I smiled at the suggestion and said nothing.

Sen added, "You would have to recommend men. We wouldn't be doin' this shit to no woman."

Good to hear that Sen abided by standards of ethics. I just kept smiling, my eyes and my real reaction hidden under the blindfold. Now I knew why they had focused on my father and not asked about my mother. Luckily, Mom was out of harm's way in the hot sun. I wondered if Dad was all right and whether he knew I was missing, as he, too, would have called today to wish me a happy birthday.

It would only be another half hour or so before my friends went to meet me for the concert and confirmed my disappearance, as Scott and Dan would not have seen me all day at work. I wondered what they would do. I didn't worry about it for more than a few seconds, though, because I was most preoccupied with maintaining my new relationships.

There were layers of risk here. Just as I was donning faux-friendliness, so, too, they could be fronting with me.

"Yo, Stanley, man, it's a shame we had to meet under these circumstances," Sen waxed philosophic. "We could have been friends."

I just kept smiling. And I had reason to smile. Sen must have been out of his mind, but this is exactly where I wanted it to go; all my friendliness and respect were paying off. Giving and receiving legal advice was a bonding experience, as a client revealed personal travails and as a lawyer you responded with guidance and strategy. Even the powerful federal judges felt the bond when I represented them in the courthouse case— you could see it in their eyes and read it in their e-mails. Sen actually did seem to like me, and that was good.

"Yeah, Stanley, man," Ren said, not wanting to be left out. "It's a shame. We could have been friends." Reptilian snicker.

"Thank you," was all I could think of to say. I wasn't going to start fawning and saying how wonderful I thought it was that I was able to get to know them, considering that they were holding the guns and my enthusiasm would have sounded hollow. I kept smiling.

I heard a match strike flint, and even before I could smell it I knew it was weed time again. These boys were in a good mood and marijuana would put them in a better mood. I should send a check to NORML, the National Organization for the Reform of Marijuana Laws, because if it had been crack cocaine or alcohol altering their moods, quiet contemplation could have changed to kung fu kicks. The pipe passed from hand to hand, as I heard one person after the next inhaling deeply into their lungs, holding the smoke, then letting it out slowly. No one spoke while the pipe went around.

Footsteps crossed the room and somebody descended on Ren's body on the mattress beside me. "Mm . . . , baby, that shit's nice," he said to whichever girl was straddling him. Sen was down to business across from me, too, as I heard the movement of two forms on the second mattress.

Ramos was left out. "I got to go to work," he said sheepishly, and I heard his footsteps leave the room. Sixty seconds later, the apartment door slammed shut.

Across from me, Sen lay quiet as another form moved above him, servicing. He was neither breathless nor even flustered when he cordially renewed last night's offer. "Yo, Stanley, it's your birthday, man. How 'bout a blow job for your birthday?"

It sounded to me like he was getting one at the moment.

Ren liked the idea and said laughingly, "Yeah, Stanley. You should have something nice for your birthday. How 'bout a blow job? These girls is nice."

"No thank you," I demurred, appreciatively.

This was very fucked up for me. I had the same problems as before— I could not afford to lose my dignity by dropping my pants, and at the same time I did not want them to think that I thought their girls weren't good enough for me. The indignity of a blow job here was a line I could not afford to cross, as both a tactical and a psychological matter.

They left it alone until after the sounds of sex acts surrounding me died down. Ren was feeling good, happy. Inches from my ear, he started to snicker and singsong affectionately, "Sta-a-a-a-nley. Stan the ma-a-a-a-n. Sta-a-a-a-nley. Stan the ma-a-a-n. C'mon, Stanley, man. You deserve a nice blow job for your birthday. How 'bout a blow job for your birthday?"

I needed to defuse the issue. I decided to phrase my refusal with more appreciation of the prize that was being offered. "I'm sure that would be lovely. But considering the circumstances, I'd really rather not."

I sat in dread that they would push it further. I could not stand to have it forced on me, so I prayed that it would not continue on that path. I prepared my next line of defense; if pushed, I would praise the girls' beauty as follows: "Listen, I'm sure they're beautiful, but given the circumstances I'm in, I'll just say no, thank you." I hoped that line would take the sting out of any inference that I was refusing because I didn't like their girls or I didn't like black girls.

But my strategy needed to take a one-eighty. Ren pushed further in a cuter way: "C'mon, Stanley. I think these girls is startin' to like you. They lookin' at your lips."

Now I had the opposite problem. I couldn't let them think that I didn't like black girls, but if they thought their women actually desired me, Sen or Ren could turn on me like a scorpion. With the velour scarf covering me from my forehead to the bridge of my nose, and with the girls never having seen me without the blindfold, I replied, "Really? The only reason they like me is because most of my face is covered."

The three young men and two very young women around me erupted with laughter. Weed-loosened Ren at my side gave bursts of reptilian snickers as he wheezed uncontrollably. Sen gave forth deep-throated chortles as he cracked up, weed having lubricated him, too. The girls shrieked out feminine titters.

The comedy approach worked. As the laughter died, my friends surrendered their zeal to push the blow job on me. Now, just as though I was attendant at an Upper West Side dinner party, or, say, a holiday meal with family, the satisfied crowd turned to impressing each other with jokes. It went around the room, starting with the man of the house, Sen, moving to Ren, then to the girls, Mercedes first, then Mystic.

I can't remember all of the jokes. Ren contributed to the party with his comic version of a Jamaican accent. "Yahmahn," he giggled next to me on the mattress. "Down't bee teallin' meah whaht to-oo doo, Sen, mahn, 'cause Aye ain't goanna pud op wid it, mahn."

He buzzed in Jamaican-accented English for a couple of minutes. I was loosened up a bit, too, from the joking around, and I weighed whether I would hurt or help myself by jumping in with my own Jamaican accent. I couldn't take the chance that they would think I was being racist. On the other hand, Ren was doing the accent. Oh, what the heck, I decided.

"Yahman," I interjected, with my own considerable ability to imitate accents. "Ire, mahn. Eets good to be in Noo Yawhk ahfter gro'in' op in Jhamaicamahn."

Ren and Sen could not have laughed harder. For them, the notion that a white guy could imitate a Jamaican was so far off their sense of reality that it was intensely comic. Chortling, snickering, tittering—it rang out in waves from the boys and girls. I thought possibly of buttering them up a little more, but decided to quit while I was ahead.

The jokes continued at various levels of perversion. I can only remember clearly one of the jokes, unfurled by the gleeful sixteen-year-old whose street name was Mystic.

"All right, so dere's this little boy whose name is Deeper," she began with enthusiasm in the telling, as would any friend or family member while entertaining at home. "So Deeper goes to school and sits in the class with his teacher. Then he raise his hand and he ask if he can go to the bathroom. The teacher say, 'Okay, Deeper, you can go.' So Deeper goes down the hall to the bathroom and he goes inside the stall and he does his business. But he don't go back to class. Finally, the teacher comes lookin' for him. She goes in the bathroom and says, 'Deeper, are you in there?' Then she open the stall door and see he playin' with himself. She screams, 'Oh, no!' so Deeper pulls out his gun, and he makes her lie down, and he start fuckin' her. He fuckin' her and fuckin' her. So while they doin' it, she yells, 'Deeper . . . Deeper.'"

Everybody except me thought this was very funny and they laughed out loud. I smiled and pretended to laugh right along. "What the hell is our society creating in the minds of these children?" I thought.

Hot 97 or maybe some other station at this point was still chugging away on Ramos's stereo in the background. A pop tune sung by some white female vocalist came up. Mystic and D exuberantly crooned in at the top of their lungs, teenage girls singing along with the radio just as any teenage girls would in any garden suburb across this great land. In that moment, I could see that these prostitutes and kidnapper-accomplices were nothing but a couple of little girls. So much humanity packed into such inhuman circumstances.

Ren's mind-altered affection for me seemed to be growing. He went back to pleasing himself with a singsong in my honor: "Sta-a-a-nley. Stan the ma-a-a-n. Sta-a-a-nley. Stan the ma-a-a-n." Again, "Sta-a-a-nley. Stan the ma-a-a-n. Sta-a-a-nley. Stan the ma-a-a-n." I sat, facing him, with a smile on my lips but no verbal response. Just listening, enjoying, like a friend.

Ren didn't miss my enjoyment of his enthusiasm. Suddenly he had a revelation. With a squeaky crack in his voice and a humorous delivery, he pondered aloud:

"What's goin' on here?

"We give you food.

"We offer you weed.

"We offer you a blow job," he deadpanned.

He delivered the punch line with rising volume and squeaky pitch:

"What kind of *robbery* is this anyway?"

Ren's own reptilian snicker was overwhelmed by the eruptions of laughter from his appreciative audience. Even I had to laugh genuinely, as he was pretty damn funny. My new friends kept snickering for quite some time. I laughed, I smiled, I kept quiet.

Suddenly, the front door opened and slammed. Footsteps sounded down the hall, and then Lucky's commanding business twang demanded, "Whus goin' on?"

Lucky was back, and with the general back on base, the party was over. The laughing stopped, dead, in its tracks. Business was business, and there had been enough fooling around. Everybody shut up immediately.

THIRTEEN

LOSS

'd be late to my own funeral.

Although I didn't know it and didn't even bother to think about it at the time, that night was anguishing a colorful cast of characters that I had collected around the world. The only thing that matters in your life is the web of human contacts you weave between the time you emerge from the egg until such time as a pair of size ten boots squishes the end. All the rest is commentary.

Two of my best friends tunneled out on Broadway and turned toward the Bottom Line, looking for Freedy and me. When the prosecutors arrived, it was past seven, and among the four friends waiting already, Darcy the Midwest Jewish dancer who looked nothing like a Jew was kvetching already. She hadn't comprehended on Wednesday night when I insisted more than once that everyone be sure to arrive on time. The tickets sat in my wallet, and there is no reserved seating at the Bottom Line, so we needed to congregate as one to get in. "If anybody is late," I had said to Darcy, "we'll all have to wait for that person. Please be sure to be on time."

Yet here it was past seven, and the birthday boy who'd insisted on punctuality had himself broken the pact. The others had varying reactions. Matt Daniels, Scott's brother, was happy to see me whenever I showed up. Dafne Alon had just started dating Scott and barely knew me, so she just observed, not knowing what to think.

Alysoun Charnoff was somewhere between Darcy and Matt; shivering in her long, red wool coat, the cold and delay loomed irksome, but she supposed I'd come along soon. I'd met Alysoun and her husband, Michael, six years earlier at a ballroom dance class that Dan and I had taken at Columbus Circle. You would fox-trot or rhumba with a succession of partners, the women circling clockwise and the men counterclockwise every two minutes when the instructor commanded, "Switch partners." Each time the circle went around, Dan and I noticed one seraph whose dance step seemed to float on the air, and who presented a warm smile atypical of a New Yorker. Dan and I each secretly suspected that this woman was flirting with us. It was not until the last day of class that we learned that one of the men floating counterclockwise was her college sweetheart and husband, Michael Watson.

Those two strands soon intertwined with a lover from a foreign venture. Some six months after the dance class, Dan and I went off backpacking to Bora Bora and New Zealand. Along the Kepler Trail of the South Island, I encountered Suzanne De Vrees, a spirited Dutch-German woman who fell in love with my singing and guitar playing as I fell in love with her live spirit, human kindness, and inner strength. Upon her return to Hamburg, Suzanne, never one to hesitate out of caution, particularly in matters of the heart, hopped on the first available plane to New York for a two-week tryst. Just then seraphic Alysoun dialed me up to suggest that I meet her and Michael to celebrate her birthday at the East Village bistro of my choosing. Suzanne and I feasted with them at

Cooper Square, a few blocks from my apartment, in a joint that served Midtown food at East Village prices. Thus commenced a friendship with Alysoun and Michael that was to take deep root over the next few years.

As for Suzanne, she had since moved to New York, and we were no longer involved but we were good friends. She couldn't party at the Bottom Line that night because she had recently become a yoga instructor and had downward dogs to teach.

Scott and Dan briefed the others shivering in front of the Bottom Line on how I had not materialized at work all day. Scott kept believing that there was some rational explanation and that I would appear at any moment. He even finagled his way past the bouncer and into the club to look for me in case I had already slipped in, but he found no Stan inside. Still, he insisted that I would appear, and he kept the others' toes freezing for at least a half hour more to see if I would come.

Standing outside, Darcy speculated, "You know, he made such a point of insisting that we all be here on time. Maybe he has something up his sleeve."

"Yeah, maybe," Alysoun said. "He was certainly acting quite mysterious. Maybe there's a trick behind all of this."

Scott said, "I doubt it. It's not like him, and why would he want to keep us waiting out here in the cold?" Though he remained optimistic, Scott finally started losing patience. "What do you want to do?" he asked Dan.

"Let's go over to his place and see if he's there," Dan responded. "Why don't the rest of you wait here in case he comes."

"Okay," the others said. Then Alysoun added, "We'll go across the street to Dojo's and wait for you in there. We'll keep an eye out the window for him in case he comes." Dojo's low-end fare featured one of the top bargains in the city—the soy burger dinner, with rice and salad and excellent carroty sauce, all for $2.95. I'd wolfed it many a hungry night. Alysoun, Matt, Dafne, and Darcy crossed over and entered the heat as Scott and Dan faded quickly down the street.

At my building several blocks from the Bottom Line, the doorman's eagle eyes had not spotted me all day. I failed to answer the buzzer from downstairs. "Do you have the keys to his apartment?" Dan asked. Negative. Although I liked the super and doormen in this building, years of the New York experience had long ago taught me not to leave my keys with the building staff. Robberies by supers or doormen were as common as mosquito bites in the summer. Having not found me, Dan and Scott decided not to push the issue further for the moment, and to return to the others waiting in Dojo's. Scott was still optimistic that there would be a rational explanation for my behavior.

Entering Dojo's, Dan and Scott plopped down next to the others around a table with a bird's-eye view of the Bottom Line, and debriefed on their reconnaissance. Alysoun was hungry. If something bad was happening, she wanted to keep her energy up. "Listen, everybody. I feel strange and a little guilty about this, but I need to keep my strength up. I'm going to order something." She placed the order for chicken stir-fry over brown rice, feeling terrible for her self-interest as the others politely declined. But when the odor of the stir-fry spread across the table, Darcy and Dafne decided to pick.

Scott, attempting cordiality, asked Alysoun, "How's the stir-fry?"

"It's okay, but I can't really taste it right now. It's like eating cardboard. Anybody else want a bite?" Alysoun smiled, but her voice cracked.

"No, thanks," said Scott, smiling, always polite and trying to remain bright on the outside. He certainly couldn't eat at a time like this. Dan already looked like he was in another world and didn't bother to respond to the offer.

"This is really strange," said Darcy, a befuddled look on her round red face. "Here we are, sitting here eating, and anything could have happened to Stan." The others ignored her because nobody really cared one way or the other about whether anybody else ate or didn't eat. Each was lost in his or her own nervous thoughts.

But the group pulled together and resolved to start calling my relatives and friends, to see if anyone had heard from or seen me. In 1998, cell phones were still a novelty as they slowly moved out of the province of drug dealers and into common usage. Dafne had a cell phone, and between it and the pay phone in the chilly entrance vestibule, they had two lines buzzing at once.

"You know," Alysoun wondered aloud, "maybe his mom or dad got sick and he's off taking care of them."

"Could be," said Dan. They knew about my dad's Parkinson's disease and how I had gone with him to the hospital twice in the space of a recent week.

"You know," said Darcy, "when I spoke to him on the phone last night he seemed distracted. It was almost like there was somebody else in his apartment."

There certainly was not anyone in my apartment, though she was right, I was distracted. In his own mind, Dan dismissed the idea that I had been threatened with Darcy on the phone: If some robber had been in my apartment, he wouldn't have permitted a phone call.

As the conversation drifted nervously about the table, people fantasized aloud that maybe Mr. Stan had run off to Mexico or the Pacific Northwest. But deep in their hearts they all knew they were grasping at straws and they were very much afraid. Things like this are supposed to happen to strangers. They're not supposed to happen to people you know.

Scott took on the painful task of calling my father. He got the number from Brooklyn information, shoved in a quarter, and heard it ring.

"Hello?"

"Hello, Mr. Alpert, it's Scott Daniels, Stan's friend," he said. "I'm sorry to bother you, but we're supposed to meet Stan at the Bottom Line and he's not here. We thought maybe you had spoken to him."

"No," my father responded with alarm. "I tried to call him all day, at work, at home, but he hasn't called me back. Is something the matter?"

"No, no, I'm sure everything is fine." Scott's heart sank through his shoes upon hearing my dad's worried voice. "He's probably just off celebrating his birthday somewhere. Don't you worry. We'll call a couple of his friends and find out where he is."

Someone tried to call my mother in Brooklyn, but her number just rang and rang.

They got my brother Josh's number in Houston from information. When Scott got him on the phone, Josh hadn't a clue to my whereabouts. He decided not to worry, yet. Life had taught him that all sorts of reasonable explanations tend to emerge when something seems weird at first. As he hung up, he conjured up a potential scenario: I had gone to lunch, either with somebody from the office or maybe with a friend who was just passing through town. It was my birthday, so one beer led to another, and I passed the point where it was worth going back to the office. Suddenly, as in Greek mythology, a fabulous feline materialized, and before you knew it Stan had a whispered invitation to get lucky on his birthday. In this scenario, I would appear soon at the Bottom Line, with a smirk on my face, and state incredulously, "What, a guy can't take a few hours off from work on his birthday without everybody flipping out?"

Of course, Josh knew his scenario was optimistic, more of a personal fantasy than anything else. I wasn't a drinker and I wasn't the type to pick up women in a bar and take them home. Josh ran his own advertising business out of his second bedroom in Houston, where he sat for a while at his computer desk and tried to distract himself with the day's pileup of e-mails. He hoped I would show up soon. A bit later, he left the garden apartment that was twice the size of what he would have gotten in New York, hopped in his shiny black Toyota Celica, and pointed it toward the gym for a workout.

Back at Dojo's, Dan called David Prosser at his home. I'd first encountered Prosser at the University of Pennsylvania Law School dining hall, where he distracted us from the indigestible by pontificating tirelessly on the plight of the working man and the evils of big capital. Penn had one of the country's top labor law professors teaching our first-year class, and David's prior life as a union organizer and his present knack for the subject made him the uncontested star of the class. With David, you tried to get a word in edgewise at your peril. But over time I'd been drawn to him by his humanity and humor. Since law school, he had mellowed and was now a fine member of the friend collection, with whom you could while away the hours in endless symposia on law, politics, Broadway musicals, or, best of all, everyone's favorite, the chasing of skirts. David had instructed me not to buy him a ticket to Freedy because he wasn't sure if he could get out of therapy on time, but he was aspiring to a fashionably late entrance.

Dan tried to keep it casual. "David, we're at the Bottom Line for Stan's party. Are you coming?"

David reacted a little defensively. "Yeah, sure, I'll be there. I told Stan I'd be late."

"No, no, it's not that. We're wondering if you've seen Stan."

"No. . . . Is something the matter?"

"No, I hope not. Who else do you know who was coming tonight?"

At that, Prosser suspected that Moretsky was not telling all. From the concern in Dan's voice, he sensed the rising temperature.

Dan wanted to know if David had Tom Byron's number. Tom and I had worked together at the law firm, and David knew him because he had worked there, too, before becoming a partner at another firm.

"No, I don't have it. Should I come down there?"

"Sure, if you want to. But I don't know how long we'll be staying here. Maybe we'll split up and send some people over to Stan's place."

"Okay, I'll come to one or the other," David said as Dan dropped the pay phone receiver in its cradle.

The two phones buzzing out to my friends and relations were yielding a big zero. Dafne was a doctor, so she went so far as to place a couple of calls to local hospitals, just in case something crazy had happened. She, too, got nothing. It was now close to nine P.M., and those gathered at the Dojo's table were starting to feel desperate.

"Maybe something terrible has happened. What if he got robbed and knocked unconscious, or what if he's sick in his apartment? We better go back there and see if we can get in," Moretsky said.

"You're right," Scott said.

"He could have fallen and hit his head in the bathtub. Or he could be sick. Let's go," Alysoun said.

"Oh, shit," said Darcy, standing up and wrapping a big scarf around her little neck and part of her face.

"I hope he's okay," said Matt.

The anxious assemblage trudged down the same Village streets that were the source of my agony the night before. Alysoun, Dafne, and Darcy split off to the West Village to get Alysoun's beat-up New York City street Honda. Sitting in the backseat was a black leather vest wrapped in tissue paper. Alysoun looked at the tissue paper and a tiny dagger went through her heart. "Will I get to give him the present?" she thought. A premonition told her that she probably would. The three women hopped in the Honda and headed east.

Back at the building, this time Scott and Dan asked for the super, hoping he could get them in. Scott thought there was no way the super would actually do it. He was wrong.

Jose Penalta had been the superintendent where I lived since 1995. The guy was tip-top. Born in the Dominican Republic to a mother who birthed eighteen children, Jose was one of triplets. Extremely competent, the man could fix anything, and he deftly husbanded 140 separate homes hidden behind closed blue doors. Not many months before, he had stepped out of his required duties, disemboweling and then reconstituting my halogen living room lamp, keeping it off the garbage heap and saving me two hundred bucks. He always wore a smile, and seeing him plus the endless flow of children and grandchildren in and out of his ground-floor apartment made me figure that he was one happy forty-four-year-old man.

But at the moment my friends approached him and asked to get into my apartment by any means necessary, Jose was reeling. He was still freaked by what had happened in the building a mere seventeen days earlier. Some tenant had reported a terrible odor on the fourth floor, one floor below me. When he went upstairs and smelled what was emanating from apartment 4K, he knew something was wrong, but no way was he prepared for what he would find. He had just seen the young girl from 4K days earlier, on New Year's Day, traipsing out of the building, boyfriend on her arm and wide ebullient smile on her face. She had a movie production job of some sort. She seemed to have it together. She was always extremely warm to Jose. One could even say they were friends.

Not having the keys to her apartment either, Jose had accessed the fire escape hugging the building on Ninth Street from above and shimmied down the metal ladders linking each floor. He'd wanted to call the police to cover himself for what he was about to do, but the building's landlord had ordered Jose to do it without the police. Reaching the fourth floor on his own, he planted himself on the grated platform outside 4K. The late-afternoon sun glared off the window, shielding the interior from view. Jose drew close and cupped his hands against the window, pressing his face into his weathered hands to peer inside. Suddenly, Jose let out an anguished scream.

A police officer buying coffee at the Korean deli on the corner looked up, startled, when he heard the outcry. Jose's 190-pound body jerked backward. The movement almost drove him off the fire escape into free fall toward the pavement, but he was caught by the thin iron rail edging the fire escape. When his eyes gazed into the girl's kitchen window, her eyes had gazed directly back into his. She had removed the kitchen light fixture, exposing a pipe, wrapped a scarf around the pipe and her own neck, and hanged herself. The police officer who heard the scream from below radioed his command that he was going in.

Jose and the cop found a note lamenting the girl's breakup with her boyfriend. It had to have happened within the past three days, as Jose had seen her with him, happy, on New Year's Day. The note also expressed her appreciation for Jose's friendship. Her apartment contained assorted sex apparatus, revealing that her movie production job was not for Walt Disney.

In the days following, Jose wondered what demons may have tormented this poor girl. Jose's life, too, was not as rosy as it appeared. Between certain marital difficulties and the loss of this girl, Jose began glancing upward at the pipes in the basement, wondering whether he shouldn't do the same himself. It was with him in this state of mind that these harrowed souls confronted him with a story about how I had failed to appear at work or at the Bottom Line on my birthday.

"Madre de Dios," he thought to himself. "What the hell is going on in this building?!" He thought of me as a nice guy, always happy and with a kind word to say. "No, Stanley, how the hell could you have done it?" he cried out to himself.

"I'll get you in," he immediately promised Scott and Dan. "But let me warn you. We gotta go through the fire escape. Two weeks ago, a girl killed herself in this building. When I saw it, I was so shocked that I almost fell off. So if you wanna come up with me, that's okay. Just make sure you hang on tight when we look in."

"Okay," Dan said. Scott nodded.

The men began their funereal ascent, three life-sized spiders crawling up the side of the building. Matt Daniels stood in the courtyard below and watched their bodies shrink as they moved farther away. He couldn't stop himself from viewing it all through the prism of his own subway encounter just two days earlier. His mind's eye painted a clear tableau of a group of young toughs who probably had picked me up, robbed me, killed me, and thrown my body near Riverside Park. His brain buzzed with the pressure. If you're alone, you can't protect yourself. You lose all control. There were some deaths he recalled around Central Park at night. The likelihood that someone had helped me the way somebody helped him, but after the sun went down, in that gloomy time in a city of darkness, was slim. The guy with a permanent smile on his lips looked up at his climbing brother somberly, the smile erased.

The three women arrived moments later and decided to take the elevator to apartment 5L, to be ready to enter when the door was unlocked from the inside.

Ascending, Scott prayed that his hunch was correct, that they would not find me. Dan expected the worst. Jose hoped he wouldn't have to see again what he'd seen two weeks before. Each of the men brought huge gulps of icy air into his lungs, exhaling puffs of visible steam, energizing the desperate climb.

They stopped at the fifth-floor fire escape landing. It was dark inside and they could see nothing. Dan took a crouched position that shielded most of his body behind the three-foot iron railing, holding on tight to the rail behind him. Dan reminded Scott, "Remember to hold on, because we don't know what we're going to find." Scott grabbed on, too. Jose raised a heavy steel wrench and pounded once, twice, three times, until finally the sound of smashing glass sent shards raining on my kitchen floor. He cleared out more glass with his gloved hand, then he reached up to the latch and unlocked the window. He slid it open and gestured for the others to enter.

Jose's feet hit the floor first, then Dan's, then Scott's. Scott knew I wouldn't be there, but if I was, the only place I might be would be in bed, either sick or, at the outer end of horror, bludgeoned. He ran for my bed in the dark apartment, and when I was not there, the inquiry ended for him. Hanging over the bed in the darkness were two Indonesian wood carvings, of a dragon and a goddess, gently swaying in the breeze, surreally framing the emptiness. Dan scattered cockroach-like throughout the darkened apartment, unwilling to leave any spot unexplored. Jose didn't look at all, leaving it to them, and stood impassive.

One of the men finally illuminated my living room halogen light. In some ways the place looked like there may have been a struggle; for example, the desk was buried under papers strewn randomly. Friends Dan and Scott quickly realized that this was nothing more than my ordinary mess. Their necks bent left and right as they scanned all corners, and it didn't look like anything obvious had happened in this apartment. But one lighthouse beacon drew all eyes until the three gathered around it; my telephone answering machine was blinking frenetically.

"Let's see if there's anything on here," Dan suggested. He pressed the play button and they all waited as the machine whirred, rewinding interminably. Finally, it beeped and voices started talking:

A mix of messages came across, some fun if a little embarrassing: *Beeeeep: "Stan, it's Dan. How yoo doin'. Hey—I went to a jump rope class at the gym today. You gotta see all the cute chicks in this class. It's amazing. Give me a call."*

Others had called to celebrate my birthday. Flora and Arlene were singing from down in Florida. My dad had called once wishing me a happy birthday, and then again, more somber, wondering where I was.

But then two bone-chilling messages appeared on the loop. *Beeeep: "Hello? Hello? Hi, this is Michelle. I'm calling . . . I found your credit cards this morning in the street about seven o'clock in the morning. It was near my work in Bedford-Stuyvesant by the car wash. Please gimmee ah call 'cause I want to give them bahck to you. It's 718-631-8473."*

Dan felt as though an icicle were jabbed through his heart. The next message made matters worse: *Beeeeep: "Mr. Alpert, this is Chase Bank calling. There's been unusual activity on your cash machine card. We would like to find out if this has been authorized. Please call the bank immediately at 1-800-734-8000. Thank you."*

"Oh, my God," Dan gasped, despite his atheism. "Okay, okay," he declared nervously. "Let's not jump to conclusions. Let's try to figure this out." A moment later, Jose threw open the front door so Alysoun, Darcy, and Dafne could enter. As soon as Matt had seen from the street that the super and Scott and Dan had entered through the window, he'd come up, too, and was in a moment later. Dan replayed the messages for them, but he deliberately fast-forwarded past the spot on the tape where he had told me about all the great girls in jump-rope class. He didn't want Darcy to hear that, since he knew we were dating.

With the messages ringing in their ears, all the Bottom Line friends gathered around my couch and coffee table. Meanwhile, David Prosser passed the super leaving as he entered the apartment.

They mapped out possible scenarios. Dan said, "All right, let's see what could have happened. I think he saw Tom Byron on Tuesday night. We have to find his number. Darcy last spoke to Stan at around seven on Wednesday."

"Right," Scott interjected. "Then he doesn't show up all day at work. He had important meetings and didn't call in. He doesn't show up for his own party, and he had the tickets to see Freedy."

"Now we hear that there was unusual activity on his bank card and that some woman found his credit cards at seven A.M. today in Bedford-Stuyvesant," Dan continued.

A pall fell over the room. Still, they played out the analysis.

"If he just lost his wallet, he would have called. Or even if he just ran out of town for his birthday, he would have called work," Matt said.

"If he was injured, he may be in the hospital somewhere," Darcy added.

David thought to himself, not wanting to alarm anybody, that my disappearance might be related to work. Without naming names or places, I had recently told him I was investigating a sneaky but intentional discharge of oil into a New York City waterway, and that there were suspicions that the company was mob-connected. David thought that either they had rubbed me out, or they had chosen my birthday to send an especially strong message to the feds. The notion hit him broadside, like he might have felt upon receiving bad results from an HIV test. David shivered as an invisible hand grasped his chest. He didn't want to talk about it for now, and said instead, "If he's in the hospital, he has to be both incapacitated and without his ID."

"Or maybe the hospital hasn't found him yet," Matt pondered. "Maybe he's lying in an alley in Bedford-Stuyvesant."

Alysoun had a keenly intuitive side and often felt she could predict things. In her mind, I wasn't even hurt. My face was as bright as it could be—I was looking right at her and I wasn't even injured. "I know it sounds crazy," she said, "but I kind of feel that he's okay." She understood full well that her feeling was against all logic.

Dan thought she was nuts. "Are you kidding? Dafne called some of the hospitals and that got us nothing. We've been through all the scenarios and they're all bad. Except nobody has mentioned the one. . . ." His voice dropped off. He was sure I was dead. From his seated position on my living room couch, Dan started to sob.

"He was held up, he fought, and he was either killed or he's lying in a coma somewhere," Dan choked out. Tears of frustration, anger, and sadness streamed down his face. The criminals he'd been fighting his whole life had now taken his friend. He got up and moved to the foyer to cry alone.

Scott said, "We'd better call the police."

"And the FBI," Prosser thought, keeping it to himself for now.

FOURTEEN

ALMOST THE END

They had good reason to worry. The wine and roses was over. These boys were back in war mode.

"Well, don't nobody hear me? What's goin' on here?" Lucky demanded again.

Sen was out of weed and mirth and reincarnated as Sergeant Sen. His voice returned to the low growl I'd heard when I was chucked in the Lexus. No more joking around. No more friendly with Stanley, not with boss-man Lucky around. He responded, "Everything fine. We been takin' good care of Stanley here."

"You all right, Stanley?" Lucky asked.

"Yes, I'm fine. Thank you. These guys have been taking very good care of me. Very cordial, actually."

My enthusiasm went a little too far. "Really?" Lucky exclaimed incredulously. "Maybe I stayed away too long."

It was my mistake; the hint of our little party made Lucky feel that maybe he couldn't trust his soldiers. He needed to regain control. "Did you feed him?"

Indignant, Mercedes crowed, "Yes . . . we fed him. Where the hell were you all day?"

"Do I have to answer to you?" Lucky snapped. "I was taking care of business and don't give me no lip."

"We was here all day and didn't have no idea where you was. We tried callin' you, but there was no answer on your phone. We didn't know nuthin'."

"There was nothing to know. I had serious business to take care of. I had to go try to get the window fixed, but they needed to order the glass so I just taped it up with some plastic for now. I have to thank Stanley for the new glass, since I ordered the window and put it on his credit card. Now we're gonna let Stanley go at midnight just so we can get one last thousand dollars off of his cash machine card. That okay with you, Stanley?"

I responded enthusiastically. "Sure, thank you. I appreciate that you're gonna let me go."

"No problem," Lucky replied. "You understand, of course, that we couldn't have let you go earlier. We'd have let you go, and the first thing you would have done was to cancel the cash machine card and the credit cards. We needed to keep you a little longer." He exited and his footsteps led down the hall to another room.

"'Bout time he got back." Mystic pouted.

"Shut the hell up," responded Sen, with characteristic sensitivity.

"Stanley, man, you gettin' outta here soon." Ren's words reassured, but his tone had hardened, too, harboring the ominous.

Lucky reentered a few minutes later. "My fiancée gave me that Social Security number. Who do I have to thank for that?"

"Me," said D.

"Thank you, Mercedes," said the businessman.

"I had it, too," Mystic chimed in, seeking credit.

"Well, thanks to both of you, then," Lucky conceded.

Lucky was standing to my left, close to the entrance of the room. After she spoke, I could hear Mystic's footsteps drawing up to him.

"Lucky . . . ," she cooed.

No response. "Lu-u-u-u-cky . . . ," she cooed again.

"What do you want?"

Mystic's voice grew quiet and imploring. "You know . . ." She faltered. It felt to me as though she was glancing around the room, wondering whether to continue with all these people around.

"Well, what is it? C'mon, I don't have all day."

"Well, uh, I know you been at your fiancée and all. But I need to say that since you and me was together . . . I mean, I got feelings for you."

"What are you talking about?" Lucky exclaimed, irritated.

"Like, I just want you to know what I feel inside for you. Like it was somethin' special. I don't know if you feel the same. I got feelings for you."

"Don't bother me right now, Mystic. We have business to attend to." I heard Lucky's step, backing away from her.

Yeegads. Lucky, man of Wall Street polish plus street-level robber and small-time pimp, was two-timing his fiancée, sampling the goods on the side. I sure hoped he wasn't eating up all the profits. And poor Mystic had fallen in love. Under better circumstances, I might have wished Mystic well or felt angry over the way Lucky was mistreating her, even lashing out with positively feminist indignation. At the moment, though, I merely gawked as this theater of the absurd unfolded before my ears.

Lucky pulled out by changing the subject. "I'm not gonna be here on Saturday. I'm driving down to Virginia. The Italian side of my family— I'm half Italian, you know, Stanley—has got some property down there that I need to take a look at. Y'all are gonna have to do without me for one night. I hope everything's going to run smoothly."

"Don't you worry," Mercedes responded, speaking as a loyal and trusted employee.

Mystic added, "We'll be all right."

This latest bit of information solidified my planning process. I hoped and I prayed that they were serious about returning me to my neighborhood alive. If so, what would I do as soon as I was set free? I pondered my scheme to float helicopters over the East River bridges. No need for it anymore; with the latest tidbit in hand, look at all that I had: I knew we were somewhere on the Brooklyn/Queens border, near an airport, probably Kennedy. It was a $16.40 cab ride from the streetwalking spot that was "downtown," either in Manhattan or Brooklyn. The Salaam Shop was nearby. A gent with the full name of Luis Ramos lived in this apartment. Granted it was a common name, but it would help. I had the first few numbers of Lucky's cell phone, for whatever that was worth. My credit card bill would show a charge for a new Lexus window, which the cops could trace to the shop where the glass was sold. And now I knew that the leader of the gang, Lucky, would be driving down to Virginia on Saturday in a brand-new black Lexus with a broken window. How hard would it be for the police alert to go out on I-95 that an African-American male in a brand-new black Lexus with a broken window taped up with plastic was wanted and was on his way down to see the family estate in Virginia? Not too hard. I knew by now that if I made it out alive, I had enough clues for law enforcement to nail these punks.

The helicopter plan was out, though, I thought. It had too much downside risk. Let's say the choppers were floated over the East River bridges and the cops spotted the Lexus but the gang slipped away. If Lucky, Sen, and Ren saw those birds of prey hovering but escaped anyway, the first thing they would do to pay me back would be to point the Lexus in the direction of my father's apartment and go blow his head off. I couldn't take the risk. I no longer needed even to consider it, given all the information I now had.

Sen interjected, "You can go wherever you want, Lux. Just so long's we get our share of tonight's money before you go."

"Don't worry, man, you'll get it tonight," Lucky assured him.

I didn't know it, but Honey was back in the room. "I want somethin' for my trouble. This here's my apartment."

"Don't you worry, Honey, you'll be taken care of," said Lucky. "Now, all you girls, I want you up, and dressed, and ready to go out and work tonight. You all need to bring in some money, too. I'm gonna drive you down before we take Stanley here home."

"All right," said Mystic.

"Fine," said D.

"I better get some money," said Honey.

I could hear the girls scurrying around gathering their scattered articles of clothing and then re-attiring their sex-ready teenage bodies.

Lucky was on to the next subject. "By the way, does anybody know if that President Street gang hangs in Coney Island on Thursday nights?"

"I think Thursday is they night," said Ren.

"I think we gonna take a cruise down there, boys, and see what's up."

I didn't know that 1998 Coney Island was still a place where bloody street gangs made war or otherwise courted the devil. I remembered it well from my youth; Coney had been the place to be for street gangs. I guessed some things never change.

"All right," Lucky announced. "I'm out of here. I'm gonna drop off the girls and pick up the last thousand dollars. When I get back, it'll be a little after twelve, and I want Stanley to be ready to go. Understand?"

"We'll do it," replied Sen.

"No problem," sneered Ren.

"Okay, see you later. See you later, Stanley."

"Okay," I replied, cooperatively.

His footsteps moved toward the door. Then they slowed, then stopped. I heard them return to a spot about six feet to my left. Lucky had been thinking.

"Yo, Stanley, let me ask you something. If you had the chance to put me away for life, would you do it?" His twang rang at a slightly higher pitch than usual.

My head buzzed with alarm. Think fast, boy. If I say yes, I'm dead. If I say no, this guy is no fool and he'll know damn well that I'm lying through my teeth and I'm dead. I took a deep breath to calm my pounding heart and then I spoke slowly, deliberately, pensively.

I said, "You already told me you know where I live. . . .

"You know where my father lives." I hesitated and dragged the speech as though I was pondering it.

"I don't know who you are.

"I don't know where we are.

"You haven't hurt me so far, and you say you're going to release me unharmed."

I hesitated some more and seemed to give it more thought. Then, with the best nonchalance I could muster, I finished the pitch, flat-voiced. "I don't think this has to go any further."

Lucky responded with a grunt of satisfaction. "Well, all right, then. Let's go, girls—move." They walked out, leaving me with the other two desperadoes. The door slammed until his return for the end operation.

I breathed a sigh of relief. I'd spent years standing in front of federal judges pounding me with the most difficult questions ponderable to trip up an attorney. I'd had to learn to respond in a thoughtful way that fully answered their questions, advocating my clients' positions while dodging the wrath of the judges. It had been good training for the night I needed an argument more than ever. Maybe Lucky really thought that he didn't have to kill me and he would still get away with this little caper.

FIFTEEN

"THE BODY"

Richard Meade, a Special Agent in FBI Squad C-30, the violent gang squad, was down in the basement of his suburban New York house doing the laundry when the phone rang upstairs. He was planning to shed his civvies and go to bed soon after a long day of work. By the time he got upstairs, the phone had stopped. Relentlessly, his beeper assaulted him a second later and Meade dialed back the familiar number, knowing he wasn't getting to bed after all.

"Yeah," he answered.

"Rich, it's Dom." Dominick Scaglione was the head of Rich's squad, a seasoned veteran of many years who had risen through the ranks to Supervisory Special Agent. "We got a situation you gotta get on right away. An Assistant U.S. Attorney from the Eastern District is missing. There may be a problem. Get yourself dressed and go straight to his apartment." Scaglione gave Meade the address and hung up.

Meade had sandy brown hair and warm yet elusive blue eyes and looked like a taller version of Barney Rubble of *The Flintstones*, but the man was no-nonsense. He was a seven-year veteran of the FBI's New York violent gang squad, which dealt with extortions, kidnappings, and assaults on federal officers. Before that he'd spent three years in FBI foreign counterintelligence. He was also an ex-marine. He slammed the door shut behind him, with the screen door doing its own thing right after, and climbed into a scratched-up, dented brown 1989 Toyota van with blacked-out tinted windows. The van was so good at not looking like the cops that one time on a drug surveillance in Washington Heights, a nonchalant neighborhood goon had pissed right on the bumper with Richie and his partner staring out through the rear tinted windows. *That's* good cover.

Within a few minutes, he was speeding south in the van on the Palisades Parkway at eighty-five miles an hour. He thought to himself that he might get arrested and that if he didn't he was liable to get killed, flying along at that speed on the narrow Palisades through the blackness of night. As the bright glow of the George Washington Bridge reflecting off the clouds suddenly loomed before him, Meade was surprised he'd made it that far without being stopped. Just then a siren blared, and red-and-white police car lights reflected in his rearview mirror.

"Shit," he thought, as he pulled over.

The New Jersey patrolman sidled up to Rich's door. "I guess you're in a big hurry, huh, guy," the cop smirked.

"Sorry, I'm FBI." Meade flashed his credentials under the officer's nose. "We got a federal prosecutor missing down in Manhattan, and I gotta get down there right away."

Slightly deflated, the patrolman waved him on. "Fine, just don't put anybody in a ditch."

Meade sped the rest of the way, just a little slower. At my East Village apartment, the doorman let him in, and he immediately encountered detectives from the Ninth Detective Squad. "His friends are upstairs," said nice Jewish boy Detective Samuel Miller, and the detectives led Meade up to my apartment.

After my friends had called the cops, it was uniformed patrolmen who arrived first. Hearing the story, they quickly realized they were in over their heads, so a uniformed sergeant had come next. Finally, the plain-clothes detectives who would lead an investigation of the magnitude of the disappearance of an Assistant United States Attorney arrived. It then dawned on Dan Moretsky that because I was an Assistant, the FBI would also be willing to work the case, so he called their New York headquarters at 26 Federal Plaza. While they waited, Dan called Michelle, who verified finding my credit cards at seven A.M., and he called a representative at Chase Bank, who, in response to Dan's plea that his friend might be dying somewhere, said they would only release information to the police.

Meade and the detectives took the elevator to the fifth floor. Inside my apartment were a pile of my friends, and two uniformed patrol officers of New York's finest. When Meade learned that my friends and the super had broken in, he thought, "Bad idea, this may be a crime scene." Equally possible, Meade thought, Alpert may have committed suicide or just taken off somewhere on a whim.

Dan took Meade through the day's events—how I was missing from work, how I had missed an important meeting, and how it was my birthday and I failed to appear at the Bottom Line. Dan played the answering machine tape for Meade, fast-forwarding again past the message he'd left about the cute girls in jump-rope class, straight to the messages from the bank and the woman who had found my credit cards that morning. Meade had had five prior assault-on-federal-officer cases in his career, all shoot-outs. Nobody made it out alive. And kidnappings in general didn't usually work out too well. Meade thought to himself that this guy was probably dead, considering he'd been missing all this time and the credit cards in Brooklyn. It was just a question of when they would find the body.

Meade asked, "Why would anybody want to kill Stan?"

Scott, taken aback and clinging to hope despite his own conclusion that I was probably dead, responded querulously, "What, you think he's dead?"

"I don't know. It doesn't look good. He's an Assistant U.S. Attorney and he's been missing a long time."

Dan responded, "He does environmental work and it's mainly civil."

Good point, Meade thought. Meade worked mainly with Southern District Assistants, and all criminal, so he didn't know me. It was less likely that a civil assistant would face the kind of creeps who might want to waste him.

Darcy told Meade that she had spoken to me the night before. "He was in a hurry to get off the phone," she said. "It's possible that somebody was there with him." No, I was leaving to go out when we spoke. That's what I get for going on a blind date when I've already got something going with somebody else. Divine justice.

My sordid love life became an issue. Meade assumed from Darcy's demeanor and the fact that she had spoken to me that she was my girlfriend. By now, someone else who'd been contacted in the flurry of calls from the Bottom Line, Janice Janofsky, had arrived. Janice had been invited to the Bottom Line but bowed out because she wasn't feeling well. My friends knew that Janice had been my good-looking, animal-loving, and PETA-promoting student intern a year or two before. At that point in time, student interns had gotten a bad rap, and I hadn't wanted to sully their reputation further. Jan had a boyfriend, anyway, and a very serious one. One day, though, I was sitting at my desk shuffling legal papers from one side to the other, when bells went off as Jan sashayed into my office in a skirt barely covering her behind and a tight shirt wrapping the sort of breasts for which men compose poetry. There had to be a reason for this change of outfit, and sure enough, Mr. Serious Boyfriend had gone south. This past Hanukkah season, she had made me up a big gift basket, with home-baked cookies and other goodies. "Hmmm . . . that's affectionate," I'd thought, and we started spending a lot of time together—just as friends. Dan and Scott both knew this, and knew I'd had a few dates with Darcy in the meantime, so despite the fact that I might be lying dead in an alley somewhere, they felt obliged as best male friends to cover me.

"Stanley has a girlfriend?" Janice reacted with surprise when she heard Meade referring to one. Pulling her aside, away from the hearing of either Darcy or Meade, Scott assured her, "No, I don't think he knows what he is talking about. He is probably referring to one of Stan's female friends."

Meade then ran through with them all the usual theories for why a person might disappear. Was he depressed? Suicidal? The type of guy who would take off for New Zealand on a whim? Into drugs? Recently broken up with a girlfriend? Family problems? Was it like Stan to miss a meeting without calling in?

No, no, no, no, no, and no, my friends assured him. This behavior—not showing up at work and then leaving friends stranded at the Bottom Line—was totally uncharacteristic. Alpert wouldn't do it. Dan wanted to bring Meade right into line. "Look, Rich," he insisted, "Stan is a guy who can take care of himself. He's not the type to disappear or get depressed over his birthday or something like that."

These were Alpert's closest friends and they knew nothing. All dead ends. Meade decided to treat the apartment as a crime scene. The New York detectives in the room had come to the same conclusion. Calls started going out to the morgues, the hospitals, and to my friends to see if anyone knew what I was doing Wednesday night. No luck, though the negatives at the morgues and the hospitals seemed to be good news. Periodically my phone would ring with calls from my brother or my father. My friends tried to reassure Dad that everything was okay. Dan fudged: "We're looking into everything. I'm sure he's fine. The FBI and police are working hard to figure out what's happening. We've got the best forces available."

Some comfort for a father. My father understood that they were trying to keep him under control and the line about "best forces" confirmed his worst fears. All day long, he'd kept trying to find me and he couldn't understand why I hadn't gone to work. His mind's eye saw me sick, blacked out, or in a hospital someplace, but not dead. Ida, his seventy-nine-year-old girlfriend, thought it was worse, that I was dead. My dad thought to himself, "If anything happens to him, I'll kill myself." Scott promised to call him every half hour, and hung up the line.

Meade placed some calls to other agents on his squad and ordered them to shed the pajamas and get over there fast. He told Special Agent Terry Mehan about the credit cards found on the street. She immediately concluded that she'd been assigned to the case of a murdered Assistant U.S. Attorney. Early in her career she'd been exiled to St. Louis and she'd worked kidnappings. There were good kidnappings—very few—and bad kidnappings. If some sicko snatched a little girl, Mehan knew that by the time she got there she was looking for a body. Actually recovering the victim in a kidnapping was very rare.

Mehan called her unofficial partner at the time, Jimmy Glynn, and then she jumped in her car and headed into Manhattan. Glynn and Mehan were both seasoned FBI agents, surveilling and harassing violent gangs such as the Latin Kings and assigned to Meade's squad, which also handled assaults on federal officers. But you could skip the "yes sir, no ma'am," straitlaced FBI career path stereotypes with these two. Mehan was an accented New York Irish Catholic kid from the burbs of Mineola. Surrounded by vinyl siding, curled up on the shag rug in front of the family black-and-white TV, she watched two cops on *Adam-12* cruising their blue sedan as random adventures popped up like gremlins on a video game screen. She thought, "That's the most exciting job in the world. That's what I wanna do for a living." She'd thought of herself as a Nassau County cop, but as life turned out, it was FBI.

Jimmy Glynn had a much rougher upbringing in a much meaner New York suburb, Jersey City. He and Mehan had never discussed it and never would, but he, too, had decided to be a cop from watching *Adam-12*. In Glynn's beat-up old wooden Jersey City house, his heart raced when the radio crackled and the black-and-white TV cops cried, "One Adam Twelve, roger," flipped the siren switch, and sped off into the night.

Glynn had become an adult when he was a kid, and now as an adult he still looked like a big kid. Watching *Adam-12* was not enough for Jimmy. In sixth-grade art class the teacher asked the students to dress up to show what they wanted to do when they grew up. Glynn put on a suit and tie and made a badge out of construction paper with the letters "FBI" on it. He freelanced in law enforcement from an early age. Jimmy's dad died when he was barely out of kneesocks, and as the oldest boy, Jimmy became the man of the house. He was a man outside of the house, too. As a fifteen-year-old junior in high school, Jimmy Glynn was standing on a downtown Jersey City street corner when a robber busted out of a local bank, hopped on a bicycle, and took off. Never once thinking or caring about the danger to himself, Jimmy Glynn raced on foot after the bike, which sped ahead of him at some distance but always within Jimmy's view. Miles later, they hit downtown's Journal Square and a couple of Guardian Angels wearing vigilante T-shirts and signature red berets spotted the strange sight of a lone kid chasing a crook on a two-wheeler. They cut the robber off, and Jimmy and the two Angels held him skin to pavement until the suits from the Federal Bureau of Investigation showed up. From that day on, there was never any doubt as to what Jimmy wanted to be when he grew up.

Jimmy's cop practice wasn't over. One day Jimmy wrestled to the ground an escapee from the local prison who had the dumb luck of showing up in the Glynns' backyard. He held the guy tight till the cops got there. Another time he was trolling Jersey City asphalt in his sedan when he spotted two thugs hop out of a car and grab an old lady's purse. He slammed on the brakes, came to a full stop behind the robbers' sedan, and torpedoed the snatcher with his two hundred pounds. The robber flew through the open window of the waiting getaway car, and his partner hauled him away fast from the wrath of Glynn. Jimmy ran after the old lady to return her purse, but she was so scared she thought he was one of the robbers, so Jimmy turned it over to the cops when they showed up, long after the excitement was over. All in a day's work.

They wouldn't let Jimmy be a Special Agent of the FBI too easily, even with all his freelance experience. He first worked nine long years, starting as a file clerk working his way through college and then as a telephone dispatcher, screening calls and calling the right agents if a matter required immediate FBI attention. He put in to be a Special Agent, but the FBI bureaucracy found it more convenient to keep him in his dispatch job, since, after all, they had him already and needed him for dispatch. The day that a last-minute opening for an agent came through and they finally said Jimmy could start carrying a shield was the happiest day of his life. He sat with his mother at the chipped kitchen table in Jersey City; they drank champagne, and they both knew how proud his dad would have been if he'd been there. Now Glynn was on the case of the missing prosecutor.

All the fifteen or so agents on Meade's squad had been alerted by a chain of calls to work on this case, and some had been told to get over to my place right away. Others would be kept fresh till morning. Mehan and Glynn finally walked in to join the others a little sheepish and a little late. They got the address and had raced over to 59 Third Street, in the West Village, while I lived at 59 Third Avenue, in the East Village. It was a common error, West instead of East. They had wandered through a pitch-black bar trying to find somebody to talk to, to find out if maybe I lived upstairs or something. Other FBI agents ended up in the same bar, persistent even if off track. When giving directions to my apartment, I would always tell people it was near Astor Place, in the East Village, so they wouldn't get confused.

So there were probably ten agents plus several detectives plus a couple of uniforms there already when Mehan and Glynn arrived. Meade was starting to feel uncomfortable with such a large crowd jamming a possible crime scene. All of Meade's customary questions as to why a guy might disappear were leading nowhere, and he was at a loss as to how to proceed, especially at this late hour. David Prosser felt that now was the time to reveal his theory to the appropriate authority. "Let me talk to you on the side," he said to Meade, gesturing him away from the others.

As they approached the foyer to my apartment, David thought Meade looked worried, and Meade muttered to him, "We've lost a few AUSAs before, and it hasn't worked out well."

"Yeah, well, let me tell you what I think," David said, his voice shaking with fear and excitement. My work was mainly civil, but David was focused on the criminal investigation I had just mentioned to him. He proceeded to lay out his theory that the mob had gone after me to retaliate for my latest industrial pollution case, an oil spill investigation of a potentially mobbed-up company. Unlikely, Meade thought. The unwritten rules kept the mafia away from prosecutors, because they knew that law enforcement would respond massively to any transgressions. And environmental investigations were the softest kind of case the mob faced, not enough to get all worked up over. Technically, dumping the guy in concrete shoes in the East River was a Clean Water Act violation, but who cared?

Meade had heard more than enough. With the ranks swelling he needed to thin out the crowd and focus people on getting something done, anything. He wanted someone to check my voice mail and e-mail at work for any clue as to where I might be, and he ordered Scott to get in a car with an attractive blond FBI agent to speed over to the U.S. Attorney's Office and work with the head administrator there.

Next, he ordered all my friends, apart from the two AUSAs, to go to the Ninth Precinct to sit and wait there for any news. As they were hustled out of the apartment past other arriving FBI agents, David couldn't help overhearing the uniform cops, standing around my big gray metal schoolteacher's desk that I'd bought at the University of Pennsylvania Law School for twenty-five dollars, referring to me as "the body." Dan heard it, too, and his hopelessness deepened.

THE ANCIENT NINTH PRECINCT HOUSE ON EAST FIFTH street, sandwiched between tenement buildings, was hearing tales of crime and woe when my dad was a boy on the Lower East Side in the

1920s and thirties, and it stood to hear the tale of the missing Assistant
U.S. Attorney in 1998. Detective Sergeant James E. Duke was the supervisor in charge of the detectives that night. Duke was a handsome
Irishman, with fair skin and a cute upturned nose. As he sat behind a big
old metal desk not unlike the one in my apartment, cluttered with coffee cups and Chinese take-out containers, he was nevertheless resplendent in a finely fitted light brown wool suit that said "detective bureau"
all over it. Duke looked like he'd been a choirboy once upon a time, but
all you had to do was talk to him and you'd get from his eyes and his
voice that the streets had made him hard notwithstanding any boyish,
handsome looks. His father had been a police captain, and his brother
was also a cop, and Duke had followed the family lead and climbed his
way up the ladder within the department. The Job was in the bloodline.

It started as an ordinary night on his 4:30-to-midnight shift, but that
hadn't lasted long. After my friends broke into my apartment and called
911 to report that I was missing, Duke got a call with a piecemeal account of what had happened. He sent Detectives Samuel Miller and others to my apartment, and they called back to tell Duke what they were
learning.

The FBI had been notified, too. Turf battles could rage between local
and federal law enforcement, but on this one Duke wasn't too concerned
about turf, because the missing person was a federal agent, and Duke
thought that it might be their responsibility under their laws.

But either way this was going to be a pearl of a case. Duke thought to
himself, "Jesus, this is going to be a good one. No matter what happened, I got a federal prosecutor missing." And nobody had asked ini-
tially what type of prosecution I did. Right then in New York there was
a big organized crime trial going on; Duke thought it might have been
something involving a couple of brothers, with one dying of AIDS, and
though Duke couldn't recall the full details, he was aware of it. He wondered whether I might have been involved with that case.

He called his lieutenant, the supervisor running the Ninth Detective

Squad, at home. The lieutenant was off that night, but on a case like this he needed to get the call at home to get the heads-up. After discussing the situation, the lieutenant said, "Get everybody the hell out of that apartment. It might be a crime scene."

"Yeah, that's a good idea," Duke said. Duke issued orders from the precinct to start taking everybody out of there, and to secure the location, just as Meade had.

As the supervising detective, Duke was point man. My father got hold of his number at the precinct and rang him up.

"Duke," Duke answered the phone.

"Hello. This is Benjamin Alpert, Stanley Alpert's father," said the nervous and strained voice of an elderly gentleman. "Do you have any information on where he might be?"

"Naw, Mr. Alpert, we just stahted the investigation. It's not uncommon for people to be missing for twenty-four hours or so. Try not to worry, and we'll call you when we hear something. Let me have yahr numbah."

My dad would call back every so often, and Duke kept telling him to sit tight. One of the greatest tragedies in life is a parent losing a child. But the calls from my worried father failed to move Duke. He was a pro, and the NYPD dealt in human tragedy every day of the week. If you let it hang you up, you won't be able to do the job.

Soon high-level NYPD types started pouring in from all over. A captain inspector doesn't show up at the precinct for just any old case, but the case of a missing prosecutor while there was a mob trial going on drew a captain inspector and lots of other top brass to the precinct house.

A gang of worried yuppies also showed up. Several minutes after Meade had kicked them out of my home, David, Alysoun, Darcy, Jan, and Matt Daniels arrived at the Ninth Precinct. Duke got to babysit them and he herded them into a basement room in the precinct house.

It wasn't long before additional friends started to appear, scurrying in worried and confused. Michael Watson, Alysoun's husband, hadn't been able to make the birthday bash because he was due at the Metropolitan

Opera, where he worked as an usher to support his volunteer community organizing. On the way down to the police station, scenes flashed through his head like those in a movie. Three summers earlier, he and I had lived our dream to busk on the streets of Europe. We strolled around Vienna and Prague, instruments strapped on our backs, till we found a promising spot where the locals and foreigners didn't look too hostile. I would pull out my guitar, he his mandolin, and we sang and played as hard as we could for enough pocket change to buy the local beers at the end of the night. Man, Pilsner goes down nice after a night of work.

When Alysoun, the concert pianist, was with us, she would join us in song and play a few notes on a recorder. We presented as a very rough Peter, Paul and Mary to the sometimes appreciative East European crowds. I grabbed the public's attention on the street by crooning "Tears in Heaven," Eric Clapton's heartbreaking ode to the son who'd died falling out of an Upper East Side window. Otherwise we'd mix it up with Paul Simon, Beatles, Bossa Nova, or whatever else came to mind. One night on the Charles Bridge in downtown Prague, a semi-crazed young Englishman heard us playing Elvis Costello's "Oliver's Army," and he appreciated the mock salute to Britain's conquerors so fervently that he ran back to us from the other end of the bridge, shouted, "Yo, England! . . . Thanks a lot, man," and plunked a handful of British pound coins into my guitar case as Michael and I kept wailing.

Our adventures flashed past Michael's eyes as he pulled into the Ninth. "Yo, England," he thought, a sob emanating from his chest. "Plus, we won't be able to go on our annual Christmas ski trip to Vermont, if there's no more Stan," he lamented. "It'll never be the same." As soon as Alysoun had called him to tell him what was happening, he hopped on the subway. Husband and wife hugged and could say very little in the cold, gray police station.

Duke, sizing up the crowd that was growing under his watch, noticed it was mixed, with some lawyery types and some artsy types. He wanted info like an addict wants smack, but he decided to do it in a casual way, not formally interviewing. In off-the-cuff conversations, he asked such questions as:

"Where was the last place you think he would be?"

"Does he have a girlfriend?"

"Does he have a girlfriend nobody knows about, or maybe one of you knows about it, but nobody else knows about it? Does he have something going on on the side? It's his birthday; maybe he's out celebrating with somebody else, then he was gonna meet up with you, he lost track of the time . . . ?"

"Did he lose any big cases recently?"

"Any reasons to be depressed?"

It all came up a dead end. Darcy was sitting right there, so from the friends it came up that I had a girlfriend, but as to whether I might be seeing somebody on the side, they said very clearly, "No, he would never do anything like that." And I hadn't had any major tragedies lately, nor was I the type to let things get me down, they assured Duke.

After talking to my friends, Duke thought I'd probably just gone out for my birthday. There was no history of behavior like this. There was no lost big case or failure to get a promotion or everything in my life going to pot, leading me to jump into the river and call it a day.

Maybe while I was out celebrating, my wallet had been stolen. Miller had told Duke about the calls on my answering machine, and he considered whether *I* was the one with the excessive activity on my ATM card—people can spend money when they're out barhopping. It wasn't *that* excessive. Duke's men were trying to track down the woman who had found my credit cards. They couldn't get bank ATM records until the following morning, and there was a long night ahead with a prosecutor missing and Duke playing den mother to his pals in the bowels of the Ninth. At this point, though, pushing midnight, there were very few leads to follow, my friends having provided nothing of any use, and the investigation was essentially at a standstill, Duke thought. Maybe the following morning would revive the stagnant trail.

SIXTEEN

WHO SHALL LIVE AND
WHO SHALL DIE

en and Sen were not talking to me any longer. A somber mood permeated the room that had been jovial a short while before. No one had put on a light, as I could not feel the warm, yellowish glow penetrating my blindfold that I had felt when Mercedes, Mystic, and Honey came home the night before and served up greasy McDonald's. My captors worked in the dark to prepare to terminate the operation.

"We got to change his blindfold," Sen said.

Three young black men escorting a well-dressed white man with a velour scarf wrapped around his head might draw considerable attention.

"I got these sunglasses. We'll use them. You got that sleep mask, Ren?"

"Yeah, I'll get it."

"We got to put his coat back on 'im. I'ma go through his pockets first." Sen grabbed my overcoat from behind me on the bed. He walked away with it. I took note: Absent gloves, his fingerprints would now be on Lisa P. Marantz's business card, on my eyeglasses, on my leather gloves, and whatever else was in my pockets.

Besides my coat, my sports jacket was still on from much earlier when I'd felt cold. My shoes had never come off. My pants felt crumply from two days of hugging my grime and perspiration. My house keys still sat in their customary location in my left front trousers pocket, unmolested. (I didn't need to change the locks.) My tie was loose around the collar of a sweaty, wilted, once-starched white dress shirt. The body beneath these rumpled clothes was tired, a bit smelly, but so far none the worse for wear.

"He got some change in here," Sen informed Ren. "We better take it, so he can't make no phone calls."

"Right," Ren agreed.

Sen commanded me, "Stanley, man, put ya coat on."

He handed it to me. Still seated, I wriggled into it.

"Planadugga otaugga akedugga blindau ithauga." Ren spoke to Sen. Even though by now I had finally figured out that, as with pig Latin, they spoke a jargon formed by the transposition of consonants and the suffixation of an additional syllable, I still could not understand a word they said. They were so good at it, as if they were brothers and had been at it for life. I figured these guys knew each other from way back.

Sen responded, "Onadugga askawugga fantouabugga disre aintouabugga."

"Where's the sleep mask?" Sen continued.

"Right here."

"Stanley, keep your fuckin' eyes shut if you know what's good for you, mah man." Sen knelt behind me and to my right, slipped the scarf off my face so it draped once again across my shoulders, and swiftly replaced it with the sleep mask. I was not about to start opening my eyes this close to the finish line.

"Gimme mah sunglasses, Ren."

I heard the rustle of Ren's sleeve as he handed them to Sen. Above the sleep mask, Sen placed a pair of plastic sunglasses. Less noticeable than a scarf, no doubt; but still, three young African-American men escorting a well-dressed white man wearing sunglasses in the middle of the night was not exactly inconspicuous. There was a real risk of getting spotted, and I couldn't afford the violence.

We sat in silence waiting for Lucky. I could hear Sen, back on the mattress across from me, breathing, steady but heavily. Ren had given up his friendly spot next to me on the mattress and sat across from me and near the door, watching, waiting. The nervous tension permeated the room, as my captors sat and pondered the final stages of their operation. I prayed that they were serious about returning me, and that they wouldn't screw it up. I prayed that they would not load me in the trunk, as I saw that as the beginning of the end.

It must have been twenty minutes more before the front door opened and slammed again. Footsteps down the hall approached our room. "Let's go," commanded Lucky's voice, without more.

Ren and Sen pounced on me, jerking me up to my feet and shoving me toward the door. They moved with speed and military determination. Down the narrow railroad flat hall we flew. Three feet farther than the distance to the bathroom, the front door opened and they shoved me through. I thought the stairs would be over to the right and diagonally across about ten feet, but I was wrong; the apartment sat adjacent to the staircase, and a left turn with a quick one-eighty, and then the hands pushing me and I were on the descent. I could feel two sets of hands on my back and hear a third set of feet walking ahead of me as we moved down to the first landing, followed by a right turn one-eighty. Scared but alert, I counted the number of steps—eight—down to the first landing. It was eight more steps down to the second floor, below, and another two eight-step flights and right-turn one-eighties landed us on the ground floor. Just as I had remembered it, a left turn did lead us down a long hallway to the front door. This time I did not have the opportunity or the presence of mind to restudy the old-world mosaic pattern of tiles that I had memorized on the way in. The door to the front vestibule swung open, we descended another four steps, the outer door swung open, and suddenly a blast of cold, arctic air reintroduced me to the world outside Honey and Ramos's little house on the prairie.

On the street, the greater risk of being spotted made the hustle even more urgent. They rushed me across the sidewalk and slightly down to the right, where the door was open for me to be shoved into the rear of the now familiar Lexus. Lucky assumed command post in the driver's position. One of the others—I do not know whether it was Sen or Ren because they did not speak—slid in beside me. The other ran around the back of the car, opened the rear passenger-side door, jumped in, and slammed it shut.

I was now sandwiched in the backseat between Sen and Ren, though I couldn't tell who was on my left and who was on my right. Their legs pressed snugly up against mine as I occupied the tight spot over the middle hump of the car. Each leg was connected to a trunk supporting a chest that sprang an arm that held a gun just inches from my life. We sat immobile during a pregnant pause, as though they all needed to absorb the latest position they had put themselves in. Then Lucky said, "Let's go," and the Lexus eased away from the curb.

We drove in complete silence. The Lexus glided smoothly across the asphalt, a calm humming punctuated intermittently by bumps in the road, which barely perturbed the fine machine's engineered suspension. As before, the faint smell of blond leather wafted to my nostrils. The Lexus moved steadily; no sudden or precipitous accelerations that might catch the attention of a member of the other side. We slowed and stopped for a red light, but when we proceeded, the regained speed was steady around a series of quite gentle curves. I thought we were headed back to Greenwich Village, because they had told me they would drive to my neighborhood and drop me off. As Lucky had mentioned the BQE on the way in, I thought we might have been headed back on the road that emptied into it from the south, the Belt Parkway. I really wasn't sure.

Suddenly Lucky swerved the car into a turnoff to the right and parallel to the road. The car came to a full stop. He killed the ignition. No one said a word. What the hell was going on? My heart raced, the veins in my neck pounded, and my head ached dully as I contemplated the unthinkable. We had driven only ten minutes and were nowhere near Manhattan, where they had promised to drop me. Why had we stopped? I said nothing and neither did they.

Lucky swung open the car door, and I heard two shoes scrape the pavement as he rose to exit the vehicle. He slammed the door shut behind him and I was alone in the car with Sen and Ren, their legs still sandwiching me, and still, despite the changed circumstances, they said nothing.

I could not hear Lucky's footsteps as he paced around toward the back of the vehicle. I did hear the trunk opening. I heard items rattling around in the trunk as he fiddled for something. The fiddling stopped, and the trunk slammed tight. Next I heard the sound of tape being stripped off a roll—it sounded like thick, heavy, industrial-use duct tape.

The time clock stopped. My life was over. I was positive that they were about to tape my mouth shut, take me outside, and shoot me dead.

SEVENTEEN

OOPS

Every one of our days on earth contains a series of small adventures, or small threads that, when woven together, make up the fabric of our lives. When you wake up in the morning tomorrow, you'll wipe the sleep from your eyes, and drag yourself into the kitchen for the first pleasure of the day, a cup of steaming coffee to pump up the energy in your veins. You may not like your job, but still, when you get there after sitting for thirty-five minutes at the entrance to the George Washington Bridge, you'll shoot the shit with Joe across the hall and your secretary, Marcy, complaining about the bills you have to pay and dreaming of the trips you'd like to take. On your break, you'll absorb yourself in the drama of that morning's newspaper; for, while the news is almost always bad, admittedly it is satisfying, gratifying, on some deep and perverse level and whether or not you are for or against it, to find that the hardworking pilots of the United States have blown away a gang of recalcitrant Iraqis; or that the Republicans are once again scheming to open up new tax breaks for the rich and the Democrats are trying to figure out how to keep up;

or that an earthquake killed three hundred people in a place you've never heard of; or that an investment banker on East Thirty-third Street was knifed dead in his lobby the night before, with robbery the apparent motive; or that the Yankees were up and the Mets were down; or that Macy's has a one-day sale and you can pick up a casual shirt on your way to Penn Station and get fifteen percent off the *sale* price with the coupon in the paper. After dinner at the kitchen table, you'll go upstairs and telephone your mother to find that her arthritis is a little worse but that she's thrilled to have won seven dollars at tonight's Bingo game at the community center. You'll watch Jay Leno or *Nightline* as fatigue overcomes you, and, with the light off, you'll hug your wife, but that's all, because you really don't have the energy anymore to make love to her more than once or twice a week. As you close your eyes, you'll have complete confidence, with the arrogance of the living, that the next morning you'll wake up to do it all again, starting by wiping the sleep from your eyes, and dragging yourself into the kitchen for the first pleasure of the day, a cup of steaming coffee to pump up the energy in your veins.

But it was all over for me. The adventure that was my life was done. I'd never make plans to have dinner with a friend or talk to my parents on the phone or complain about my long-distance bill or go on a blind date, ever again.

The fear from the tearing duct tape hit me like a sledgehammer. It started deep in the stomach, at the level of my navel; a blackness commencing low and rising quickly through my chest, my neck, my face, all the way to the top of my head, the blackness of fainting, filled with dots and little psychedelic sparkles and a welling sense of loss of consciousness and almost nausea. But I didn't faint; it passed quickly, and still not saying a word, I braced myself. If they took me out of the car, I would try to make a run for it.

Again, I heard the sound of duct tape tearing and I braced myself for the final moments.

Then, as quickly as I thought I had lost my life, it rebounded. I could hear Lucky applying the tape to the plastic that was covering the front passenger window broken overnight by the thief who had stolen Lucky's car radio. It was blowing with the wind and making a lot of noise, so he was taping it to silence it and perhaps keep out a bit of the icy night air. I silently breathed a sigh of relief, wounded by my mistake but not out yet.

Lucky reentered on the driver's side and pulled the Lexus out of the turnoff without comment, and the other two gangsters guarding the prisoner also remained mute. Again we cruised along at a steady speed of perhaps thirty miles per hour, following gentle curves in the road, stopping for the occasional red light.

Only ten minutes or so more and we were still nowhere near Manhattan. The car slowly rolled to a halt. I still could only postulate as to where we were; in my mind's eye we might have pulled up on one of the patches of grass that frame the Belt Parkway in the vicinity of the Verrazano-Narrows Bridge, which is on the way from the Kennedy Airport vicinity to Manhattan via highway, thanks to Robert Moses.

Lucky finally punctuated the silence. "Okay, this is it for our friend Stanley."

The voice to my right, it may have been Ren and it may have been Sen—too few words uttered for me to know—said, "Should we give him twenty dollars to take a cab?"

"Who's going to give him twenty dollars?" Lucky demanded.

"We got twenty dollars left over after the split of the last of the money that we could give to him," said the voice to my right, in a low, unrecognizable growl. I couldn't see in the moment how a thousand dollars split three ways would yield an integer plus a twenty-dollar remainder.

"But I didn't get us the last thousand dollars yet," Lucky countered.

"Tch," complained the voice, making the noise of frustration formed by percussing the tongue against the roof of the mouth. To my right, he grumbled under his breath, and I could feel his body shift against my leg as he dug into his own pants pocket to pull something out.

"Here," he barked disgustedly, as he handed me a twenty-dollar bill out of his own stash.

"Thanks," I responded meekly, still not sure where all of this was going, even though the twenty dollars for a cab was a good sign, if it wasn't a ruse.

"Get out of the car," growled the voice to my right, with an air of sadism reminiscent of Sen, though I was still not sure. He opened the right-side passenger door, stepped outside, and I followed on his heels.

Still blindfolded, I felt the cold air bracing on my cheeks as I stepped from the vehicle.

The voice stood behind me and ordered, "Don't say a word. Put your hands up over your head."

I complied.

"Now just start walking, straight, and don't stop."

Hands in the air, I took a faltering step forward with my left leg. I took a faltering step forward with my right. They still had me blindfolded with Ren's sleep mask and Sen's sunglasses. To me that was a negative sign. It seemed to me that youngsters like these like to keep their few possessions and that they would have wanted their sleep mask and sunglasses back. Which could easily be collected after shooting me. I took another blind step forward with my left foot, then one with my right. And again. I heard the soft sound of the Lexus gently pulling away, with the meekest acceleration, but I never heard the door slam. Was Sen still standing there behind me while I walked, preparing to put a bullet in my back? I continued; one step with the left, one right, one with the left, one right. Then I did it one more time.

I finally felt that I had gone far enough. Not knowing where I was, I thought that I might fall into the river or down an embankment if I continued walking blind. I stopped. I stood. Hands still up in the air like one of the hapless bank tellers in *Dog Day Afternoon,* I sang out in a soothing baritone: "Are you the-e-ere?" My voice rang out against the silence of the cold winter's night.

Upon hearing no response, I spun quickly around and ripped the sleep mask and sunglasses from my face. I stared back to where the Lexus had been. The smoky haze of midnight air hung over trees surrounding a lonely road without cars and without people. I looked left and right. There was no Sen and no Lexus. They were gone! I had my life back! I was free!

EIGHTEEN

ISN'T ANYBODY HOME?

Silently, I screamed at the top of my lungs in sheer joy. The tiniest of tears covered my shell-shocked and exhausted eyeballs. It was the happiest moment of my life.

I immediately recognized the location. It wasn't a grassy knoll on the side of the Belt Parkway at all. It was Brooklyn's Prospect Park. I grew up in that park. Every Saturday I would lead my dog Maggie, a spunky little wire-haired terrier, on long ambling journeys over the few green hills Brooklyn still had to offer. At times she, lacking inhibition, would plunge spontaneously into the dirty gray-green waters of Prospect Park Lake for a swim. I reached into my trench coat's left pocket where a happy hand slipped around my trusted eyeglasses, still sitting right where the muggers had allowed me to leave them twenty-five hours earlier. I slid the glasses behind my ears and rested them on the bridge of my nose. Now with clear vision, I could see that I was in the park about one hundred yards off Prospect Park West, the boulevard framing the racially integrated but yuppified neighborhood of Park Slope, home to one of New

York's largest lesbian populations, a sixties-style food cooperative, beautiful brownstones, and Seventh Avenue, a respectable commercial promenade of cute restaurants and cafés and the constantly humming real estate outlets. It was a hip alternative to Manhattan. The neighborhood of my childhood was on the other side of the park and about a mile away, a million miles away. As with so many New York neighborhoods that changed radically even from one block to the next, my old one was still a crime and drug haven. And here I was in the middle of Prospect Park at twelve o'clock at night—I had better move, and move quickly. Prospect Park at night is dangerous. I could get mugged.

I was disoriented. Regaining vision after so many hours and with the shock that my body and my psyche had been through, I was a little bit dizzy and a little unsteady on feet that had not walked in a while. But I needed to get out of the park, fast, and I also had business to attend to. The helicopter plan was off, but I wanted to rush to a phone and call the bank to cut off my ATM card and deprive the stinking bastards of their last thousand-dollar theft of my money. There was one big problem, though; I needed to find out whether my dad was at home or staying at his girlfriend's. If at his girlfriend's, where the gang could not find him, I would cut off the card immediately. If he was home, though, I couldn't afford to take the chance that they would gasp and go to my father's apartment for a little blunt payback.

As soon as I gathered my wits, seconds later, I began to race toward the edge of the park and the street beyond. My feet ascended across hard dirt and dead-packed grass until the sidewalk was beneath them and the gutter just beyond. I was on the south end of the Slope, and I headed down Second Street toward Seventh Avenue. My breath grew heavier and heavier till it moved toward a wheeze, as a late-night sprint in suit and trench coat and dress shoes strained my lungs. The street was as deserted as the one I had walked on in Greenwich Village the night before. Trees grow in Brooklyn, and my run was canopied by grand old oaks and framed left to right by the stoops of splendid century-old brownstones. I crossed

Eighth Avenue without event, and my free feet kept running all the way up to the commercial Seventh Avenue.

At Seventh, I turned left and half a block up landed in a pizza shop, one of the few places still barely open at that empty hour. I blasted past the orange plastic seating up to the counter, huffing and puffing, surely looking crazed as a banshee. Behind the counter was a young Italian guy, who looked at me with the hardened nonchalance so powerfully overdeveloped in the toughest city on earth. His eyes stayed hard and his face revealed no expression, not even surprise.

I was quarterless. I would not spend the twenty dollars because it might have fingerprints on it. I needed to get through to this ice-man. "Ex . . . cuse me, c-can I use your phone," I stammered. "I was kidnapped. They just released me and I'm fine, I'm okay. But I need to make some calls. Please."

He stared at me expressionlessly.

"Look, I don't have any money. I was kidnapped. I need to call my father and tell him what happened. Please. I'll pay you back."

He seemed to understand my words and he may have been moving toward relenting, but it was painfully slow.

I gilded the lily. "Look, I was kidnapped, but they got the wrong guy. I'm a federal prosecutor. I remember a lot of details and the cops or the FBI are going to be after them . . ."

His eyes moved downward. He hesitated. Shit! I seemed to have thrown him off with that last remark. Could this pizza place be mobbed up? My being a fed could be reason enough for him to throw me out on my ass.

He hesitated a moment longer, but then grudgingly relented. "Ahright, go ahead, but make it quick. Weah closing."

"Thank you," I gasped. First call: Daddy. Was he okay? Had they hurt him? Was he at home or at his girlfriend's? I punched in the seven numbers. Damn! It was busy. What now? I felt the urgent need to get out of Brooklyn and stay out of Brooklyn. I certainly couldn't go home—they had my address and could come after me there at any time. I felt like a hunted animal, with Lucky, Sen, and Ren Lexus-roaming, gun-toting, and still hanging on to my wallet, ATM card, and driver's license telling them exactly where to go if they wanted to see me again. My best safe house would be at Scott Daniels's on the Upper West Side, far from Brooklyn and far from my Village apartment. I dialed 1 plus 212 and Scott's seven digits. It rang and then clicked. "Hello," came on Scott with nasal enthusiasm. "You have reached . . . I'm not home at the moment, but please leave a message." I exclaimed after the beep: "Scott, it's Stan. I was kidnapped but they let me go and I'm okay. I'm in a pizza place in Park Slope. I don't know where you are." I abruptly hung up.

Where the hell was Scott at past midnight on a Thursday night? Shit. What now? My German-Dutch ex-girlfriend, now friend, Suzanne, lived a few blocks away in Park Slope. I desperately wanted out of Park Slope and out of Brooklyn, but I supposed I could go to her house, make a few phone calls, and then get away. I confirmed her number in my address/date book, and then dialed her seven digits. Lucky break; they had not touched or taken the book, which had sat in the breast pocket of my sports jacket during the entire kidnapping, meaning they did not have a list of my friends to threaten or kill. Suzanne's number rang and rang, till finally it, too, was picked up by voice mail. I didn't bother with a message. Where the hell was *she* at this hour?

Full circle, I punched in for another try at my father. Miraculously, the phone rang. On the second ring, it came off the hook.

"Hello?" my father answered, sounding weak, weary, old, sad.

"Dad?!" I cried out. "It's Stanley. I was kidnapped, but I'm okay."

"What? Where are you?"

"I'm in a pizza place in Park Slope. I was kidnapped. They held me for twenty-five hours but they let me go. I'm fine."

"I'll be damned," my father said. He had seen it all in seventy-eight years on this earth but this was a new one. Never in his life had he been happier to hear a voice. "Are you all right? Do you want me to come down there?"

"Yes, I'm fine. Has anybody bothered you?"

"No. What are you talking about?"

"Nothing. As long as you're okay. Just stay in your place with the door locked, okay?"

"Call your apartment."

"What?" I replied. Why would I call my own apartment? I certainly didn't need to pick up my answering machine messages at the moment.

"Call your apartment. There are people there who are looking for you."

"Okay, Dad, I will. I'll call you a little later."

"Okay, son. Thank God you're all right. I don't know what I would do if something happened to you."

"Bye." I hung up. I glanced up to see that the Italian ice-man was getting impatient with all my calls.

"We gotta close," he admonished me.

"All right, just one more."

I dialed the numbers as familiar to me as my own name. Back in the apartment, it was less than an hour after Meade had arrived. The phone rang. Dan Moretsky, sitting on my couch with his head in his hands and feeling as though he was in a morgue, looked up; it was probably another friend with whom they'd left a message, calling to say he or she had no idea where I was. Rich Meade, professionally dour as any fine agent investigating the likely killing of an Assistant U.S. Attorney should be, lifted the black receiver off its art-deco base where it rested on my gold-colored coffee table with the dark faux-marble top. With practiced lack of emotion, he said, "Yeah?"

"Hi, it's Stan," I screeched excitedly. "Who's this?"

"Stan?" Meade responded with disbelief, practically in a whisper. Meade's voice was somewhat muffled by the chatter of voices in the room. Meade's hand went up in the air with two fingers extended in an effort to hush people. Dan heard Meade use my name and did not believe his ears. The whole room went dead quiet. Dan raised his dejected head with no joy, only disbelief. It was inconceivable to him that it was me. "Stan?" he mumbled quietly as though being brought out of a trance, his face still reddened and streaked with tears. And if it was Stan, Dan thought, he was either in a pool of blood or crippled or otherwise in need of immediate life support.

"Stan?" Meade repeated. "It's Special Agent Rich Meade of the FBI. Are you okay?"

"Yeah. I'm in a pizza place in Park Slope," I burst out manically, jabbering. "I was kidnapped, but they let me go. They gave me twenty dollars to take a cab, but it might have fingerprints on it so I didn't want to use it. The guy in the pizza place is letting me use his phone." My eyes moved up and met the still-unsmiling eyes of the pizza guy.

Dan ran up to Meade and, inches from his face, demanded to talk to me. "Is that Stan? Is that Stan? Put me on the phone," he yelled desperately. Meade nodded hesitantly and waved him off.

"Whoa, whoa," Meade responded on the line. "Hold on a second. Stan, what's your home address?" Meade was testing to see if I really was who I claimed to be.

I gave it to him without considering why he wanted it. "Fifty-nine Third Avenue, apartment five-L," I said.

"Are you all right?" Meade inquired.

"Yes, I was kidnapped, but they released me. I'm okay."

Dan interjected forcefully, impatiently, "Let me talk to him."

"Where are you?" Meade asked me, ignoring him.

"I'm in a pizza place on Seventh Avenue in Park Slope."

Dan again: "Is that Stan? Let me get on the phone."

Meade kept focused on me, ignoring Dan. "Do you need medical attention?" he asked.

"No, I'm all right. They didn't hurt me."

"Looks like it's Stan and he's okay," Meade announced to the expectant room.

Dan was ready to explode with a burst of excitement and joy, and he began a sprint toward my apartment door and the outer hallway where some of the friends had been exiled by the police. He wanted to share the great news, to scream at the top his lungs, to hug anybody in sight. Meade put the brakes on him. "You're not going anywhere. You're staying right where you are. I got a job for you."

"So why don't you let me get on the phone?" Dan asked.

Dominick Scaglione could see that a little supervisory influence was required. "Listen, Rich. Let Dan talk to Stan. He can identify the voice."

Meade was finally ready to relinquish the receiver.

"All right, hang on, I'm gonna put somebody on. Dan." Meade summoned Dan to the phone.

Dan grabbed the receiver and screamed into the phone: "Stan? Is that really you?"

Dan would tell me later that I responded in a shaky, exhausted voice. "Yeah, Dan. It's me. I was kidnapped, but I'm okay."

"Oh, my God. Thank God. Buddy! You're alive!"

"Yep, I'm alive."

"I love you, buddy. I love you. I love you," he shouted excitedly, not caring who was listening. "Where are you?"

With some leftover energy, a small smile crept across my lips, though don't think I was letting my guard down for a second. Lucky, Ren, and Sen could drive by in the Lexus at any moment, for all I knew. "I'm in a pizza place in Park Slope. These guys are gonna kick me out in a minute. It was tough enough convincing them to let me use the phone." I looked at Pizza Man for any sign of shame; there was none.

"Are you hurt?"

"Nope. I'm fine."

"What's the address there?"

I asked Pizza Man for the address and gave it to Dan: 189 Seventh Avenue. Dan announced to the room, his voice rising, "He's at one eighty-nine Seventh Avenue in Park Slope. One eighty-nine Seventh Avenue. One eighty-nine Seventh Avenue. Is anybody getting this down?" Dan shouted to the congregated law enforcement mass, even though several agents had already written it down.

Still speaking off the phone, Dan told Meade, "It's him."

"All right, we'll send out a car to pick him up. You're going to get him, Dan."

Back on the phone, Dan told me, "Okay, Stan, we're coming to pick you up. Just sit tight."

"Okay, Dan. Thanks. Put the agent back on."

He did. "This is Special Agent Meade."

"Listen, you gotta send somebody out to my dad's house right away. The guys who kidnapped me threatened to kill him. I gotta know he's okay and you gotta protect him. Please."

"All right, we'll take care of it. What's his address?"

I gave it to Meade and then we both hung up. I called my father and told him that FBI agents were on their way over to his house and to let them in when they came. That night two FBI agents, an attractive blonde and a man, spent the night sitting on my father's couch. Although my father lay in his bed, nobody slept a wink. My father would feel nervous for many months after it happened, his head throbbing with a constant feeling of tension. He could not stop thinking of what could have been and the eulogy he was composing before I called. The FBI agents watched TV all night, and my father recalls them watching a murder show.

Meade was shocked that the story had a happy ending and that Stan was not dead. He was glad, but as a pro he needed to get to the bottom of why I had been missing. Meade wasn't going anywhere. He had an investigation to lead.

"Terry," he said to Special Agent Mehan, "you and Jimmy go pick him up. If he needs medical attention, take him to the hospital. Otherwise I want him back at the Ninth so we can get to the bottom of this." Mehan and Glynn took Dan in their car. Miller picked up Duke at the Ninth in his, and the two cars sped through the night.

Off the phone, the icy pizza man still looked at me like, why did I take so long with his phone and when the hell was I getting out of his shop, which was closing, anyway? I spotted a refrigerator full of cold Snapples and other refreshments. I needed something to drink, desperately, and I had no money, just the twenty-dollar bill with potential prints. I said to the guy, "Can I have a Snapple? I'm sorry, I don't have any money, but I will gladly pay you back."

He kept looking at me like I was nuts, asking for more than I was entitled to. I didn't think I was getting it. Then I reached down into my right pants pocket and, miraculously, in addition to the twenty-dollar bill, pulled out two wadded singles that had gone untouched.

"Wait, here," I urged the guy. "I just found two dollars. I can pay you for the Snapple."

In shame or in disgust, he replied, "Here, take the Snapple. Fawget about the two dollas."

"Thank you so much." I opened the fridge and pulled out my first Snapple Peach Iced Tea since the mattress. The gulps went down smooth and cold.

Outside, the street was deserted as I downed the rest of the drink. All the neighboring shops had been long since shuttered for the night. I stood in front of the pizzeria as its gate swung down, too, and realized that I was much too vulnerable just standing there on the lonesome street. The boys could still be cruisin'. Although I was supposed to wait at the pizza place for the Bureau and the NYPD, I started up the block, south. At the next corner I spied a car service storefront, which, upon entering, was somewhat filled with an assortment of Russian and other Eastern European arrivals, waiting for the next call for a pickup on X Street and a drop-off on Y Boulevard.

"Excuse me, do you mind if I sit here and wait?" I implored excitedly. "I'm getting picked up."

They looked at me like I was a little touched. "Look, I was kidnapped," I burst out. "They let me go, but now I'm waiting to get picked up by the FBI. Can I just sit here and stay warm while I wait?"

"Holy sheit," said a Russian accent. "What de hail heppened to yoo? Sure, sure, you ken ssiht."

I plopped down on the hard wooden bench. All eyes were on me, disbelieving but not unsympathetic. Car service drivers, like cabbies, know about crime. They would get a fare to a rough neighborhood and a gun to the head. They would consider themselves lucky if they got to drive themselves home, penniless but unhurt. Many new immigrant drivers, including many of color, were no longer willing to pick up blacks, for fear that the ride would take them to one of those neighborhoods where the guns came out. And black lawyer friends of mine couldn't hail a cab even in a high-priced suit.

I explained myself. "Look, I was walking last night in the Village when some guys came up to me in the street with guns. They took me in a car and held me in an apartment until now. Luckily, I made it out. I just gotta wait to get picked up. They got the wrong guy. I tried to tell them that." I hesitated. You never know; these Russians—some of whom might be illegal aliens—might not be happy with me, either, if I told them I was a federal prosecutor. I left it out. They didn't need to know everything. I just needed a safe and warm place to sit until Dan and the agents showed up.

"Holy sheit, mahn. Yurre locky dey didn't keel you."

"Tell me about it. That was close."

Every five minutes, I would go out in the street to look for an unmarked car in front of the pizza place. Then I'd go back in and the drivers would look at me and shake their heads. It seemed interminable—how long did it take to drive from my apartment to Park Slope? I was very antsy, and I wanted to get out of Brooklyn.

Meanwhile, on the way into Brooklyn, Dan grumbled to himself that the agent driving did not put a brick on the accelerator and was not using the siren. The round red police warning light was up, but the agent only gave a brief *whoop* of the siren to pass through a red traffic light. Dan thought, "Why don't they move faster? Until we get to Stan, God knows what could happen." Though irritated, he held his tongue.

After at least a half hour, on one of my runs outside, I saw two dark, beat-up sedans pull U-turns up the street. That was them. I raced out of the car service, shouting, "Thanks," as I ran, and hop-skipped up the street to the cars. On the two cars, five doors opened simultaneously and out stepped my old friend Dan Moretsky and four new friends, Detectives Samuel Miller and Sergeant James Duke of the NYPD, and Special Agents Terry Mehan and Jimmy Glynn of the FBI. I hugged Dan. Terry Mehan was a pretty, solid-looking woman a few inches shorter than me. Though she was a total stranger, I gave her a big, round hug, too, and then Jimmy. I would have hugged a dancing bear if he had FBI credentials on him.

"I'm very happy to see you," I said.

"We're glad to see you, too," Mehan responded.

Mehan asked me again if I needed medical attention. I didn't. She wasn't bothered that I'd given her a big hug as if I knew her. She would later recount: "It's not unusual. I've gotten hugs from all kinds of people for all kinds of reasons. You get hugged from victims, from parents. You're the first non-bad person. I expect I was the first non-criminal he had seen in a few days."

In the street, Dan saw that I looked bedraggled, disheveled, exhausted, with a drawn face. Standing with the cold wind of Seventh Avenue blowing up the tail of my long trench coat, I bore a sickening resemblance to a newsreel concentration camp survivor. My cheeks were fuzzy from not shaving, and Dan noted the terrified look in my eyes. I had devolved to a creature appearing more beast than human.

When I spoke, I sounded weak, but Dan couldn't help but admire what he said was the remarkable composure his friend exhibited. Dan kept hugging me, but I had a sudden realization and pulled away, explaining, "Sorry, Dan, I would hug you, but they handled my coat and there may be fingerprints on it."

I showed Dan the scarf. "Look, this is what they used to blindfold me. My own scarf." I handled it by the edges so as not to mess up any prints.

Finally, I pulled the twenty-dollar bill out of my pocket, handling it by the edges, and showed it to Dan. "Look, they gave me twenty dollars to take a cab. This may have prints on it also. They gave me the money, then they told me to get out and walk, still blindfolded. I did it. I thought they might kill me, but they drove away."

The agents led me into one of the cars and put Dan and me in the backseat.

We pulled out of the Slope and headed for Manhattan. I was home. On the way back to the East Village, Dan and I hardly spoke; we were both in shock.

Sergeant Duke was in the front seat. He started casually asking me questions about what had happened, so I wouldn't have time to fabricate anything. The cops didn't know what had happened until they knew what had happened.

NINETEEN

WHO CARES?

Meanwhile, Scott Daniels sat in the U.S. Attorney's Office at the desk of Ellen Conrad, world-class word processor, and began to compose a eulogy to his friend Stan. They were there to see to it that our administrator Rosemary would hack into my voice mail and e-mail to look for clues to my whereabouts.

Scott looked up from the desk and a pretty blond face was staring back at him. She fit one of the typical FBI agent profiles: peaches and cream, middle America, how-ya-doin'-John, slap on the back, success, apple pie. Blond hair, blue eyes, any man's dream. But these FBI women were tough. Very tough. You had to be for that job.

"What?" Scott asked.

"They found him. They're bringing him in," she replied.

" 'They found him. They're bringing him in.' What the heck does that mean?" Scott thought. "What do you mean?" he said to the agent.

"They found him. They're bringing him in."

To Scott, it sounded like FBI-speak for, "The dude is dead. Let's wait until everybody is together for us to describe how he was mutilated first and then murdered." He still didn't want to accept that one of his best friends was dead.

He was mad. "What the heck do you mean 'They found him, they're bringing him in'? Is he okay?"

"I don't know," the attractive blonde responded.

Scott's voice was rising steadily. "What do you *mean* you don't know? Is he dead or alive?"

"I don't know. They found him. They're bringing him in."

Scott had had it. A good litigator has a ferocious side when pushed. "All right, let me tell you," he bellowed. "I am not moving from this spot until you find out whether he is dead or alive."

She walked away. Scott picked up the phone to call the command post in my apartment. The first three times netted him a big fat busy signal. Time number four it rang, and a female voice answered, laughing. "Hello."

"Hello," Scott reverberated. "It's Scott. What happened? Is Stan okay?"

"You mean you didn't hear? He's fine!" the voice said. "He called in from a pizza place in Park Slope. He was kidnapped, but he wasn't hurt and they're on their way over to pick him up."

"Wow. Thanks a lot. I'll be back over there in a little bit." As he hung up the phone, Scott threw a little dance into his step as he absorbed the joy and relief. The thing had ended well and Stan was not dead, just damaged. Thank God. He donned his puffy down coat and grabbed the FBI agent and pulled her out the door toward her government-owned car. He wanted to see with his own eyes the guy they were "bringing in." Alive, not dead.

PART TWO

CAT

TWENTY

REASONABLE DOUBT

The investigation had begun. I didn't know it at the time, but the cops added insult to injury. They marched me into a small interrogation room with two FBI agents, Rich Meade and his fellow squad member Terry Mehan, and two NYPD detectives, Sam Miller and Larry Riccio. Miller looked sharp in a suit and tie, just as Duke did; it was a thing for these NYPD detectives to dress smart. It was the uniform. They felt that when they investigated a murder in a $4 million town house or even a $400 crack house, the fine suit would set them apart and earn them the respect a New York detective needed to unravel the crime. Meade and Mehan had pulled on jeans.

It was late and there was serious business at hand, so both feds and locals looked mighty somber. I had, after all, gotten them out of bed, and they were now at work. Telling the story, I felt empowered, even self-impressed, with my ability to recall so many critical details that ought to lead to the gang in a matter of days. I mean, for God's sake, I knew the pattern on the tiles in the entranceway; I knew the first few numbers of

Lucky's cell phone; I knew Ramos's full name; I knew we were near the airport because I'd heard planes, and near water because I'd heard gulls; I knew Mystic and Mercedes and Honey were local young hookers who might be known on the street; I knew how much a cab cost from hooker-land to kidnapping home base; I knew Lucky would be on the Jersey Turnpike Saturday in a black Lexus with a broken window covered by plastic. It went on and on. For hours.

It was a damn good thing I didn't know at the time that my recall of the details was a little too good. After about an hour, I remember we took a break in the proceeding; I figured maybe so people could go to the bathroom. And I had a big treat, because anytime the door would open, even for a couple of seconds, little hives of my close friends would buzz in the vestibule, smiling, waving, giving high fives, and even, if the agents let them get close enough, giving powerful hugs with a couple of tears to boot.

What I didn't know then was that after the first run-through of my story the interviewing agents gathered in a room outside with the other NYPD detectives and brass, and FBI agents who were all drawn to the case that night like bees to honey. Miller and Riccio and Meade gave the rough outline of my account, but their heads were not held high because of a creepy feeling in their guts. Sure enough, when they gave it over, a top-level NYPD detective unabashedly jumped to the conclusion that the others were grappling with.

"Dat staw-ree?" he exclaimed in his detective Noo Yawk-ese. "Dat's da biggest piey-ahl a shit aye evah herd."

The other detectives and agents gathered around the aging steel police desks shook their heads. Most of them agreed with the big honcho's call. The details didn't fit any of the cops' patterns. Jamaican drug lords shooting it out over a couple of kilos; innocent gets caught in the crossfire—okay, been there, done that. Kidnapping with this MO was not a recognized category of crime in New York City. Even my dating habits didn't make any sense. A blind date followed by meeting a girl on the subway? "Who meets a girl on the subway?" thought the detective sergeant in charge, James E. Duke. I told how I then walked her home and stopped to buy cookies. "Who meets a girl and goes to buy *cookies*?" Duke thought. I also said I'd walked her to her door and invited her out for a cup of tea. This seemed incredibly odd to Duke. "Who asks for a cup of tea? 'We can get a cup of tea sometime.' Who says that? It's a cup a kawfee, or a drink—who says a cup a tea?"

They knew it was my birthday, as Duke later related, "so we started talking about could this girl have been some girl that he met somewhere that maybe either he shacked up with, or, ya know, maybe, who knows. Could portions of this story be true, and then, ya know, he's filling in blanks to make it sound a little more, ya know, sanitized, and, ya know, humanitized. Was he out partying for the last three days and he finally comes back now, realizes he's gonna get screwed, he doesn't show up to work, his friends are lookin' for him, it's a big, ya know, everybody's out . . . lookin' for him, he's in a little bit of a bind, and now he's coming up with a story, so he takes a little bit of the truth, and he fills in the gaps. . . ."

Even the fact that those phone calls were on my answering machine from the bank and the woman who found my credit cards did not, in and of themselves, establish my credibility. Duke would later tell me: "Well, one of the points we brought up was, was he out partying, maybe he was out partying somewhere and got rolled by somebody. Maybe someone picked his pocket while he was drunk somewhere. He could have been with a prostitute, was he out smoking crack all day, ya know, he was with a prostitute, he passed out, she took his wallet and went out and tried to party with it."

The fact that I was an Assistant U.S. Attorney did not shift the balance in favor of my credibility, particularly for the cops. Local police tend to be a little less cozy with prosecutors than the feds. When you deal day in and day out with the sewer of street crime, you sometimes cross the line. There's the law in the court but there's also the law of the streets.

So institutionally, the police force has too much experience being prosecuted by the same DAs they work with to build too much trust. Just being an AUSA would not get me over the hump with these guys.

Plus, the story was way too crazy no matter how you sliced it. Duke: "You look at the totality, not just the specifics, at that time. And the circumstances. Combine that with the statements his friends had made. We asked, 'Where were you that night? Could he have been out with a girl?' They said, 'No, he wouldn't've been out with a girl, or he wouldn't've met a girl.'" And as it turned out, "Where was he? He was out on a blind date with a girl that they didn't know about, ya know, or that they weren't tellin' us about. They're tellin' us, 'No, there's no way he was out with a girl.' So now we're sayin' maybe they don't know him that well. Maybe there's a side of this guy that they don't know. Now he's tellin' us this grand story of this elaborate kidnapping, and abduction, and robbery, and bein' held, and the guy can remember the tile on the floor, ya know, *tunnel, phone numbers.* It's to an extent where it just seems too fantastic."

Meanwhile, Abe Lebewohl, owner of the 2nd Avenue Deli, just two blocks from my apartment, had been murdered recently in the morning on his way to the bank with the prior night's deposits. Detective William Glynn (no relation to Glynn the FBI agent) sat at one of the metal desks focused on the Lebewohl investigation. Glynn was one of the most experienced and accomplished detectives on the force—that's why they'd put him on Lebewohl. He had extracted more confessions—in high-profile cases—than a Catholic priest. Glancing up from a pile of papers, he noticed that the yuppies pouring in looked like "very legitimate, concerned people, who were very concerned about their friend."

But Glynn had heard it all before. "A good number of missing persons—of course we get into teenagers that have taken off and don't want to go home—when we go out lookin' for them, they actually hide so that we don't find them. They don't want to be found. You'll find most people over twenty-one, when they're gone, are gone because they want to be, whether it be a girlfriend or a boyfriend, a lover, whatever. Usually the 'missing' part is a smaller part of what's going on."

Earlier that night, before I emerged from the dead, Duke and Miller had sidled up to Glynn's open-air station and asked the voice of experience what he thought about the missing prosecutor case.

Glynn said, "It's bullshit. This guy is where he wants to be. He's partying somewhere."

Much later, with me in the station and snippets of the results of my interrogation wafting across the squad room, it smelled like garbage to him, but Glynn kept his thoughts to himself. He'd been with the police department for more than twenty-seven years and a detective for more than twenty, and he'd never experienced anything like this. "They're in some bag of shit over there. A black Italian guy, he's got Ren and Sen, he's got prostitutes, ya know, everyone comes up with a little story, but this was really blown out of proportion. I figured the guy was doin' something— he was on somethin'—I figured snortin' some coke or something. I thought really it was far-fetched—this was really stretching." Glynn had also never heard of a case where the criminal offered the victim cab fare to get home.

Glynn had one consolation. "I was just grateful it wasn't me that was assigned the case. As you get older, you don't have as much patience. I've heard the shit. Yeah. That was pretty much it." Little did he know that as this thing ballooned he would end up having to put the Lebewohl file down for a couple of sleepless nights.

Feds normally give Assistant U.S. Attorneys more slack, but Meade wasn't buying what I was selling, either. They brought me back in the room and grilled me once more, this time with pointed questions instead of the narrative I had given them before. I never had a clue that the interrogation room was filled with skeptics. I just thought they were doing their job.

Once they finally put a stop to the whole interrogation, and I'd told my story three times, they finally let me out of the room. Now, as I waited in the detective work area of six steel forward-facing desks with phones but not much else on them, I bounced around from sitting to standing and smiled and whooped and said things like,

"Whoa, was that one insane ride. I mean, they threatened to kill my dad! Thank God he's okay! And all those nutso sex acts going on around me! And hour after hour and I had no idea what they were planning to do to me. And at the end I thought for sure they were about to shoot me. The whole thing was nuts!"

Scott and Dan sat at two of the empty detective desks and shook their heads sympathetically. The pretty blond FBI agent sat looking at me, impassively. I wondered if she was single. Duke sat there in his fine-looking suit, shaking his head and giving an occasional perfunctory smile. If I had had any idea what he was actually thinking, or that there was any doubt about the true-to-life, sick-as-hell, life-or-death roller coaster I had just gotten off of, I would have hit the roof. But the thought never even crossed my mind.

TWENTY-ONE

LOTS OF REALLY WEIRD PEOPLE COME INTO THIS BANK

Poor Carrie Skashosa. Twenty-five years old, she was still considered the new kid on the block at the Chase Bank branch on the corner of Eighth Street and Broadway. It's bank tradition: The youngest one always gets the challenging cases. I pulled in with Scott as soon as the bank opened, a little after nine A.M. I had very serious business to attend to. My cash machine card and my Social Security number were on the street. I had to protect the rest of my stash.

Skashosa looked up from her desk next to the window facing out on Eighth Street. She observed Scott and another man—me—wearing "obviously a big long hair wig and a baseball cap and looking like he's upset, distraught, and a little bit crazy or something." The men sat down across from her and explained that they needed to change all the account numbers and PIN security codes on Mr. Alpert's accounts.

"Look," I blurted at Skashosa in an agitated state, "I gotta be careful. We can't be seen. People might see me looking through the window. I was held at gunpoint. I was kidnapped, and you can verify it and you can call the precinct and they'll send you a police report. I need to change the accounts really fast. They had my information—Social Security number, everything."

Skashosa could see that the window really drove me nuts, heightening my strange presentation. She grew up on a farm in Pennsylvania and had only been in New York a couple of years. Chase had positioned its young service representative at the East Village branch, and while it was located west of the pink hair, bone-through-the-nose zone, it was the eastern-most Chase Bank, so it drew an unusual crowd.

Skashosa: "Here at the branch we have a lot of artsy people that come through. They are very diverse in their likes and what they do. It's normal here to have people come in not just in business attire."

Still, my appearance and demeanor and psychotic explanation that morning were pushing the limit, and as she pulled out the necessary paperwork, she mumbled to herself, "Oh gosh, why me?"

She was right to conclude that I was a little unstable. The cops had finally let me go at dawn on Friday morning. The last time I'd had any real sleep was Tuesday night. Accompanied by several friends, I finally arrived home at about six A.M. to a full house.

Unbeknownst to me, Suzanne and Darcy had decided to clean my apartment to kill time as the night became morning, and they delicately compared Stanley notes. For Suzanne, my disappearance was Act II in the Theater of the Macabre that day. At lunch, a colleague at her electronic publishing job had related the horrible story of how his father had just killed himself by putting a gun to his head in his car and pulling the trigger. The colleague had been relegated the ghastly task of cleaning out the car. When she heard the bad news about me, Suzanne thought of Jonathan Levin, and how his student had forced his PIN number out of him and then killed him in the end anyway. "Why Stanley? He's a good guy," she thought. In her mind's eye, she saw me lying on a street somewhere in New York, unconscious, and no one was doing anything, figuring I was just a bum lying there. She thought that if I had been kidnapped it was 98.5 percent certain that I was dead, because it was well known that the best witness to the kidnapping always gets killed. Images of my funeral flashed through her mind. What would she say? She prepared a brief eulogy: "Stanley was a great guy. He tried to do the right thing, and he devoted his life to fighting for the right stuff. He was honest and decent. I loved him and will always miss him." She almost jumped through the ceiling when she got the call from Dan that I was okay.

When I arrived at my apartment, Darcy grabbed me and pulled me into the bedroom, to hug and kiss me and tell me how happy she was that I wasn't dead. As Darcy closed the door to my room, I could see the disapproval in Suzanne's eyes that someone whom I had only just started dating casually three weeks before should get priority in the order of people who cared for me.

After a few minutes, I was able to break away and rejoin the group in my living room. The night was drawing to a close, with the steady press of morning light creeping in through the sooty windows. My friends were tired and subdued, and they would hug me and get bits and pieces of the story that spurted out of me as though I had Tourette's syndrome. I couldn't relax, as I was still hard at work protecting my life. At a bar in Texas, where I'd been attending an environmental crimes conference, a friendly local had given me a baseball cap with a fake ponytail at the back. I found it in a closet and perched it on my head, and also donned a pair of my own sunglasses this time. Dan thought I looked demonstratively paranoid, as every ten minutes or so I would nervously peer out the window in my disguise to see if a black Lexus with guns was waiting to fix the mistake they had made in letting me go. That fear would end up lasting a long time.

A phone call came in from one of the people who hadn't slept well that night because of me. The United States Attorney for the Eastern District of New York, Zachary W. Carter, had been notified by a call from the Bureau the night before at his suburban home that one of his assistants was missing. Zach led a charmed life, and had had a stellar career that followed traditional prosecutorial paths plus paths open only to a few: He went from being a well-paid associate at a large private Manhattan firm to assistant prosecutor in the Brooklyn DA's office to Assistant U.S. Attorney to state court criminal judge to United States Magistrate in Brooklyn to the first African-American top federal prosecutor in the Eastern District of New York. Zach had tossed and turned a good part of the night, always caring about his people and worrying who could have done it. He had just learned I had been released unharmed.

Although I can't claim we ever spent enough time together to become close, Zach had been very good to me. Two years earlier, he'd made me the environmental chief. Plus, just months earlier, Zach had put me up to receive the Stimson Medal, an award for outstanding performance bestowed each year on an assistant in the Eastern District and one in the Southern. The Cy Young Award. When I had my five minutes in the sun at the ceremony at the Association of the Bar of the City of New York, I feted Zach as the chief prosecutor who always wanted to know not just whether we were *winning*, but whether we were also *doing the right thing*. (The award recipient for the Southern District, Pat Fitzgerald, then got up and quipped insistently that his U.S. Attorney, Mary Jo White, cared about whether they were *winning*. Fitzgerald later became the U.S. Attorney in Chicago; he was one of the government's most aggressive terrorism prosecutors, and he prosecuted Scooter Libby for the outing of CIA agent Valerie Plame.)

As he dialed the phone to call his still-breathing environmental assistant, Zach was thrilled that I wasn't hurt but worried about how his award-winner would react emotionally to the incident. Zach considered himself a bit of an amateur Freudian psychologist. Scott answered the phone and chatted with Zach for a minute about how I was right there and doing fine; then he passed the phone to me. I felt a pitter-patter of excitement. It's not every day that you get a call from the U.S. Attorney, especially at home.

"Hullo," I said in my tired tone.

"Man, am I glad to hear your voice," the United States Attorney for the Eastern District of New York said, with genuine joy. "Are you all right?"

"Yes, Zach, I'm fine," I responded. "It was a pretty wild ride I went on, but I got through it okay. I guess you heard about it."

Zach could not believe how chipper I sounded despite the circumstances.

"I got a few of the details. Thank God you are safe," Zach said. "We're here for you. If there's anything you need, you just tell me."

"Okay, Zach," I answered quietly. "Thanks a lot. And thanks so much for calling."

As he hung up the phone, Zach had serious doubts about how fine I could possibly be after an experience like that. If he had seen me wearing the ponytail cap and shades, he would have worried even more about my stability.

At Chase, Skashosa could see the strange man with her own eyes. Noting her look of skepticism, I obligingly pulled off the cap with the fake ponytail. "Look," I said, "it's just a fake cap. I need to keep them away from me."

"Can I see some ID?" Skashosa implored gently. There had been some fraud cases at the branch, and she couldn't be too careful. Most of my ID was still on the street, so I pulled out my passport and plopped it on the desk.

The next hour or so was spent trying to freeze my bank account, freeze any transactions, and set up security codes. I traded in the ATM PIN that had traveled with me for most of my adult life for a new one. Skashosa, filled with the sweet kindness of rural Pennsylvania, worked hard "to try to show you that we *could* do it, too." She instinctively strove to reassure me "'cause I think you'd kinda lost faith in everyone and everything at the moment," she explains in her soft voice. My story was "out there," but she believed it "just because of the way you were acting."

The kernel of detective in this service representative also pored over my accounts to confirm I was telling the truth. "All I had to do was go through the system. I could see where you'd been, what transactions, you know, large transactions. And I could look through your account to see that had never happened before." A man's bank transactions reveal the story of his life and definitely map out the crimes.

Skashosa was with me for more than two hours, checking data, filling out forms, running to the copy and fax machines. Her supervisor and coworkers were a little miffed that it was taking so long just to open a new account for a weirdo. When all my cash was in new accounts, my PIN number had been changed, and Scott and I finally hopped in a cab for the Upper West Side—subways were out, as I was too scared—she was finally able to explain calmly to her colleagues that she had just assisted a kidnapping victim protect his life savings from further robberies.

That's when the jokes started. "Yeah, Carrie got a guy that was kidnapped. Uh-huh. He came back in disguise with a detective. He was afraid they would spot him without that ponytail. Yahhhh." Everybody at their desks burst out laughing.

They were like, "Yeah, you're gullible. That Carrie would accept any story somebody told her."

Then they used a standard joke coined just for her. "You'll believe anything. Oh, yeah, you're just the Amish girl."

The whole bank staff was cracking up, even though Carrie was not Amish. "Not all farm girls from Pennsylvania are Amish," she thought.

Later, in a business meeting, Carrie got a phone call from an FBI agent. She reviewed with the agent the unusual transactions on my account, and quickly advised the agent to call Chase's security number to obtain ATM cash machine videotapes, as a way of spotting their man.

Even the call from the FBI failed to convince her coworkers that the "Amish girl" was not just plain gullible. "Uh, uh—stop—you paid somebody to call you. You just want us to stop kidding you," said one.

"Ye-ah ri-i-ight—the FBI's gonna call the bank. What are you gonna do—catch the kidnapper?" said another. It was crazy, but Carrie ignored them with the calm satisfaction that she had helped somebody in need.

On Monday morning, one of Carrie's coworkers brought in a newspaper article on the kidnapped fed. "Ya know, guys, Carrie wasn't lying."

Carrie kept that clipping in her desk drawer to prove that she wasn't crazy and neither was I. Still, over the coming months, when the dingiest of the East Village black leather outfits would sidle in to open a checking account, Carrie's coworkers would say, "If they've got a wig on, maybe Carrie will take care of them. Maybe Carrie will believe 'em."

TWENTY-TWO

GATHERING THE BITS
AND PIECES

Whether or not the cops would believe me was another question. For me, Friday morning meant protecting my remaining assets. For others, there was a job to get done. As the sun rose over New York on the morning of January 24, 1998, about 120 NYPD detectives and FBI agents gathered for a briefing at the Sixth Precinct house in the West Village on Tenth Street. The case had attracted a small army because law enforcement looks after its own. Even if they had their doubts, they still needed to find out. The back of the precinct house bordered Charles Street, overlooking the tenement apartment with a bathroom the size of a tanning booth that I used to live in when I first started at the U.S. Attorney's Office.

Cops are highly territorial creatures. I lived east of Broadway, and therefore the Ninth Precinct led the charge in the A.M. hours of January 23 after I was released. When they learned that I had been abducted west of the border with Broadway, the cop code required the case be moved to the precinct where the crime took place, the Sixth. Sergeants James Duke and

Samuel Miller's misfortune became the good fortune of a teddy bear turned fighter, Sergeant Georgie Wich. George was a burly ball of Irish enthusiasm, his handsome round features framed by a large blondish mustache and straight hair parted in the center and a little long for a cop. That middle part and 'stache made him look like he could have been one of the extras on the album cover of *Sgt. Pepper's Lonely Hearts Club Band*. He dressed nicely in a natty tweed sport jacket and nondescript slacks, but he was nowhere near as stylish as the finely suited Miller and Duke I'd met the night before in the Ninth.

George's commanding officer, Detective Sergeant Ronni Haas, would later tell me what he thought about the less stylish George. "I knew that George was a really great detective," Haas explains. "George is quiet. He's not a very flashy detective but he's very, very competent. He's also like a dog with a bone. If you give him a case, you know that if it's something that he believes in, he's not gonna let go until the case is solved." Wich would run the investigation under Haas's supervision.

On *Law & Order*, it is all exciting leads and snappy banter. Not so the plodding, methodical nature of a typical investigation, even if it is for a kidnapped fed. No stone too small to turn over. There were more than enough leads in the FBI 302 report of my interview to keep everybody busy. Sergeant Haas ordered his men to get the stock videotapes of Washington Square Park. Just in case. They checked with the security guards at the NYU dorms and the videotapes on the sides of their buildings. They canvassed every parking garage in the area and spoke to each manager. The cops visited every doorman in the neighborhood; doormen are the silent eyes and ears of the city, even when it sleeps. Nobody saw nuthin'. They went to the cleaning service company to talk to whoever might have been cleaning the Chase vestibule at 671 West Twenty-third Street at approximately 2259 hours on January 21. No dice. The owner of a grocery on West Ninth Street, the manager of Greenwich Brewery on Sixth Avenue, the manager of EJ's Luncheonette, and the manager of the French Roast café all saw nothing unusual. At Sammy's

Noodles, a customer saw a car accident involving a taxicab on the corner of Sixth Avenue and Tenth Street and reported it to the Sixth Precinct. Nothing more.

One item early Saturday morning at least had meaning for the head of the FBI squad, Richie Meade. FBI agents went to the A&P supermarket on Sixth Avenue and Twelfth Street where I bought the cookies. Amazingly, the manager remembered me and the woman, and was able to provide a copy of the receipt for the two boxes of cookies. While this seems inconsequential, it actually convinced Meade that I was telling the truth. In the experience of FBI agents, small details are difficult to manufacture accurately, and Meade was amazed to learn that the time he was about to spend on this case over the next few days would not be wasted.

The doorman at my building on Third Avenue, Sylvester Quarto, recalled with uncanny clarity having seen me enter the building at approximately 1730 hours on the twenty-first. He called out to me in his soft Filipino voice: "Stanley, you have a package—laundry." He gave me the hangered shirts and saw me walk to the elevator. The victim was alone. He did not see me leave the building. But I did anyway.

Another team contacted the command of the 63, 67, 70, 71, and 77 Brooklyn detective squads and precincts to see if there had been complaints of criminal mischief to an automobile, in particular a late-model black Lexus. I sincerely doubted that Lucky had called the police on Thursday morning to report that someone had broken into his car. The leads on automobile tampering that came back from the 63, 67, and 70 were all dead ends. Another cop looked at Sixth Precinct parking summonses to see whether Lucky had gotten snagged before snagging me. Nope.

One detective called the Larchmont Police Department and obtained the details of the theft of a 1997 black Lexus. It was stolen on the night of January nineteenth from the owners' garage with the alarm activated sometime before the husband and wife woke up the next morning. Wrong Lexus.

As I had suggested, the FBI put out a National Law Enforcement

Telecommunications System (NLETS) bulletin for the Lexus to all Eastern Seaboard law enforcement agencies. It read:

BE ON THE LOOK OUT FOR A BLACK LEXUS HEADING SOUTH ON I-95. VEHICLE INVOLVED IN A KIDNAPPING/ROBBERY. THE FRONT RIGHT PASSENGER WINDOW IS MISSING WITH PLASTIC OR TAPE COVERING THE EXPOSED AREA. THERE ARE POSSIBLY 1–3 BLACK MALES IN THE LEXUS WHO ARE ARMED AND DANGEROUS CARRYING AUTOMATIC WEAPONS THAT WERE USED IN THE KIDNAPPING/ROBBERY IN NEW YORK CITY. SUBJECTS POSSIBLY GOING BY THE NAMES LUCKY OR LUCKS AND ALSO REN OR SEN. SHOULD ANYONE SEE THIS VEHICLE PLEASE CONTACT SPECIAL AGENT RICHARD MEADE OF SQUAD C-30. . . .

If Lucky drove to Virginia as he had told me he would, the long arm of the law could reach out and touch someone.

Bank records showed a cash withdrawal at a Chase branch on Utica Avenue in Brooklyn. An FBI agent and a detective visited the branch to arrange to pick up the ATM videotape. Two other detectives drew a four-block grid in the area of the bank and walked it, looking for a black, late-model Lexus with a broken passenger-side window and missing a radio. They met with negative results. Another agent and detective visited the Chase Bank at 6510 Avenue U, Brooklyn, where another withdrawal had been made on my card. They talked to all the tellers. Results: negative.

My credit card records showed purchases of auto glass, a car stereo, and a computer. But the credit card companies would not be able to give precise locations until later, when the vendor submits the paperwork. A useless lead for now.

Special Agent Confrey and Detective Rogers spoke to the cute head of hair from the subway, Lisa P. Marantz. She confirmed the Entenmann's, the Chips Ahoy!, and the offer of tea, for which she took a rain check. "I told him maybe another time. We exchanged business cards and he left me at my building," she related. Mr. Alpert left her location between 10:30 and 10:45 P.M. She never expected that chatting up a guy would land her a visit from the FBI. From the Bureau's perspective, she was a suspect until proven otherwise.

Cavorting with known prostitutes left a trail of bread crumbs that the cops would try to follow home to Lucky. The cops quickly found a rap sheet on a girl named Mercedes showing an arrest for working at an unlicensed restaurant. Detectives Cronin and Walsh visited a man in Woodhaven, Queens, who openly admitted to being Mercedes's boyfriend. He claimed that on Thursday the twenty-second he went to work at a restaurant on Fulton Street and then went shopping for a rubber piece for the front of his car, accounting for his whole day. More important, he claimed that Mercedes went to work with him at the restaurant on Thursday and that she stayed there until ten P.M. An obvious lie, since I was with Mercedes all day on the twenty-second. When they caught up with Mercedes herself a little later, she confirmed the boyfriend's story and insisted she did not need an attorney, had never seen a shiny black Lexus, and had done nothing wrong. There was only one problem with this lead. The cops were interviewing the wrong boyfriend and the wrong Mercedes.

Inching closer, Detective Suschinsky found a beat officer, O'Brien, in the 7-1 who had seen a female named Mercedes in the area of a burnt-out building near Grafton and Livonia Avenues. She'd been seen in the company of a black male who worked on cars on that block. O'Brien had also heard the name Mystic but did not remember seeing her.

The records for the Kings County Criminal Court looked promising. They referred to a Mercedes who had been arrested on December 9, 1997. She was due in court on January 22, 1998. She failed to appear, and a warrant was issued for her arrest. Try finding her.

Of course the small army did SOP lab analysis. Special Agent Meade vouchered over to the crime lab the following items that he got from me:

one twenty-dollar bill USC; one pair of sunglasses; two dry cleaner receipts; three business cards; one velour scarf; one necktie, "Cocktail Collection," multicolored; one Bill Blass pin-striped suit jacket; and one green Stanley Blacker trench coat. They were to be scrutinized for latent prints, and would undergo hair and fiber analysis. Many hours later, tech Joseph Fritz of the Latent Print Unit reported to Detective Suschinsky that the lifts from the business card and the twenty-dollar bill were of no value.

Cops get a bad rap, sometimes justified but usually not. The painstaking detail work with multiple dead ends they pursued on my case was done not because these guys couldn't land jobs as accountants or insurance brokers. There were two core agendas in the hearts of these cops: solve the crime and help the victim. Supervising Sergeant Haas explains: "I have a really hard exterior, but inside I'm a real softy. I think a lot of good detectives and a lot of good police officers and a lot of good FBI agents are."

Haas gives the example of a sergeant in the Seventh Precinct who handled the homicide of a little girl in Manhattan. The investigation went cold. There was no prosecution. To this day, Haas says, "I know that he still keeps a picture of that girl on his desk." Tough guys on the outside who keep pictures of unavenged child victims on their desks. Think twice, Al Sharpton, before you mouth off at the cops again.

In my case, Haas wanted it done and done quickly, if only for my sake: "It was definitely only a matter of time before these guys killed sometimes. Life is cheap to a lot of people. . . . They don't care about anything except material things for them, their stature in whatever group they're hanging out in, and nobody else means anything. The fact that you might have been traumatized, or your father might have been traumatized, doesn't enter the picture at all. They don't care. Ya know what, selfish people like that—it's only a matter of time before they say, 'Okay, let's kill 'im. Hey, let's see what it's like.'"

As the methodical detail work continued relentlessly during Friday afternoon, tiny jigsaw pieces belonging to the right puzzle started to float in. A police officer from the Fifth Squad in Brooklyn knew about a couple of prostitutes driving around his beat in a black sedan. Definitely worth following up.

Agent Bendetson and Detective Cronin followed up with Michelle Jones, the woman who had left the message on my answering machine that she found my credit cards on the street in Bedford-Stuyvesant. Michelle, an immigrant from the West Indies, was very, very concerned that something may have happened to me. The investigators visited Midwood Car Wash on Utica and Midwood Avenues, where Michelle worked. The manager directed them to a hermetic glass jar behind the cash register where Jones had left my credit cards and told everyone not to touch them. The investigators transferred the cards from the jar to a property envelope. They called Jones from the car wash and she agreed that they could come over and talk to her. At her home on Crown Street in Brooklyn, twenty-nine-year-old Jones informed them that she found the cards at seven A.M. lying faceup in the street a few feet from the entrance to the KFC on the corner of East New York and Utica Avenues. She took the cards to work, put them in a jar, and called the credit card companies and me. The agent and detective took elimination prints from Michelle so they could distinguish her fingerprints on the cards from the perpetrators'. Then they vouchered the cards and the elimination prints to the crime lab.

Other cops picked up still photos from the ATM machine cameras. You withdraw cash, you get your picture taken. This generated some frustration because at first the bank provided the wrong pictures. The banks were not skilled at calibrating the transaction with the photo. Later they fixed the problem. I was told over and over by cop after cop that the photos alone would not have easily led to the villains, especially without known priors. In fact, one detective showed a still photo of Lucky to a registered federal confidential informant, and the CI had never seen the dude. Still, it's awfully nice to have a framed black-and-white of Lucky for when you eventually run into him. The cops did post Lucky's mug at the 71 and the 77 precinct houses, just in case. Others got negative recognition on the pics from the squad, RAM, Anti-Crime, and Burglary units in the 73 and the 75. At the 61, 63, and 69, the detective squads were asked to show the photos and debrief prisoners to see who might recognize the Lucky man. Nothing.

The tech boys generated the best leads. Sixth Precinct Robbery Squad Detective John Fitzgerald ran the nicknames "Ren," "Red," "Lucky," "Sen," "Cen," "Honey," "Mercedes," "Dee," "Misty," and "Luis Ramos" through the cops' BADS, CARS, BETA, and FORCE FIELD photo databases.

Bingo. This time the right Mercedes and her photo came back "with a phenomenal amount of prostitution," says FBI Special Agent David Biddiscomb, cool enough and tough enough to be an NYPD guy himself. Biddiscomb came from investigations pedigree—his dad was a CIA agent who eventually climbed to the highest civilian levels in the CIA—but Biddiscomb also came from street blood; his uncle Gary was a sergeant in the NYPD who stood guard at Fort Apache in the Bronx during the 1970s. Unlike some of the others, Biddiscomb did not immediately jump to the conclusion that I was lying. But he sure had his antennae up. The very fact that I had come out alive was a bit much to take, especially when he heard about the area of Brooklyn in which I'd been sequestered. "One of the first things that they told us was that you were alive," Biddiscomb says. "I was shocked! Because I know that area. We knew the areas and stuff and it was hazardous. . . . What *didn't* happen to you— it was kinda weird. Everybody gets kidnapped gets killed." Biddiscomb had been tracking the Latin Kings seven days a week, twelve hours a day, since September of '97, and the Brooklyn ghettos were a familiar place, as was the typical criminal behavior.

"I go to neighborhoods everywhere. I'm a Brooklyn guy, I go to

Brooklyn North, Brooklyn South, really crappy areas. I go to the Bronx. Particularly with the gang stuff, I'm in really crappy areas in the city. All the time, to me it's just another place."

Biddiscomb speculated that I may have been robbed randomly by guys who eat dogs at Gray's Papaya at the corner of Sixth Avenue and Eighth Street. "I spoke with a friend of mine at the hot dog stand right down in lower Manhattan, in the area, and basically they say a lot of subjects—perps—hang around down there," he explains. "They come from Brooklyn and they hang around in there. And that's where a lot of robberies jump off from the hot dog stand. The guy was telling me. I go down there all the time and see these guys. A lot of them don't belong in the neighborhood. They do robberies but usually don't take their victims with them."

It was still Friday the twenty-third of January when Detective Thomas Hayes of the Homicide Squad on East Twenty-first Street, Manhattan, and Special Agent Biddiscomb set out together to track down Mercedes. She had a lot of arrests in the 73 Precinct. They printed out the addresses corresponding to her arrests and started at 289 MacDougal Street, Brooklyn. That location was an empty lot. They asked the owner of the building across the way, on Granite Street, if he knew her. "She used to stay in an empty apartment on the top floor," he related. "But I haven't seen her in four months."

The apartment on the top floor was the home of a lovely middle-aged woman, Rosie Vasquez. Hayes was a very nice guy, and Biddiscomb tried to be polite, letting Vasquez know there was a problem and that they really needed to speak to Mercedes. When Mrs. Vasquez saw the picture she said, "Oh, that's Dee. I seen her maybe three weeks ago—she was stayin' down the block."

She directed the men to an apartment on the eleventh floor of a building on MacDougal. When they knocked, a black male, Leon Johnson, answered. The apartment was filthy, with clothing covering the floor and the furniture in disarray. The lawmen could hear other people in the apartment, making it a hazard. A couple was in the back bedroom just hanging out, in the middle of a weekday afternoon. "You don't know when you gotta pull out your gun 'cause somebody is gonna come at you," explains Biddiscomb. He made Johnson walk in front of him, shielding as they swept through the apartment. "You have to be very careful," he explains. "It's kinda like a waltz. What if he's got a gun stashed in the place? What if he's got dope stashed somewhere?" But he and Detective Hayes calmed down when they saw an infant child. "It was kinda like it can't be that bad."

Johnson stated that he last saw Mercedes at a party on Saturday. Johnson could see that these cops were not narcs, that they were just looking for someone and he didn't have to put up with them for long. Biddiscomb relates, "He was a little startled, but at the same time he was also very kinda like . . . A lot of times you have people when they know they haven't done anything and they know you're not gonna find anything, particularly as it pertains to them, then they start getting a little more hostile. He was basically back there having sex with this girl and once we kinda gathered everybody out, he kinda got his wits about him and then he was kinda, *Fuck you*." The detective and agent saw no value in antagonizing him and left.

Meanwhile, another male from Johnson's apartment, Jabbash Douglas, was taken by Detectives Biddell and William Glynn back to the Sixth Precinct in Manhattan for an interview. He said he knew somebody by the name of "Dee" but not by the name "Mercedes." He also mentioned having been arrested that past summer along with a male named Tuck and an unidentified black male, for kidnapping. Douglas told Glynn and Biddell that he was asked to take the two males to a rental place and when he got into the car with them he saw a white male sitting in the car. Douglas thought the other two were robbing him. Somehow all the charges were dropped in court.

Back at the Sixth, Wich was pissed off because he had been trying, unsuccessfully, to reach me all afternoon. I still had not slept, as calls kept coming in from friends and well-wishers and from the U.S. Attorney's Office and a million other professional relations. In midafternoon I broke free from it all, and Scott took me downstairs to swim in the Olympic-sized pool in his elegant building on Sixty-seventh and West End Avenue. With my bare flesh surrounded by the bluish-green luminescence of chlorinated water, I floated peacefully in a world a million miles from the Brooklyn ghetto apartment I had visited just a day earlier. Murder and mayhem and raw sex and guns and clothing on the floor and gangsta rap promises of pummeling were replaced by a soothing baptism of healing waters in the indoor heated comfort of a sun-drenched pool overlooking the Hudson. I thanked God for preserving my life.

Finally, Wich reached me and convinced me to come downtown to talk again. He had Special Agent Diana Parker drive me, and although he had not slept, either, my buddy Scott insisted on coming with me. At the precinct, Wich and Special Agent Dave Burroughs took me through the whole thing one more time. I actually enjoyed telling the story, but this was getting a little ridiculous.

Burroughs seemed particularly warm and caring for an FBI agent. When he heard what had happened to me, "it just sort of took my breath away," he says, although he, too, was probing to find the truth. "There's a certain fraternity in the law enforcement community, and when we were told it was a missing U.S. attorney, it just heightened your concern." He was so anxious to get moving on the case that he couldn't sleep Thursday night. He showed up at the Sixth the next morning two hours before everybody else. There was something deeper in Burroughs. He had left a smart career in banking for the Bureau. He is a devout Christian whose powerful faith "helps me keep a balance." In one case he worked, a woman was abducted in Connecticut, driven to New York, and burned alive in the trunk of a car. She was twenty-five years old and had a seven-year-old son. The woman's boyfriend, who was the boy's father, was one of the coconspirators whom Burroughs busted and locked up forever. But for Burroughs, with his deep Christian beliefs, there was no anger at another of God's children. "As much as he had done a horrible thing, he's still a human being, and I couldn't hate him for what he did." I could see the kindness on his face when he interviewed me, thorough and incisive though he was.

Wich and Burroughs interviewed me for several hours. As they wrapped up the first repeat of my interrogation, the prey couldn't resist participating in the hunt. "Look, George," I said, "all ya gotta do is find that pay phone where Mystic went downstairs to call Lucky. It's near the Brooklyn-Queens border, and it's near a deli called the Salaam Shop. It should also be right outside the building with the tiles I described to you in the hallway. Then you subpoena the phone records for that pay phone, and you'll find the number that starts with 917-69, which she called Thursday afternoon, and BOOM! you'll have Lucky's cell phone number. Then just subpoena the records of that number and that will lead you right to the man."

As I spoke, Wich nodded his head in agreement and wrote down every word I said. He had never had a victim prosecutor before, but what the fuck, take the help from wherever you can get it. On this case he felt like Columbo for the first time, and don't think he wasn't excited about heading up a team of FBI agents along with his NYPD guys in the highest-profile investigation of his career. That morning, with FBI agents pouring in, Wich says it was "like a fuckin' invasion. I hate to profile, but they have like a special kinda bag, with all their good stuff in there. Ya know, like an L. L. Bean bag with a nice cell phone, this, that, all these gadgets. They're all coming, they ain't fuckin' kidding." As a victim, I provided a smashing law-enforcement opportunity. He would make his thirty-three-year cop father, who died three years before, proud.

The confirming details coming in meant that at this point the men no longer harbored the previous night's doubts about whether some kind of a robbery had really happened. Still, my saga was a big mouthful to swallow. "I remember George and I looking at each other when you were saying that the prostitutes were offering sex on you and all this stuff, and we're sorta looking at each other like . . . sorta weird," Burroughs explains. "Here's a guy, ya know, they have a kidnapping and they're offering, 'Hey, by the way, ya want a sandwich? Oral sex? Anything?' Ya know, we sorta looked at each other going, 'How weird is that?'" But from my eye contact and the way I handled myself during the interview, Burroughs was convinced, and by the time they were finished all he said to Wich was, "Come on, let's go get 'em."

TWENTY-THREE

THE CELL PHONE

While I returned, exhausted, to Scott's, back at the Sixth, Wich was pushing a lead of far greater inspiration than any I had suggested. A citywide inquiry had gone out from the desk of the chief of detectives for any information concerning similar ATM robberies. According to Wich, there had been two similar robberies in Brooklyn. And one they tried but failed to do in Manhattan, earlier on the same night they grabbed me.

My friend David Prosser also had a lead on an almost-robbery he'd heard about that was probably the same gang. At work on Friday, his associate Liza Kaplan had told him of a harrowing experience she'd had a few nights before when she was walking her Maltese in the West Village. That night, Liza, a powerful lawyer but a diminutive five-feet-zero-inch presence, noticed a slow-moving black sedan with several men in it cruising the street, the car windows open despite the bitter cold. She felt relief when they passed her by, but seventy-five seconds later she was shocked to see the car behind her again. In order to return to her, given all the one-way streets, they would have had to drive north several blocks, then purposely swing back and onto her street. She knew then without a doubt that they were prowling for prey, and she and her Maltese made a fearful dash for her building just in time.

Prosser called me, agitated, and said, "Stan, you're not gonna believe this. I think your gang almost did the same to a woman I work with a few nights ago." He told me her story, but the robbery that never happened lacked details beyond some hoods cruising around and looking bad.

As a result of Wich's search of the robberies that did happen, Hayes and Biddiscomb were handed the plum lead on a robbery in the 67 Precinct in Brooklyn. Because Biddiscomb had worked real street cases cooperatively with the NYPD, he knew Sergeant Kevin Butler of the 6-7. Good thing, Special Agent Biddiscomb explains: "You have to really bridge your credibility gap with the police and the FBI a lot of times, because a lot of times they don't trust you." It's "the jack-in-the-box theory. You feel like, at what point in time when they're spinning the wheel does the FBI demon come popping out and it's like, see, you're a fuckin' fed? Because they always feel you have a certain way of taking over things—the feds come in, they take everything over, things like that." Biddiscomb was ready to roll out to Brooklyn again. His federal job placed no specific limits on his discretion to pursue. Hayes was at the end of his shift and hopped in the car for the drive out to Brooklyn with Biddiscomb only after his overtime was authorized.

The two men climbed the five steps to the door of the precinct house and asked the desk cop where they could find Kevin Butler, who was the squad supervisor in the 6-7. Butler knew and trusted Biddiscomb, and he turned over copies of the files of robbery cases #66 and #71, both with similarities to mine. One of the files from this Brooklyn precinct house— the precinct in which my mother used to yell out the windows to me— bore an intriguing resemblance to my situation. It occurred on the nineteenth of January. There were two male perpetrators with guns. They drove a black Lexus. They demanded the complaining witness's

PIN number so they could withdraw cash. The victim's name was Steven. *And they stole the victim's cellular phone.* Hayes and Biddiscomb thanked Butler and beat it out of there.

Driving back to Manhattan, "Tom and I are talking on the way back," Biddiscomb says. "It's the same robbery. The guy's not hurt, taking money, they do what they do. Goodbye, see ya . . . use him up. We were feeling really good. Great lead. We got the Nitrosystem. Now we have a picture. Now we're like, okay, let's put this together and get the person. We're kinda marching methodically through these different things following these leads. We're only a couple of days behind them."

When briefed, George Wich, running the show from the Sixth, immediately requested that Detective Ross from TARU (the Technical and Reconnaissance Unit) perform a dump on Steven's stolen cell phone to determine if calls made from that phone went to another cell phone beginning with the numbers 9-1-7-6-9 as described by the complaining witness in this case.

Wich also asked Ross if he would check to see whether calls had been made from the 9-1-7-6-9 number to Chase Bank at around eleven P.M. on January 21. Finally, he wanted Ross to tell him whether there were calls received by the 9-1-7-6-9 number from a pay phone somewhere in Brooklyn near the Queens border. Ross said he would look into it and hung up the phone. Ross knew his stuff, and he knew how to work the phone companies so he could get answers in just a few hours. This was an unusual case—a kidnapping saga with a "victim" safely returned. Quite often, Ross worked under real-time pressure, when an Asian gang member's girlfriend had been kidnapped for revenge and was still being held; lost minutes could cost the girl her life.

A few hours later, the fax machine at the Sixth was humming subpoenas for phone records to Detective Ross. Those subpoenas would prove to be more powerful than any police bullet.

At the same time, back in Brooklyn, Hayes doggedly stayed on the trail of Mercedes. He spoke to a lieutenant of the 4-1, a sergeant of the

1-0-8, and a detective in Brooklyn North Vice. The subject, Mercedes, had been arrested in each of those commands. Hayes was advised that canvasses would be made for her at each location. He and Biddiscomb finally went home to get some sleep, hoping the next day would hold promise.

Into the wee sleepy hours, Ross finally called Wich and then dropped off the printouts at the command center by four A.M. on Saturday, January 24. The dump from Steven's stolen cell phone revealed a single wireless call from the stolen phone to a number beginning with 9-1-7-6-9. The number 917-692-5858 had received a call from the stolen cell phone. Pay dirt. The phone belonged to one Terrance Micelli, residing at 485 Linden Boulevard, Brooklyn, New York.

Subsequent investigation also revealed that there had been two calls to Micelli from two separate pay phones in the vicinity of Howard Street and St. Johns Place, Brooklyn, between 1500 and 1800 hours on January 22, 1998, as described by the complaining witness, Stanley Alpert. The two pay phones were located in front of the Caribe Grocery at 1715 St. Johns Place. A separate check for prostitution locations at Howard and St. Johns came back negative.

Oh, yes, one more thing. At 2303 hours on the night of January 21, the 9-1-7-6-9 number had called Chase Bank. The call originated, as close as the technology could pinpoint, from the vicinity of West Twenty-sixth Street and Seventh Avenue, almost the exact location and time described by the complainant and verified by bank records.

It was now just a matter of time.

Other tidbits fell right into place. The cops compared the home address of Mr. Micelli with the Department of Motor Vehicles list of Lexus owners in Brooklyn. A 1998 Lexus was owned by a Betty Johnson, residing at 485 Linden Boulevard. Betty was the name of Lucky's grandmother.

A background computer check on Terrance Micelli found one such person with a date of birth in 1946. A lot older than Lucky. According to the police report, that Terrance Micelli had one arrest—no conviction—on file, for forgery, from 1974. Other than that one official record, it appeared that Lucky's father had stayed out of the law's grasp.

By six-thirty A.M. on Saturday the twenty-fourth, two members of the police detective squad, Leser and O'Keefe, were in the vicinity of 485 Linden Boulevard looking for a black Lexus. The address was a two-story home with a two-car garage in the rear. A search of surrounding streets proved negative.

Leser and O'Keefe also visited two buildings at 553 and 563 Howard Avenue to view the lobby tiles and building layout. The building at 553 Howard had a white tile lobby with red and black trim tiles; two steps to get in and then two more steps up to the lobby; a set of stairs to the right rear of the lobby with seven or eight steps up to a small landing, then a left and the same number of steps to the second floor. "This building generally fits the basic description from the victim," Officer Leser wrote in his report to Wich and Haas. It was close, but they were looking at the wrong building.

Meanwhile, in an attempt to close in on Luis Ramos, Detective Suschinsky spoke to anti-crime units in the 71, 73, and 77 Precincts. Nobody there had heard of Loo-iss. Not one to skip a beat, Suschinsky asked the Postal Service police at which address in the vicinity of Howard and St. Johns a Mr. Luis Ramos received his mail. I'd worked with the postal cops and investigators on more than one case, including one against mining giant Phelps Dodge. They are very, very good at what they do. They quickly came back to Suschinsky with a Luis Ramos at 1945 Union Street, just a couple of blocks away. By contacting Kings County Hospital, Suschinsky found another Luis Ramos address on Ralph Avenue. All leads to follow as the new day unfolded.

Wich never went home. To him, the suspects were true "gangsters." He says these were "bad guys. They're gonna rob people. They have whores. They have young little girls, all these young guys are running these young little girls, ya know." His feeling was that Lucky the leader "had the most potential for killing someone, ya can just tell, instinct." Yet by the time the sun rose over the West Village, Wich was finally snoring with his feet up on the desk, feeling cautiously optimistic about the whole thing. He honestly thought that within about a day, "we're gonna have every one of these fuckin' assholes in custody."

TWENTY-FOUR

MONICA AND ME

Apart from two naps in Ramos's apartment, I had been up for fifty hours straight. Back at Scott's, I finally hit the sack at around one A.M. on Saturday the twenty-fifth of January.

I slept peacefully. In the morning I felt like a new man as Scott and I ventured down a sunny but cold West End Avenue to pick up some bagels and the Saturday morning papers. Never before had the simple exercise of taking a morning walk to buy bagels and the paper felt like such a privilege. But the newspaper was a shocker. Staring up from the cover of the *Daily News* was a smiling Monica Lewinsky, looking sultry under a "She Kept Sex Dress" headline. Right above her was a banner headline announcing "Kidnapped Fed Freed—Somewhat Poorer."

I was livid and ready to kill. Who in law enforcement with shit for brains had decided to deliver my story to the papers when the investigation had just begun? Lucky and his gang, or a friend or relative of theirs, might see the paper and, knowing they were facing a manhunt, slip out of town on the next bus to Elmira or some other obscure place, perhaps

207

never to be found. Sen had been arrested in D.C. and so might have been on the lam in New York; nothing would prevent him and his buddies from doing the same thing one more time. A publicity-hound cop might have just wrecked what I believed were excellent odds of tracking down the gang.

"I can't fuckin' believe it," I said to Scott. "Whose bright idea was it to publicize this when they aren't caught yet?"

Scott looked troubled, too, but he wanted to keep me happy. "They must have a good reason for what they did. Anyway, look at this article," he said, flipping the paper open to the large article on page 38. I read over his shoulder:

FED KIDNAPPED IN VILLAGE:
U.S. ATTORNEY CAPTIVE 26 HOURS

An assistant U.S. attorney was kidnapped near his Greenwich Village home Wednesday night and held captive for more than 24 hours before being released yesterday in Brooklyn's Prospect Park, authorities said.

During his captivity, Stanley Alpert, 38, chief of civil environmental litigation in the Brooklyn U.S. Attorney's office, was forced to reveal the numeric password of his bank card, which his abductors used to withdraw large sums of money from several banks, authorities said.

Alpert, who was not hurt by the kidnappers, apparently gained his freedom after telling his captors he is a federal prosecutor. Law enforcement sources said Alpert warned that if anything were to happen to him, federal agents and police surely would hunt them down.

"The odds were sort of against him being released unharmed," a law enforcement source said. "Your opportunity to escape is in the first minutes. Once you get in a vehicle, it's usually the last anybody sees of you."

Alpert is a popular official in the office of Brooklyn U.S. Attorney Zachary Carter. Co-workers described him as a hard worker and an extremely productive assistant federal prosecutor whose cases included a $21 million judgment against a copper refinery company for failing to clean up land it sold to the government.

There is no pattern of similar robberies in the area matching the method of operation, sources said last night.

Naturally, as often happens, the press got some of it wrong. I sure as heck was not so dumb as to warn my trigger-happy friends that if they left my body in a Dumpster "federal agents and police surely would hunt them down." A man with no power must find alternate means to prevail.

Ignoring the inaccuracies, after reading it, I said, "I cannot for the life of me believe that they are telling the kidnappers that the FBI is after them so that they can run and hide before they find them. This is so bone-headed. If they get away because of this . . . ," I groaned.

Scott's focus was someplace entirely different. "Wow, look at this," he exclaimed. "A popular and extremely productive Assistant! This is great! Hey, I could use some good press like this. What's the name again of that guy that did this to you . . . Sven?!" Scott delivered this with comic glee.

We had a good laugh. It was also funny that I ended up on the same page as Monica Lewinsky and her blow-job sex dress. Riddle: What's the difference between me and Bill Clinton? Answer: He took what I refused.

TWENTY-FIVE

ROUNDUP: GIRLS

When they got to work on Saturday morning, Biddiscomb and Hayes were juiced to tighten the noose.

Biddiscomb's rep with the cops came in handy. "We come back Saturday morning, and the first thing, I'm sitting down in this meeting room and the first thing that happens is the person from that squad comes down and he's like, 'Where's the guy who got the photo and was looking for Mercedes?'" Biddiscomb explains. "I go, 'That's me.' He comes over and says listen, 'I really think that you're onto something with this. I really want you to really push hard and try to find this woman.' Now that's him coming to me and saying that. He's not going to one of his detectives, he's coming to me."

The universe of possibilities was starting to narrow. Not only did they have a general area in which Mercedes was known to hang out and occasionally get arrested for prostitution, the phone dumps now told them the location of the pay phone from which Mystic had called Lucky in the middle of the day to find out when he was coming home.

The men followed the playbook I had written. "We went out there and just sort of tried to check out the different neighborhoods, and I remember we went into three or four different buildings," Biddiscomb recalls. "We go in, look at the tiles in the ground and try to get an idea, as far as going in, how many steps up, which way you turn, and things like that. What happens is that we go into four or five of these buildings, and then we do some other checking of leads—this, that, and everything else—and the day is kinda going on."

They started canvassing the neighborhood in the late morning, energetic and hot on the trail. They drove up and down Eastern Parkway and the side streets over and over with no luck. Some buildings were similar to my uncannily precise description, but failed to match the Ramos homestead for one reason or another. Biddiscomb: "Well, we found stuff that looked like that. But it wasn't the same place and we knew it wasn't. We'd say, 'Look at the tile here, blah, blah, blah, and that's close but that's not really the same thing.' And then there isn't the number of steps that he went up and turned to the right, things like that. It just never really fit. And then we started doing other things. I can't remember half the shit I did that day."

Stymied by the tiles, Hayes and Biddiscomb and another agent settled in to watch, hoping something would break the surveillance, like a cruising black Lexus, perhaps. "We wind up sitting on a corner of Eastern Parkway and this cross street, not far from where we had gone into those different buildings. It's getting later now, and then what happens is that the guy I'm sitting in the car with, he's driving around with a couple of different agents, and they kind of did a lap around the block. And we were looking for certain cars, I remember that, too. So we're on Eastern Parkway, and if we saw a car that fit—we had a black Lexus and a partial license—we would try to follow some of those cars to see if we could find anybody."

The weak winter sun slowly descended over the distant brick buildings and the trees, and the men felt no closer. As the second day of the investigation drew to a close, Biddiscomb sat behind the dashboard of a cop sedan pointed east on Eastern Parkway, not far off Howard Avenue, wondering how many more days this Stan Alpert thing would keep him away from the Latin Kings. Lost in thought for a moment, he glanced in the rearview mirror and something caught his eye.

"I remember that all of a sudden it's getting later and we noticed these two females standing in front of this place. We're almost at the corner of this cross street and Eastern Parkway and there's a building behind us, and they're probably about twenty yards behind us, to the back and to the right of us."

The cops from the other car came around the block, pulled over, rolled down the window, and one of them said, "Hey, what's your story with these two over here, these two women?"

They all leaped out of the cars—Biddiscomb, Hayes, and the detectives from the second sedan. They walked over to the two women standing in front of the building. "And as soon as we're walking up to them, I can tell this is Mercedes," Biddiscomb relates excitedly. From her PIMS police database picture. It actually required considerable skill for Biddiscomb to recognize her, because the database had seven pictures of her and they all looked different. "And then this other woman with her, we start talking. And I think somebody actually said to her, 'Hey, are you Honey or Butter or whatever it is?' And she goes, 'Yeah.' Honey told the officers that she was out there waiting for her friend Sen.

"I'm like, this is a friggin' home run," Biddiscomb says.

"So we're like, 'All right, come on, let's go.' And they're like, 'What's goin' on?' So we separate the two of them and put Mercedes into the other guy's car and we put Honey . . . Butter . . . whatever the frig her name is, we put her in our car."

Then they noticed the building where the girls were standing, which had been sitting a few feet behind them as they whiled away the afternoon hours. Biddiscomb couldn't fuckin' believe it. "We were right on that block. Right on the corner. When I got out of the car, I literally didn't even have to move the car. I just got out of the car and walked over.

"We were there for hours going up and down Eastern Parkway. And the whole time we're there, this is the building we're looking for the whole time. We're talking twenty yards, tops. I mean, the whole friggin' time, we're right on the pot of gold." They had looked at a lot of other buildings nearby but not at this one, 1430 Eastern Parkway. "It's funny about the building. This building was a little more isolated—over. There was a lot of business on the corner. The houses are kind of distinct the way they are. It's kind of isolated when you think about it."

Once it was pointed out, it became clear as day that this was the scene of the crime. With the girls sitting securely in the cars, Biddiscomb and a few detectives examined the layout. "We can tell just looking at it that the tiles are the same color, just the way it was described, and for some reason there were a couple of steps and then you turn in, either a sharp turn to the left or the right or whatever, and it's right up on the first flight. Something like that. So what happens is we kinda check it out real quick and call people in and the sergeant winds up going up with his group and says, 'Yeah, this is the door.' So definitely we knew we had the right location."

For an investigating machine like Biddiscomb, it wasn't Miller time. The workday had just started. He was happy to a certain extent, but he had no time to waste giving high fives. "Now you know you gotta get down to business," he says. He also needed to move fast because he was afraid the male perpetrators might show up at any minute.

Biddiscomb got in the car holding Mercedes, while Honey was with detectives in the other sedan. Biddiscomb's professional routine was not unlike a surgeon grasping a scalpel or a carpenter a hammer. He got right into it. "To me, she's the one we're looking for. Basically what happens is there's a new agent in the car and she's in the backseat with him and I get in the front seat. There are lots of things you can do, you can be very sweet, you can be whatever. I started talking to her, and you can tell right off the bat that she's not a happy camper. I started cursing at her a little bit. I told her, 'Look, you're in fuckin' trouble and you really screwed up this time. You have no idea what's gonna happen to you now. You kidnapped a U.S. Attorney and you can go to jail for twenty, twenty-five years. I said, 'Don't if you don't want to, but now's the time to talk to us. We need to know right this second or forget it, you go to jail and forget about it.'"

Mercedes was nothing but attitude to start. She shouted back at the pushy FBI agent as soon as he started talking. "What's this shit all about? You can't arrest me. I didn't do anything."

Biddiscomb was slightly taken aback. "She was cursing a lot. Fuck you, blah, blah, blah, blah, blah, et cetera. Things like that." Biddiscomb was convinced that she had a drug problem.

Mercedes was no Latin King, and Biddiscomb knew how to push buttons. He hit Miranda's "right to remain silent" and some other speeches the Supreme Court hasn't mentioned in its written opinions.

Biddiscomb: "You use basically all the fed bullshit. It's like, 'You're gonna go to jail forever.' It's like the gang members. 'You goin' upstate? Well, guess what, now you're with us. Now you're going to Kansas. Now you're gonna go to Florida. Now you're gonna go to Atlanta. And now you're gonna go there for twenty years.' It's a great tool. And a lot of times it doesn't work out so well, but especially, in some of these cases, you tell the guy he's gonna go to jail for ten years . . . it's still a lot worse than what they're used to."

He hit hard and fast. "'Hey listen, you kidnapped one of us. You wanna screw around, you picked the wrong people.' That's part of what you do. You wanna send a message to these people to think about it. Also scare the shit out of them. That's really what you wanna do. That's part of what it's all about."

Confronted by a man with the one-on-one power of this street-tough FBI agent, Mercedes's belligerence and cursing dissipated like air from a balloon. She stopped and breathed heavily. There was an awkward moment of silence as the agents in the car glanced at each other without expression. Then Mercedes started crying.

"You saw her change from the street prostitute into a little girl," Biddiscomb says. "A little kid—absolutely. As soon as she started crying, it was almost like she melted away. And then you realized she was just a little kid." She *was* a little girl. Sixteen. And ready to flip on her pimp and his gunmen.

But now the call came in from a sergeant at the Sixth. He wanted the suspects transported back to the nerve center for questioning. Biddiscomb was apoplectic. A few blocks away at the 73 Precinct, he could get the job done before the girls had second thoughts, and he didn't want some bureaucratic friggin' rule getting in his way.

"The sergeant comes on the scene and he comes up to me and says, 'They wanna take them back.' I said, 'No. We got them here—we're gonna talk to them. We got them, let's just do it. Why should we leave here? We got the apartment secure as well. This guy may show up.' He's agreeing with me, don't get me wrong. We're all in agreement that this is what we should do. So he goes to me, 'This is out of my hands.' I said, 'Yeah. I could understand—I could imagine everybody is really hyped up.' I call Rich back and I guess he was talking to Dom, and Dom sorta straddled the fence. I just said, 'Rich, I promise you that we take the interview, you'll have the information you need within forty-five minutes. I promise you it will happen.'"

Rich Meade ignored the turf battle and decided to let his guy do his job. "No problem," he said. He'd worry about the fallout later.

Biddiscomb hung up on Meade and told the sergeant, "We don't have to take them back; we'll take them to the Seven-three. You know what you wanna hear."

The sergeant smiled conspiratorially and said, "Absolutely."

Biddiscomb's play worked. They took the girls to the 73 and the girls gave up the whole scheme—names, beeper numbers, phone numbers, everything. Biddiscomb switched over and interviewed Honey. He found her to be a real pleasure. "She was really a nice kid. I mean really a nice kid. I remember talking to her, she kept talking about Leonardo Di-Caprio, and he's so sweet-looking."

They bought Honey a soda and just chatted. She acknowledged that she was there. She acknowledged that she knew Mercedes. She acknowledged that she knew the other guys and told how they met. And as for one of the guys, Honey was enchanted. She kept saying about Sen, "He's so diesel. He's like really well-built, nice-looking."

Biddiscomb: "Yeah, I think she had intercourse with him—I forget. I'll be honest with you—I can't remember. She really was infatuated with the guy. Then she talked about Leonardo DiCaprio and things like that. It's a whole different way of talking to someone. Here I was trying to scare this other girl right off the bat, just because I wanted to shock her into reality a little bit. I didn't need to do that with Honey. She's scared. She definitely now knows who we all are and that this is a bad situation she got involved in and she's so young. So we sat and talked to her for quite a while."

From Honey's childlike pitter-patter emerged one icy detail. The cops were correct in their expert view that I should have died.

Biddiscomb is matter-of-fact about it, just like with everything else. Emotion is not on the table when you do this kind of work. "She just said they were talking about what they should do with you, and I forget who she said," explains Biddiscomb.

"But one of them said, 'We should just kill him.'

"Then they were all like, 'Nah, nah, nah—he's a nice guy.' It was just one of these things. . . . The conversation was sort of whimsical the way she talks. She's a young kid. But what happened is that she walked us through the fact of what it was like in the apartment, what they were doing as to maximizing the amount of money they would get, going to the bank, to the ATM, getting you to withdraw money to give to them, this, that, and the other thing and anything else. They were worried about getting caught. There were definitely discussions about the fact that you were a U.S. Attorney thing, this must really be serious. So one of them had sort of said, 'Let's kill him.' There was more of the fact like, 'Hey, look, let's just take what we can get and then get rid of him. Just let him go.'"

Lucky for me.

Once back at the Sixth with the girls, Honey's mother showed up, according to Biddiscomb. "Her mom was furious, just furious." At Honey, and at the cops. The woman looked like she had just gotten out of bed.

Now that Biddiscomb and Hayes had worked their magic, the cops had two subjects and a confirmed kidnapping. Back at the Sixth precinct house, the mood shot up. Another agent gave Biddiscomb what passes for a compliment in FBI talk: "We knew if anybody could find him, it would be you." The dominoes were falling and the boys were next. Biddiscomb went home and had no more involvement with the case. All in a day's work.

TWENTY-SIX

ROUNDUP: BOYS

Other teams were busy tracking the male masterminds.

While the girls were being rounded up, an agent and detectives sat for hours in an unmarked car across from 485 Linden Boulevard, looking for a Lexus. The waiting time is a chance for cops and FBI agents to trade law enforcement yarns and play the cop version of Jewish geography. Above all, surveillance is boring. Hour after hour went by with no more action than cops getting to know one another and littering the floor of the backseat with coffee cups.

Detective Glynn describes the stakeout: "There were four of us in the car—the driver was an FBI guy." Glynn remembers the mundaneness. "We needed to find a place to piss, and we ended up taking turns going and pissing behind a truck. The FBI guy was getting ready to get transferred back to Michigan. Nice guy—real sharp. These FBI guys were street-smart guys. They weren't like yokels—they seemed to know what they were doing. As a matter of fact, it was the *FBI* guy who spotted the plate when the car went by us in front of the grandmother's house."

218

Special Agent Burroughs, who had interviewed me on the second run-through with Wich at the Sixth, sat in another car up the street, and so did Special Agent Mehan and more detectives, chatting.

The drudgery finally paid off. Special Agent John Kohler of the FBI violent gang squad was the first to spot the Lexus as it sidled by at an inscrutable rate of speed. It was approximately 2100 hours on the twenty-fourth, and the Lexus was headed east on Linden Boulevard toward Utica Avenue. There were three males in the car. Presumed armed.

The cops pulled out slowly, tailing them first to Utica Avenue and then to the corner of Lenox Avenue. They pulled over the suspects, guns drawn but without incident. They put Terrance up against a fence. There were two more men in the car, Sen and another guy who wasn't involved.

Terrance was quick to assert himself: "I know my rights. This car isn't stolen."

Glynn laughed to himself at Lucky's yapping. But then Glynn had to take care as the situation grew a tad more complicated. The cops narrowly avoided a scene.

"We were cuffin' 'em, another car pulls up, and a bunch of people get out of the car and it was his father and his girlfriend," Glynn says. A friend of Lucky's sitting at McDonald's had seen what was going on and ran over to Lucky's house to tell the family. The girl may have been Lucky's sister, not girlfriend. "Girl's cryin' hysterical. She kept sayin', 'He didn't do nuthin'. The car's not stolen,'" Glynn remembers.

"At this point we wanted to get some sort of backup—I don't know what's gonna go down. The father kept sayin', 'He didn't do anything wrong. The car's not stolen. It's his car.' I said, 'That's what we're gonna have to look at.' The father did look concerned."

"What's gonna happen to my son's car?" the father insisted. A detective told him it was going to be impounded.

Lucky seemed to be the mouthpiece. He kept talking. Sen was quiet. Then a uniform van pulled up. Glynn wanted the two perps separated—he did not want them talking to each other at that point. They were put in separate cars for transit. Bullets were found later on the floor of the police van, which Glynn figures must have come from Sen's pocket. Detective Di Shiavi recovered from Sen and vouchered in another five rounds of ammunition, $350 in United States cash that belonged to me, and a pager.

More cops, including Jerry Bayrodt and his guys, closed in. The teams at that moment were caught up in the midst of different investigative tasks. Some were touring the streets in a van that could pick up and trace cell phone activity, giving the location of the phone. Others were out at Kings Plaza, where Lucky worked. One detective went into Sears at the mall and was shown the record of a laptop computer purchased with my credit card, so they knew this was a hot spot. Agents went to every department at Sears asking if anyone knew an employee who fit Lucky's description. Only one worker thought he sounded vaguely familiar. Also, agents Jimmy Glynn, Burroughs, and some others were running a grid pattern in the parking lot next to Sears. For forty-five minutes, they went around in circles, up and down, checking out every car, looking for a black Lexus. Radio transmission was fuzzy in the parking garage, but when they got the news, they hightailed it to Linden Boulevard. Within minutes— ten minutes tops, maybe—everybody had congregated at the bust.

The cops were excited, but "We played it cool because you had the family members there," Detective Glynn explains. "This was nuthin' but a bullshit car stop kinda thing as far as they were concerned. A crowd started to gather—people were watching. But it was startin' to rain, too, which was good; that worked in our benefit. That area could be a little explosive if . . . ya know. We told the father, 'Go back to the Sixty-seventh Precinct and we'll meet you over there. We'll explain the whole thing. We'll just straighten out this car thing and then we'll be done with it.' So they took off for the Six-seven and we took off for Manhattan."

Sen rode to the Sixth in a car with agent Jimmy Glynn and then sat with him and some cops in a room at the precinct. He went quietly with no struggle. Glynn could see he was a pro. "Because he was so calm, I felt he was in trouble with the police before." Sen said little, but he was clear that he had not been hanging around with Lucky and Ren and he had nothing to do with any kidnapping. Wilbur Davis was his name, and no matter how hard the cops pushed him to own up to the name Sen, "he denied that to no end. He said he never went by that name." Jimmy Glynn would have bet his life he was lying. "He could not stare at us and he could not look us in the eye. Every time he answered, his foot would come up and down. Then he'd come back and talk to you."

Detectives Di Schiavi and McNeely drove the Lexus back to the Sixth Precinct. In addition to being evidence, the Lexus could be forfeited to the ownership of the People of the State of New York. I had done many forfeitures as a fed. Hit 'em where it really hurts. And for the two perps who were involved in criminal activity, things were going to get mighty hot back at the Sixth.

Later that night, at 4:30 A.M. on January 25, Detectives Stewart of the Sixth and Rosario of Manhattan South Homicide visited the home of Ren—Kenyatta Bandule—and his sister on Hawthorne Street in Brooklyn. They got easy permission to search, and Ren was quick to point out that he had two guns in a Timberland shoe box on the floor of a closet. The detectives vouchered one 9mm Luger and one Haskell .45, the instruments of my ordeal. A subsequent Police Laboratory Analysis Report detailed results of a ballistics examination. The 9mm Luger looked bad, but the "gun [was] inoperable due to [a] weak main spring." The .45-caliber automatic Haskell worked just fine.

Fifteen minutes later, McNeely of the Sixth led a team to execute the search warrant signed by Judge Finnerty for 1430 Eastern Parkway. Detective John Flynn of Manhattan South Homicide had to laugh on the way into the building as he pointed out to Detectives Bayrodt and Biddell, "Look at the tiles," in disbelief. The door to the apartment was exactly where I said it would be, and was decorated with Wu-Tang Clan stickers. No bullets flew during the search, as I had feared. But the only evidence the team got to voucher were two McDonald's paper bags and two apartment keys. The cops also lifted latent prints from three beverage bottles they pulled from the kitchen trash and forwarded them to the police laboratory for analysis.

At 10:30 A.M. on Sunday the twenty-fifth, the cops executed another search warrant for the first floor of 485 Linden Boulevard, the home Lucky shared with his grandmother and the floor where he resided. The cops vouchered over two—count 'em, two—Nokia cell phones, a money clip engraved with the name "Sen," an envelope with hair and fiber samples, and another envelope of tape taken from the car window.

By 2:15 P.M., they were also combing through the apartment of Sen, or Wilbur Davis, on Hawthorne Street. At the door, Davis's mother demanded to see the search warrant, and her other son John looked on. They searched the whole place, including the bedroom Wilbur still shared with John. The cops, including the resplendent Detective Sergeant Duke in his fine suit, removed one telephone book, miscellaneous papers, and one artist's sketch book. Even the viciously violent Sen had good potential, if only it had been channeled properly. He could have been showing his sketches in SoHo one day.

The only live-body holdout at this point was Ramos. A team of four detectives and agents visited with a known acquaintance of his, Tino Melendez. Tino said Luis was an old friend whom he called a cousin even though they were not related. They had had a falling-out three weeks earlier and Tino had not seen him since. They fought over a woman, but Tino did not want to get into it. Tino knew Luis was living on Eastern Parkway, and told the investigators he could point out some other locations where Luis hung out.

The same team also visited a young lady on George Street in Ridgewood, Queens. At 7:00 A.M. on the twenty-fifth, Veronica Puentes owned up to having been Luis's girlfriend until about two months earlier. They broke up because he was cheating on her with another girl, who Veronica thought Luis was now going steady with. The girl was sixteen, light-skinned and light-haired, and worked in a retail clothing store on Fulton

Street in downtown Brooklyn. Veronica also said that Luis used to work at a Honda dealership in Manhattan and that he currently worked at JFK Airport doing maintenance.

Then they visited the home of a friend of Luis's mother. The woman had just seen Luis, on Friday the twenty-third, had known him since he was a little boy, and stated that Luis was good friends with her son. Luis was not looking for money or a place to stay when she saw him. The woman identified another friend of Luis's the cops could talk to and gave them his address on Howard Avenue.

At the apartment of another friend who was identified by Tino, on Pitkin Avenue, the cops learned that Luis had lived there until February, when the friend threw him out for not paying rent. He, too, had seen Luis in the afternoon of the twenty-third. Luis had asked him for a place to stay, but the friend said no.

Naturally, whispered but imploring phone calls were placed after the law enforcement visits. It was only a matter of hours before Luis could stand the heat no longer. He turned himself in at the 73 Precinct in Brooklyn. Duke, Sammy Miller, Detective Malktenos, and FBI Special Agent Doyle transferred Luis Ramos to the bomb squad office at the Sixth. He was not questioned on the way over. That job would fall to the cop of cops who could convince Mother Teresa herself to confess, Detective William Glynn.

By the end of the day on the twenty-fifth of January, George Wich wrote his last report on the investigation. In view of the arrests and the fact that there were no outstanding subjects, Wich ordered that the case be marked CLOSED at that time. Special Agent Mehan asked for permission to be relieved of further duty, such as interrogating the defendants. She had worked eighteen hours straight and wanted to go get a piece of her sister's homemade chocolate cake with peanut butter filling. It was their father's birthday.

With the perps in custody, the FBI agents loosened up with cracks about the case. My dating life was a hot topic, especially for the women, like Mehan. The FBI press guy thought I had more dates in one night than he had before he met his wife. Jimmy Glynn thought I should find some interests: "All the years talking to victims, witnesses, normally you get a height, weight, and age of a guy. Maybe a clothing description. But as for seagulls and airplanes and tiles on the floor there, I was really baffled by that." He thought I "must have been pretty bored watching the tiles on the floor there." But Mehan notes that when I called in, and they realized that "Stan got himself free! Stan escaped!" I became "Stan-the-Man," and the agents would joke from then on about the Stan-the-Man case that worked out. No dead AUSA. Back to the Latin Kings.

TWENTY-SEVEN

REUNION

I had a safe house to hide in, and friends to comfort me, but I remained very nervous. The gang that had hit me hard was cruising around in the Lexus—pimping, whoring, robbing, and potentially coming after me. They had my driver's license, home address, and Social Security number. Psychologically, I had been violated, and could not truly rest until they were behind bars.

Supervisory Sergeant Haas was determined that his team would deliver. Haas was haunted by the police's inability to bring comfort to the victims in another case he had worked. "I mean, there was another series of rapes in the West Village. It was tough for me, too, because I realized that these people are traumatized for the rest of their life. In my heart of hearts, I thought we grabbed the guy, but we could never prove it, but not having that closure—even for me and for the people that these people raped—I mean, this is something that's gonna be with them for the rest of their life." Haas was dead on about what it was that I needed.

So it was with wonder, excitement, relief, and almost tears that I got the big calls. They started coming in on Saturday evening. Scott fielded them, and the word was that our troops were starting to round up the enemy. "We're bringing 'em in," an excited Wich told Scott. "Tell Stan to hang tight."

Amazing; they were good, real good. Sure, I gave them a lot of clues, but to start rounding up the gang a mere forty-eight hours after my release? That was impressive. The men in blue or in blue suits were way too powerful and way too determined not to leave the threat out there, and many literally did not sleep until the matter was wrapped up.

It was Super Bowl Sunday by the time we heard that all the perps were in custody. That night, as annual tradition held, Scott's sister and husband were throwing a Super Bowl party with an eight-foot-long mixed cold cut hero for the beer drinkers to ravage. But Scott, Dan, my brother Josh, and I would not get anywhere near that hero till its remnants were soggy, or near the chips and the drinks or the game till it was over.

Wich wanted me down at the station house at seven P.M. to view line-ups. He placed us under strict orders not to enter the building until he gave the word. The police station on West Tenth Street was small, and there are a lot of logistics involved in setting up a lineup that the com-plaining witness cannot be permitted to see or the lineup will be tainted. They planned to show me three lineups, and for each one, Wich and company needed to roll in not just the suspected defendant but also five innocents. That takes arranging. Some of the lineup participants are cops; some are crooks. Some are homeless people off the street who get paid ten bucks for their trouble. Some will be back in a lineup soon when they will be the subjects of the lineup, not the presumed innocent of to-day. For three lineups, Wich needed fifteen extra bodies to sit and stand and face left and face right, and that takes a lot of shuffling people in and out of the precinct house, none of which I was allowed to see.

Waiting outside for Wich to get ready, I was acutely aware of how careful I needed to be. Who says that some homeboys of Lucky's or Sen's didn't get a call to stand on the corner of Hudson and Tenth and wait until a guy who fit my description walked by on his way to pick 'em out and to blast the motherfucker with a TEC-9? Lucky was connected; he had money and a family with money and access to guns and probably friends and definitely a fiancée who could be counted on to make arrangements for him. Carefully, my handlers drove me up to the corner of Hudson and Tenth, where I stood, disguised in ponytail hat and shades, in the cold, nestled under a building overhang at an auto service station. Josh spoke by cell phone to Wich, who told us to wait because they were still setting up. It was like a big surprise party, and hopefully the surprise would be on them, not on me. While waiting, Dan, Scott, Josh, and I got hungry, so we stopped at a pizza parlor on the corner of Charles and Hudson for a quick slice. It was familiar terrain. I had spent three years living in a tenement walk-up on that very corner.

Eventually we got the call, and my bodyguards surrounded me as they whisked me like a rock star through the front entrance on Tenth Street. Upstairs, we had to sit tight for next to an hour with an agent from the Bureau, in a cop room lined with file cabinets of unsolved cases. Wich would pop his excited head in the door every fifteen minutes or so and say, "Now just hold on, Stan. We're settin' everything up. You just sit tight till we're ready, all right, buddy?" Wich looked like he was worried about his big witness's mental health. I was nervous and looked strange in my costume, but I knew I had gone through enough shit in my life to stay strong through just about anything.

"Yup. I'm not goin' anywhere," I responded. I wasn't going anywhere. In that room, time stood still for me, waiting Super Bowl party or not, because I really had nowhere to go with my life, short-term or long-term, until I got closure on the events of the last few days.

Finally, the door swung open and Wich came over to me. "All right, Stan buddy, we're gonna show you three lineups. Just make sure you're absolutely certain before you say that one of the people you see is one of the people that did this to you. All right?"

"Sure," I replied, upbeat but definitely frightened. Wich grabbed my arm and led me out into the hallway. The place was teeming with cops and detectives, a beehive buzzing with activity. I glanced nervously at their faces to see if I recognized any of them, saying nothing, as Wich pulled me into a tiny, drab-looking six-by-four room. There was a guy sitting inside—I guess he was a cop serving as witness—and a darkened glass panel, revealing nothing. He slammed the door shut.

"All right, Stan, do your best. Just tell me if you see the people that did this to you, but only if you're positive." If I picked a dud out of a live lineup, that could kill the case against that particular perp.

The possibility of choosing the wrong guy in a lineup is real. The curtain came down, and behind door number one, Wich as Carol Merrill had six African-American males for me to choose from. Naturally, the idea is to try to get five innocents who look something like the guilty party, so the victim is really forced to choose and the police can see whether he can distinguish his oppressor. But there are issues with the process. Some of the men sitting there, staring straight at you, knowing you can see them although they stare at a blank slate, look nervous. A victim might decide to pick one based on his nervousness, but that look might be innocent or maybe the guy is nervous because he committed another crime in another part of the city, having nothing to do with you. By contrast, some of the men sitting and then parading before you look relaxed and confident, which means they could be cops, or they could be crooks who are good at it. After all, some brands of crooks, like con men, are good actors by trade. Plus, you try picking out people you've seen for just a few minutes in a dark car from a crowd of similar-looking men; it ain't easy.

Staring out at me in lineup number one, and then parading, looking left, and looking right, was a guy who looked an awful lot like Sen. I thought about picking him. I had seen Sen in a dark car, with a woolen crook's cap pulled all the way down to his eyebrows, concealing certain features of human distinction such as hair and forehead size. This guy I was staring at looked a lot like Sen, but it didn't feel a hundred percent to me. The Sen I remembered, even though the car was dark, had a lighter complexion than the guy before me. Though I was tempted to pick him, I left it alone and didn't pick anybody out of lineup number one.

"Sorry, George," I said. "One of these guys looks very familiar to me, but I really can't be sure."

"All right, buddy, don't worry about it," Wich responded. "If you're not sure, we'll just move on to the next one." Wich was disappointed, but in his heart he thought I could do it in the next lineups.

I felt bad about it, but there was no way in my life that Stan Alpert was going to accuse a possibly innocent man; I'd come too far to sink so low, despite what I had just experienced.

In lineup number two, there was a guy who looked even more like Sen than the one I'd thought might have been him before. His skin tone matched, and I picked him with certainty.

In lineup number three, a guy paraded up and down before me doing an overacted faux-gay routine—strutting like a rooster, pouting, and swinging his arms like a man who would like to get to know me. He looked a little like I thought Lucky might. I had spent a lot of time looking at the back of Lucky's head, and the hairstyle from the back seemed to match Lucky's. I thought to myself, "Ya know, Lucky is one clever and conniving dude. He's putting on that gay routine purposely to throw me off the track. I should pick that SOB." Still, I really wasn't sure I recognized him, so I had to disappoint Wich one more time.

I learned later from Wich's police report that Ren was in lineup number one, not Sen as I had first suspected. I didn't pick him, and it's a good thing I didn't. Sen was in lineup number two, and I picked him. Positive ID, no doubts. Lucky was in lineup number three, although I could not be certain enough to pick him out. I just couldn't recognize him.

I also learned later that Sen was the one defendant who refused to talk to the cops in the early interrogations, while all the others gave it up. Wich prayed I would pick him out of the lineup "because this fuckin' guy makes no confession. You don't ID this guy, ya know, he's fuckin' maybe gonna walk." But I did manage to pick Sen out of the lineup, making his conviction a near-certainty despite no confession. "Mother-fucker, you got big eyes. I should kill you for those big eyes," he had said to me in the car. He had big eyes, too, large and almond-shaped, and those eyes were seared into my memory in the back of a 1998 Lexus.

As I went down to the Sixth for the lineups, I imagined that I would pick out all three suspects, since I had seen them for about ten minutes before they blindfolded me and shoved me down in the seat against Ren's leg. But afterward I realized that the only one I had really faced enough to get a solid look at was Sen. I didn't look to my right to catch Ren's features because I didn't want to provoke them, and most of what I saw of Lucky was the back of his head. As for the faux-gay act I thought Lucky put on, I was wrong. It wasn't an act because I found out later it wasn't Lucky at all. It was a good thing I had the strength to admit my failure and not pick the wrong guy, which in itself would have been a crime.

TWENTY-EIGHT

SEX, LIES, AND VIDEOTAPE

He's honest. "I love the hunt. It's a challenge. The hunt is man's natural instinct. It's how we started out. People go out and they'll go skydiving or they'll go out to the woods and look for deer or something like that. But once you hunt, man—there's nothing greater."

He waxes eloquent. "Sometimes the confession is the only thing that's gonna make the case," says Detective William Glynn, who against his will had been pulled off the 2nd Avenue Deli murder investigation to deal with my thing two nights earlier.

He's friendly. An admiring FBI agent once asked Glynn, "Is there anyone you can't get a confession from?" Glynn smiled wryly and responded with due modesty that he was only so good at getting confessions "because I like to talk to people."

Well, sort of. "What I learned working in the ghetto is that most of these people have been beaten down, abused, all their lives. When they come into a police station they think it's just gonna be an extension of that. But what they can't deal with is empathy. What I like to project is that when I'm in the room with somebody and I'm looking to get—or solicit—a confession, I build a relationship where it's gonna be 'us against those people out there,' and we got a problem and with two heads we can work this out. Somehow we can work this out. And most of them are always looking for a way out."

Relationships. Glynn had built a lot of those over the years with the lower echelons of society. Directly across the street from where Lucky, Sen, and Ren kidnapped me, at 14 West Tenth Street in the Village, the Lisa Steinberg case defined depravity in 1987. Joel Steinberg and Hedda Nussbaum were adoptive parents, and Joel had abused his daughter, Lisa, to death while Hedda let it go. Detective William Glynn led the charge in that most famous of cases.

In 1992, the year Giuliani came into office, New York was still a hell-hole. I flew home that summer after drinking in the peace of New Zealand to a strange Twilight Zone where yuppies were being shot to death standing at phone booths in Greenwich Village. They called on William Glynn to crack the case of the yuppie shot dead on the corner.

"John Reisenbach was the fella at the phone booth in the Village," Glynn explains. "His father was the assistant vice president of Warner Brothers. He was on the phone for fifty-seven minutes, and somebody came up and killed him. I landed up arresting a homeless guy, based on information from witnesses who found out that these psychos were involved. The case is still being investigated ten years later." One of very few Glynn failures.

March 1, 1994. An Arab gunman in a car opens fire on a van carrying more than a dozen Hasidic students as it begins to cross the Brooklyn Bridge from Manhattan, critically wounding two young men and injuring two others. The lone gunman, driving a blue Chevrolet Caprice equipped with a submachine gun, two 9mm guns, and a "street sweeper" shotgun, pursued the van full of terrified students across the bridge. He fired in three separate bursts, spraying both sides of the van. He then disappeared into traffic as the van came to a stop at the Brooklyn end of the

CITY OF LIMERICK PUBLIC LIBRARY

bridge. Young Ari Halberstam died hours later from severe brain injuries. Giuliani erected the sign "Ari Halberstam Memorial Ramp" as a permanent "fuck you" to terrorists on the entrance to the Brooklyn Bridge, but it was William Glynn who built a relationship with the terrorist, Rashid Baz, so he could send him to prison for 141 years.

"That's why when I talk to people I like to get background information, I like to find out about their family members and what have you. For example, with Rashid Baz, during the early part of the interrogation, I got the feeling he was very close to his uncle. Then hours later, when I'm tryin' to get this confession out of him, I says, 'Ya know, problem is, I got a funny feeling we're gonna hit your uncle's house, and I got a feeling those guns are gonna be at your uncle's house. I'd like to avoid it. The only way we can do that is if somebody told me where they put the guns in the house—then I could believe in them.'" Baz confessed. He'll die in prison. Thanks, Glynn.

Poor Lucky was on his way to the jaws of this blue-coated lion. In the car on the way over, Lucky had quite a brainstorm. *He* was the one who had been kidnapped. That story wouldn't last long; yet again the NYPD sent William Glynn into the room to crack the bad guy, together with Special Agent William Confrey of the Federal Bureau of Investigation.

Glynn: "Roger Perino said I want you to go in and talk to him—interrogate Terrance. I said, 'This kid's a little sharp, he might lawyer up and what have you.' But I go into the interview room and what I normally do is go in, I say I want to talk to you, I want to get some information. I get a whole background on 'em—father's name, mother's name, where are you born. Because what that does is creates conversation. Those are easy questions and people love to talk about themselves."

In *The Book of Laughter and Forgetting*, Milan Kundera says that people love to talk about themselves so much that they even like to be picked up and interrogated by the police because it gives them a chance to talk about themselves.

In a concrete-walled room surrounded by Glynn and FBI Special

Agent Confrey, "Lucky was sayin', 'This hasn't been a good day,'" Glynn says. "I advised him of his rights—I don't want to fuck around with that. So I said, 'You want to talk to us?' He says, 'Yeah,' so I says, 'Tell us about your day.'" Glynn also mentioned, in a friendly way, that he had video pictures of Lucky using a stolen bank card. Please explain, kind sir.

Maybe Lucky should have been a lawyer and maybe he should have been nominated for an Academy Award, the way he boldly embraced his cock-and-bull story. "Let me tell you exactly what happened, Detective," our very cooperative businessman gangster said. "I'm not sure which day it was, maybe Tuesday or Wednesday, and I had just gotten off of work at around nine-thirty P.M. I walked to my car in the parking lot of Kings Plaza when a black male approached and pointed a gun and ordered me to get into my car. He then told me to drive to Canarsie Pier in Brooklyn and told me to park my car there. He said he knows where I live, so I better not tell the police. He then got out of the car and walked away."

Glynn was chuckling inside. His voice was pure gravel, almost sleepy. A lot of nights of lost sleep. "Well, ah, remember, we got you on videotape, so exactly how are you explaining that with that story?" Glynn queried.

"Oh, yeah, yeah," replied Lucky. "I forgot to mention the rest of it because, frankly, I'm embarrassed that this happened and I wish I could just forget the whole incident."

Glynn had to keep himself from laughing. "Things weren't makin' any sense," says gravel Glynn. "I mean, I know what he was doin'. It's show business. Once you go in there, it's show business. I absolutely kept a straight face. He went through his story—on how he was taken off and they robbed him.

"Go on," said Glynn. In building a relationship, one needs first to experience the other's narrative. Glynn listened attentively and nodded respectfully, agreeably, while Lucky explained his own kidnapping.

"Yeah, so . . . uh . . . the black male forced me to lie down on the backseat of the car and he drove the car. He drove down Flatbush

Avenue—the way I know that is I looked up at one point and I saw Junior's restaurant. A little while later, he pulled the car over in the area of the Fort Greene projects, and another black male got into the car. They drove around for a short time and then they pulled over. The second male who had got in the car then gave me a bank card and told me the PIN number to the card. He said they were going to drive to bank machines and withdraw cash from the account. They told me if I did what I was told, I would not get hurt. So I went with them to the banks and took out the money and gave the money to them. The two male blacks then drove me home and they told me if I did not tell the police they would return my car in a few hours."

"By the way," Glynn asked, toying with confirming details. "Do you own a black-and-white shirt or sweater, and were you wearing those colors when you used the bank card?"

"I own a black-and-white sweater, but I don't remember what I was wearing when I used the bank card." Hedging.

Glynn: "By the way, how'd you get the name Lucky?" Friendly.

"Oh, when I was a young kid, my family was financially comfortable and I always had money. All the other kids would tell me, 'You're lucky,' and that's how I got the nickname."

By then Glynn knew from police reports that both Mystic and Honey had affectionately referred to Lucky in their signed confessionals as "Luciano." Lucky Luciano was closer than lucky kid. I guess he fancied himself a real live gangster. But Lucky had no priors, unlike his compatriots Ren and Sen, who came back with juvenile records.

"So what'd ya do next?" Glynn asked.

"What do you mean? I went into my house and I went to bed. When I got up in the morning, my car was parked out front."

Glynn looked at Lucky sideways. "Oh, yeah, yeah," Lucky said. "I also . . . well, they didn't take the bank card from me when they let me go, so I tried to use it once myself. But I wasn't able to get any money out of the cash machine."

Needless to say, Glynn was not buying it. The defining moment in any classic interrogation is when the good cop suddenly is very, very dangerous and the accused begins to suffocate on his own lies.

Glynn said, "That's a very, very bad thing that happened to you. But let me tell you what I *got* here, and maybe you can help me out a little bit. I got Ren, I got Sen, I got the Puerto Rican kid, Luis Ramos. I got the girls—Honey, Mercedes. They're tryin' to put all the weight on you. They say you're the boss and that you grabbed the white guy off the street and you were using his bank card. Maybe it was Ren and Sen— they look like the type with criminal records."

One, give him an out. Two, make friends. "You're a very well-spoken young man, you seem to come from a good family," Glynn continued. "I'm havin' problems believin' you, but you're the only one that can tell me. You're talkin' about doin' some heavy time here. I gotta ask you, are you gonna tell me about it or are you just gonna let them testify against you?"

Lucky asked, "Well, what are you referring to?"

Glynn: "The white guy you grabbed off the street, called Stanley. Tell me about Stanley."

Glynn could see the change coming as it swept across Lucky's face. The entire story was about to shift radically. No transition and not a hint of contrition at the one-eighty, and that was no surprise. "I know when I sit down in the room that his job is to lie to me," Glynn explains. "And we just see who comes out better. It's like a chess game. Everybody wants a back door out. Everybody never sees themselves as the bad guy. The *other* guy is the bad guy—'He made me do it.' So you give 'em that out. Ya give it to 'em. I'll take that. That's good. It's like makin' themselves a little pregnant—*there ain't no such thing*. You give them an out by sayin' that 'I believe it was Ren and Sen—they had criminal records.' That's what I laid on him. You could see a look come over him and you could see this kid's gonna roll."

With the DA introduced in the room, the videotape started to roll. The new story incorporated many elements of the truth but, as they all do, Lucky tried to minimize his leadership role and stick the whole misadventure on Sen and Ren. After all, how could *he,* a respectable community member who had never been involved in any crime, and who was a financial wizard in possession of vast financial resources from a fine and well-to-do family, *possibly* have instigated such a crime? He just went along for the ride, and his main reason was to protect Stanley and make sure the other loose cannons didn't shoot me. What a nice guy. Such a classy pimp.

Here's how it looks on videotape.

He sits with his arms crossed, looking down, tired at first, wearing a black shirt and a loud, patterned tie. Big eyes, outraged at the accusations. Real name? Terrance Micelli. Says he's eighteen years old, and he goes by the nickname Lucky. This brings him a chuckle. Living with his grandmother on Linden Boulevard in Brooklyn. (Not a bad commute from where he held me at 1430 Eastern Parkway.) He is a full-time college student at the College of Staten Island, in his first year. He is studying criminal justice. Classes include history, political science, and criminal law, and he is pursuing a minor in business.

Well, the cops in the room naturally want to know, what are your aspirations in terms of a career, Terrance?

He responds: "I wanted to do law enforcement for a very long time. But I've given myself up to either be a history teacher or something. I'm fascinated by that." It's true that a lot of prosecutors become criminal defense lawyers, but the law enforcement thing is a little too ridiculous.

He also works selling communications. Until recently he was stationed at Sears in Kings Plaza.

Kings Plaza is the first shopping mall I ever saw as a kid, when it opened in Mill Basin, Brooklyn, close to the ocean. Around the time of my parents' divorce in 1972, my father's weekday job as a stockbroker moved directly across the street from Kings Plaza. I used to visit him, watch the ticker tape for an hour or so, and then my dad and I would saunter across the street to forage in the bargain bins at Alexander's department store.

But Lucky had recently left Sears Kings Plaza for a better opportunity. Now he was a sales representative at Cellnet Communications. He was a full-time retail representative for AT&T and MCI. A full-time student, a full-time cell phone salesman, a nighttime pimp, and a part-time kidnapper. Gotta love that entrepreneurial spirit and energy.

His personal life was also a success. "My fiancée is Sandra Adobe. She's nineteen. She works in a theater. I don't know the details of exactly what she's doing, because I've been busy lately." No shit.

The members of the gang were new friends. Explained Lucky: "I met Mercedes through another young lady, Mystic. Known her two months. Mystic, same thing. I haven't known any of these people for a long time. I don't know any of their real names. It's not something I ask, like, hey, what's your real name and your Social Security? [Laughing]. It was something I was just rushed into with no second thought. Sen is an acquaintance I met through his older brother, a guy whose street name I know but I can't remember his real name right now. The brother asked if I need a few good guys to be security for the ladies. He recommended Sen. Ren is Sen's sidekick. I guess his partner in crime or whatever you would call him. Ren is young. Due to the way he grew up, he has aged really fast. They were a bodyguard type of presence for the ladies. I did not do security at all. I arranged for their security."

And fine security it was. Lucky was matter-of-fact: "Ren and Sen are strapped when they are guarding the ladies. Guns are very easy to get. Sen knows a guy who sells these weapons. This man meets with him on Sen's block, Hawthorne. I heard a three-eighty goes for about two hundred and fifty dollars. People go to Virginia and get them down there for up here."

When Lucky heard from his security guards about a little scheme to grab people on the street and escort them to the cash machine, at first he was *not* impressed. "Sen had brought it up previously. I didn't think he could pull it off. It sounds ridiculous. There are so many risk factors involved that it's not even funny. I wasn't very impressed."

But then he was. "I believe I was at work when Sen came to me. After he pulled it off, I was like, wow, they did that. He showed me what exactly he made or whatever. The following day he showed me after he got off of work. I was impressed. Told me four days after the first robbery. At my job. He's a well-known person at the mall; he's not really allowed in the mall. He has these other side jobs—he's a booster—you know what that is." The *American Heritage Dictionary* defines booster: "*Slang.* One who steals goods on display in a store."

As for the kidnapping-robbery scheme, a fateful pitch had been made at Kings Plaza. "Sen said it would go a lot quicker if you drove us away from the scene."

And Lucky said okay.

Allegedly, Sen made the arrangements. "He got what he needed to get as far as weapons go. A semiautomatic. Ren was carrying an automatic—what is that, a MAC-10, MAC-11, or whatever. I didn't have anything on me. It wasn't my job to get out of the car and say, 'Hey, you.' Sen said we're going out tonight and pick an individual out of the crowd. Taking Stan and holding him for numbers of hours was not part of the plan as I understood. They would abduct people for about an hour to do whatever they had to do."

Then came the night before my birthday. Lucky continued, "I picked them up at his house. I get off of work at nine-thirty and picked them up at ten o'clock. In Manhattan, I was just driving around, there was no mapped-out course. Sen spotted what he said was a good pick. A good guy to rob. Anybody that he can measure up to and see himself doing something to. Height, weight, possibility of resistance. But it's not something that I do. A good pick is a guy that won't resist as much as a guy who would resist, like a bodybuilder. He explained to me that the least crowded it is, the better it is; the darker it is, the better it is. I have no idea where Stan was actually abducted from. In the middle of the block. He was carrying cookies and something else. Probably a book or something like that. Suit, tie, I believe glasses, black trench coat."

According to Lucky, I was lucky to have Lucky. From the outset, he considered it his responsibility to protect me from the other goons. "I was there for one reason only, and that's to keep Stan happy and alive. It didn't matter to me—whatever couple of hundred dollars that I did get from the guy, I didn't need it. It's fifty thousand dollars. I've seen fifty thousand dollars three times over. Fifty thousand doesn't impress me. I'm an eighteen-year-old with an eleven-thousand-dollar watch on his hand. I was impressed with how easy the money came; that's why I said, well, okay I'll try it out. It doesn't matter to me as far as financial needs go.

"I'm doing this because he asked me to do it, and it's . . . uh . . . I guess it was a new experience for me. I've never done anything like that—criminally-wise, in any way. I guess it was kind of exciting with all of the—you know—guns or whatever."

When they pulled over on West Tenth Street, according to Lucky, the other two "were ready to go out there and I guess literally *get* the guy. I told them two . . . uh . . . you can't literally go out there with your guns in the air and try to blow the guy's head off. You might give the damn guy a heart attack. So I got out and I said, 'Listen, can you please come over here?' He jumped a little bit and I said, 'Listen, can you come over to the car.' Me and Sen both got out. I wasn't happy with two trigger-happy people both getting out of the car. I didn't have a gun. Sen had a gun. It's big—not a three-eighty—I mean it's big, black color. Sen had it in his waist, and as he walked over he pulled it out and reached it toward the guy. I put the car in park and I got out. They were gonna jump out and I said, 'Listen, guys, this is not the way this is gonna happen here.' I don't know them and don't exactly trust them. They were trigger-happy, and I wasn't prepared to be in that type of situation.

"We were coming from an angle where Stan didn't notice us—from a diagonal. That's when he jumped and he saw Sen and he got panicky. I grabbed his arm 'cause I didn't want him to run—Sen would have chased him. I stopped Sen from yelling at him. Sen and Ren was trying to put the fear in him—yelling we'll kill you and all that.

"I said, 'Hi, where you going?' He said, 'Well, I was going home with my cookies to go eat.' I said, 'Stay calm.' He said, 'I can do that.'"

But the investigators in the concrete room with the lineup numbers on the back wall demanded a fuller confession. Wouldn't Lucky admit that they really did present a terrifying threat when they put guns in Stanley's gut and face on West Tenth Street the night of January 21, 1998?

Lucky didn't deny it. "If he were to scream and . . . say . . . were to have pushed Sen, I don't think Stan would be breathing right now."

Lucky, you chill my bones. I thank God I'm alive. I thank God I took you off the street so you couldn't do this to another sorry motherfucker like me. I'll live with it for the rest of my life, but the next guy might have died.

Embellishing, Lucky continued, "You get a feeling about people. Sen is the kind of person who is not wrapped too tightly in the head. And the only reason that Ren does it is because of Sen. I wouldn't say they take direction from me. I'm the one who always keeps a cool head. It's something I have a good knack of doing—advising people of their actions."

But, insisted the inquisitors, isn't it a fact that in the apartment, Terrance, you yourself specifically threatened to break every bone in that man's father's body if he didn't cooperate?

Well, of course, Lucky agreed. "Basically what I was doing was ensuring his safety with his own fear." What a sweetheart. He also made me feel good: "Anytime I was there talking to him, he was a lot more content with what was going on."

He thought about his last statement and adjusted. "Well, how content can you be, but, you know."

And he was helping because he genuinely liked me. Referring to the victim, Lucky explained, "I enjoy his company, believe it or not. He's a very nice guy. He's so nice, like, to the point that I felt sorry this was happening to him. Um . . . that's basically what the conversation was about—I was talking about society to him. His family . . . We got to the apartment and I asked Stan if there was anything I could do to make him more comfortable. He says no. . . . But . . . we got him a Snapple."

The miracle of the advocacy I had used to save my own life also shone through in Lucky's warm confessional about me. He preened, "Me and Stan . . . I believe, considering the situation like this, I trusted Stan to the fullest. . . . He saw that I wasn't going to do anything to hurt him, so I don't think he was going to do anything to hurt me."

I guess I'm the one who should get the Academy Award.

Despite Lucky's pure and noble intentions, God chose to punish him that night with the misfortune of kidnapping a fed: "When I found out how much money he had, I was like, Oh my God, what does this guy do? When I got back to the car, I was talkin' to him. I go, 'Stan, what do you do for a living?' He tells me he's the . . . uh . . . Assistant U.S. Attorney General or something. My eyes popped out of my head. I literally almost stopped the car. I was like, 'Why didn't you tell me this before Sen grabbed you because I was . . . let you go?' And he was like, 'Well, you didn't ask'—and he was tryin' to be funny—'you didn't ask.' I turned around and I said, 'Oh my God, this is ridiculous . . . you really serious?' and he goes, 'Yeah, yeah.' Then Sen shows me his American Express card and it says Justice Department, so I look at it and I am really fascinated about it and I says, 'This is unreal.' I said, 'Oh my God, this is unreal.' The night I decide to go, you catch a fed. This is unbelievable."

Some people write books about Why Bad Things Happen to Good People. God works in mysterious ways. God had more in store for Terrance that night. Somebody broke into his car and stole Lucky's stuff— his car stereo, a black bag, and his radar Fuzzbuster. I was very familiar with the break-in and the loss of the radio that put the plastic on the window and made me think I was about to get killed as we drove toward Prospect Park. On the confession video, Lucky further reveals that the robbers in Gang Number 2—the FBI suspected they were Russians— that busted into his car actually stole *my* wallet from Gang Number 1 because the idiots had left it on the dash. Which explains why Michelle

Jones found my credit cards at seven A.M. on the street in Bedford-Stuyvesant. Luckily for Gang Number 1, they had pulled my Chase ATM and credit card out of the wallet so after *they* were robbed they could keep robbing.

Later in the day, Lucky and Sen drove over to Sears and Sen bought a laptop with Stanley's credit card. So, asked the cops, why did Sen buy the computer instead of you?

That's easy, Lucky replied, "because I used to work there," with an are-you-kidding tone in his voice.

Okay, the cops asked, did you report the break-in to your car to the police and your insurance company?

Again with an are-you-kidding tone in his voice: "The reason I didn't report it is that I have a one-thousand-dollar deductible and I would've had to pay for it anyway."

All this decent, hardworking-businessman rhetoric was starting to grate on the investigators as they stared at a man, little older than a boy, who had just held a federal prosecutor hostage for twenty-five hours, threatening to kill him and to break every bone in his father's body if he failed to cooperate. We're not buying this, they pushed. *You* are into something big to have all this money. How do you explain all your money, the fancy watch, the fancy car, and access to $50,000—how are you so *Lucky*?

His big brown eyes stare at the camera while he ponders the fact that having so much money cuts as a double-edged sword. He waits, and then launches into his effort at an explanation. "Where do I get it from? I work very hard. You mean for my Lexus?"

"I'm gonna tell you," he continued. "My watch was an anniversary gift—Christmas—from my fiancée. Okay, it came out of her Macy's card; she maxed it out—I think it was very sweet of her to do that. Okay. The bracelet with the matching chain I have on was my six-month anniversary gift. Okay, a couple of months before I got engaged, okay. And the car? That was a Grandma thing. That is a Grandma thing."

Well, Mr. Lucky, how is it that you told us a few minutes ago that you have seen $50,000 two to three times over?

Lucky kept spinning. "Yeah. My grandmother—well, not exactly fifty thousand dollars, but a lump sum—I do her banking. And some period of time her bank has twenty thousand in there. I'm a financial wizard—put it that way. I can put something in CDs for twelve months and turn it over. I have my own money—I had a lawsuit—it's in a CD."

They weren't buying the beneficent-relative routine. The inquisitors raised their voices. *You* are a very professional robber. *You* are ripping off somebody, it seems to us. Ren and Sen refer to *you* as the boss.

Lucky started to squirm. He parried, "That's bullshit. Ren and Sen refer to me as a smart guy who knows what he's doing."

Then he thought maybe he could dime somebody else out to deflect the heat. "Can I ask you a question? What are you looking for?" That got him blank stares from the DA and the detectives. Then he thought maybe he could turn to his friend Stanley for help. If they didn't believe what a minor and supportive role he had played in the drama, referring to me, Lucky practically shouted, "Why don't you ask *the guy?*"

They had asked me already. The cops pressed harder, repeating, "Who are you ripping off?"

Lucky exploded under the pressure. He raised his voice and accelerated his speech, raving, "You got to understand something, okay? I didn't know it was gonna be a *kidnapping* abduction for twenty-four hours. 'Smatter of fact, I didn't even know that they was gonna *hold* the damn guy for twenty-four hours. I was impressed. That's what the hell it is—it's an abduction."

His legal parsing between abduction and kidnapping left the interrogation team a little flat. Lucky defended his position: "No no no no—you misunderstood me. In my book, abducting a person is taking them for a joyride or whatever and doing what you . . . [pondering] . . . whatever you want to do with them. *Kidnapping* to me is a whole different thing. It's an abduction, don't get me wrong, but you're talking about taking someone out of their . . . environment—okay?—and leaving them there for a number of hours. I haven't done it before, God honest truth. I'm saying it right in front of the goddamn camera."

He gesticulates toward the camera, throwing his arms up as though ready for a fight.

The cops were relentless. So what *have* you done, what *are* you down for? There's a grand lie here, they insisted.

Still speeding, ducking, dodging, and weaving, Lucky spat it out. "You have permission to go in my house. You can go in my car. If you want, you can go on my roof. You can go to my ranch in Florida. My *family* has a ranch in Florida.

"Listen. What I'm trying to tell you is this, okay. I'm not rich. I'm not well off. But my family presents an image that they are. I'll put it to you that way. Okay . . . I was sixteen years old, my grandmother bought me a brand-new Acura V. I had an E-420 Mercedes-Benz just six months ago—'ninety-eight—the buggy-eyed one, the sixty-thousand-dollar one, okay. My grandmother leased that for me, okay? I can give off an image like I'm filthy fuckin' rich, when in reality I'm just makin' like an average person—I just know how to give off that look. I'm not into anything else, okay? This is my first . . . taste of crime? All right. I'm not into any money laundering. I'm not into any financial scams. No pickpocketing. No credit card scams. That's not something that I do, 'cause I don't need to do it. Okay, I'm goin' to college, I'm a full-time student. I don't need to do that. I told you I was impressed by that. I'm not gonna sit here and lie. He came to me, he said, 'I made over five hundred dollars in less than fifteen minutes.' I was impressed by it. I don't know a job where you can do that except selling drugs, and that I'm not gonna do. I'm not saying that *kidnapping* people is the right thing, either, but I was impressed by it. An eighteen-year-old would have to be impressed by it. 'You made over five hundred dollars in fifteen minutes?'"

He was digging his hole deeper and deeper. Glynn was laughing inside. The DA was sick of it. They pushed even harder. Did it ever occur to you that you changed that man's life forever? Did it ever occur to you that that man thought a thousand times that he wasn't gonna make it home? Did it ever occur to you?

The human interest pitch softened Lucky Luciano for a moment. He calmed, and became reasonable. Of course. "It did. To be honest with you, it did occur to me, and that's why I tried to make him feel that he wasn't threatened."

But dammit, the DA insisted, we've got five other robberies using a black Lexus. Their ATMs were used and then they were dumped on the street. This was just a little longer than your usual MO. You got the car in October—that's exactly when these robberies started.

His back got way up. Don't dare try to pin any similar robberies on him. He was too sophisticated. Yelling: "I went to law school for two damn years. I have nothing to fucking hide. I got my own attorney. I'm getting questioned on camera because I have nothing to hide. I'm sorry about what I did, I'm sorry about what happened.

"I fuckin' gave the guy money to get home, for crying out loud. *Criminals* don't do that shit, man. Why don't you ask *him* that. . . . I gave him taxi money to take on home. Sen and Ren started acting crazy when I did that. I then told him, Stan, to walk straight into a well-lit area and go home. I wished the best and I then drove home. . . . Ask him what I said when I dropped him off. I said, 'Here's twenty dollars for a cab, have a nice night.'"

They can ask me. I was there. It's a lie, along with so much of the rant. It was either Sen or Ren, whoever sat on my right in the car, street tough and with no money, who had the kindness to care if I made it home. Claiming poverty, as far as Lucky was concerned, I could have walked from Prospect Park to Manhattan.

The DA, the NYPD, and the FBI had heard enough bullshit. He'd already hung himself even if he wouldn't own up to his other gangster raps. They cut the taped interview short and stormed out of the room.

The tape ends with Lucky breathing hard, licking his wounds. He sits in the chair in front of the concrete wall applying lip balm. Keepin' that skin smooth.

The big question is, if Lucky was so smart, so rich, so well versed in the legal system, and already had his own criminal lawyer, why did he waive the Miranda rights that were repeated to him by both the detectives and the DA and why did he yap?

Glynn had a good time with the whole thing and he has a ready response. "There's a saying, 'If these kids had brains, we'd be out of business.' The average guy or girl that you have sittin' in there has committed one homicide or one kidnapping in their life. I do this every day. I'm at an advantage. I know what they're lookin' for. They're lookin' for a way out."

TWENTY-NINE

RASHOMON

I want to give him a hug and make him feel better. Ren sits in front of the camera in the same concrete room where Lucky sat, a scared young man, almost sweet-looking, left earring and wisp of a mustache adorning him, shaking his legs nervously, holding a black Yankees baseball cap between his legs, then perching it over a knee, then back between the legs. His real name is Kenyatta Bandule. He's had the nickname Ren since 1992. He's sixteen years old and attends City Challenge High School. It's an ordinary high school. He's in the eleventh grade. He goes to school regularly. He has two girlfriends, named Takeshia and Julia. He lives with his father, two sisters, brother, and sister's baby on Hawthorne Street between Flatbush and Bedford in Brooklyn. Sen lives in the same building. He hadn't kidnapped anyone before, though Lucky and Sen said they did. Ren doesn't usually boost, but he did once and got caught at Woodbury Commons.

He looks contrite, sad, caught up in the storm. He understands each and every Miranda right and is willing to talk without a lawyer anyway.

He speaks with respect, quietly, calmly, looks like he is trying hard to tell the truth. At least some of the time.

One truth quickly came out, unfortunately for Lucky. Sen wasn't the ringleader. Lucky was. Sen didn't get the guns. Lucky did. Sen didn't plan the hit. Lucky did. Ren could not have been clearer. Referring to Lucky:

"It was his idea, his car, his gun."

Here's how the story went. Sen was a good friend of Ren's. They'd known each other for about seven years. Lucky they'd known for about two and a half weeks. "One night I went up to Sen's house and he had introduced me to Lucky. Sen met him through Sen's brother, and I met him through Sen and his brother. I've heard that Lucky was a manager or something. But recently I went to Sears—my first time seeing him at work was yesterday—and he was selling cellular phones."

He met the girls the same night. "I met them the same night I met Lucky because they was leavin' Sen's house."

Ren denied that his fighting and knife-wielding résumé had landed him a spot on Lucky's ho security squad. Sen was said to be the one with the security contract, and Ren purportedly decided not to bid on the subcontract. He merely enjoyed driving around in the Lexus. He admitted openly to knowing that the girls were prostitutes, and his eyes jumped from floor to ceiling while his lips pursed, expressing something unseemly about the honest answer.

When I sat right next to him that night on the mattress, there was lots of business goin' on, but Ren allegedly did not get involved in the prostitution ring: "No. I *saw* where they do business. I took a drive. I wasn't *involved* in they business. Lucky had told Sen that he was like some type of head of security. And because I was with Sen, I guess maybe they figured that I was one of his security people, too. But they were other people who were security. I used to go just to drive around in the Lexus.

"I never actually stayed out there. I went out there . . . it's like this White Castle. Like I went out there and I got out the car and I looked around. And then we drove around where the prostitutes are—it's like a long strip and it's like between buildings. It's all dark. And I saw them doin' all kinds of crazy things, ya know, tryin' to sell their body. Lucky and Sen was with me. No one was payin' me for security. We had spoke about it like that since I was with Sen at the time, just drivin' around, that maybe if I was security then I would be getting paid by Sen—like, Lucky would pay Sen and Sen would pay me. . . . But then the time that we was together it never really clicked like that because, like, I have school to go to and I have other friends, so I'm not always quick to call Sen to social- ize or to go anyplace with me. When I seen him, he had something new to say. I knew him for a long time. We used to always play games, but he got older and he started hangin' out with different people."

Despite the nice employment offer, Ren said he was not interested. "I wasn't into it like that, not standin' around with a gun on me and waitin' for somebody to do somethin'. I wasn't like run up on them and shoot, if it was 'cause they just hit a prostitute or anything. . . . It'd be crazy. I don't carry a gun ordinarily. Not just walkin', playing on the street."

But then a new gun-related opportunity arose. "Sen approached me and he was tellin' me about, uh, you can make two hundred and fifty dollars in less than an hour and it's just so easy. It's a new scam, it has to do with an ATM machine. Sen came to me and he was like it was sweet. He only explained once. He said it was sweet, the guy was comin' out of his car. I'm thinkin' it was in Ma'hatin' 'cause, I don't know. 'Cause we live in Brooklyn and I don't think they'da done anythin' in Brooklyn. The conversation happened last Monday or Tuesday."

Well, the investigators wanted to know, if Sen raised it, how did you know it was Lucky's idea? Lucky insisted in his confession that Sen had done it before and had brought the fresh new scam to him.

Ren rattled off Lucky's braggadocio: "Lucky talked about it like . . . uh . . . 'Don't I got a good mind? If I'da never thought of this, you wouldn'ta got any money.' When we was drivin' around, he was talkin' about how it was his good idea and how he should get a bigger cut 'cause it's his idea."

Well, whoever really deserved origination credit, Ren confirmed that my kidnapping had not been planned with military precision. "Lucky and Sen, they was like . . . we was supposed to get just anybody who was comin' out of the ATM machine. But I guess there's sumthin' about Ma'hatin, and like . . . uh . . . a lot of lawyers, and people who make a lot of money live in Ma'hatin, in the city. So it was go after a person with a trench coat.

"We didn't talk about the . . . abduction. We didn't talk about . . . like what took place? It wasn't discussed. It was more like the time is now and we just hit jackpot and things like that were said. . . . The plan was to get the guy in the car. Like it turned into. At first we was supposed to go find somebody—this is the way they explained to me—find somebody with an ATM card, take their money, and then go get money out of the ATM machine. . . . It was . . . I thought that we was just gonna hold him and then bring him back."

But it played different. Snagging the prey was intravenous adrenaline, propelling them toward a much larger crime. They rolled up behind me in the Lexus on West Tenth Street—me feeling good about the girl and the cookies and seeing nothing—eyes narrowed, focus intense. Ren said it went like this:

Lucky: "That's the one, that's the one."

Sen: "I feel it, I'm feelin' it, okay, I'm feelin' it. He looks like he has money."

Ren minimized his role in the command structure. "So I'm like . . . all right." As he spoke, Ren moved his head from side to side in a yoyo neck explaining he was down with it.

Ren explained further. "Then I'm sittin' there. And Lucky just gets out the car, walks up to the guy, 'cause we're across the street and he's here. And . . . um . . . I heard the guy scream. I heard him scream. I was right by the car. It was double-parked. Lucky got out first and then Sen went right behind him. . . . I wasn't really carrying a gun. Lucky had the forty-five and Sen had the—I think it's a TEC-9. . . . Lucky grabbed

251

Stanley and sort of like took his shoulder. Stanley like shoved away and fell and dropped his cookies and the book. Sen didn't have to go all the way to him, but he got up and went into the car. Sen had a gun when he got out of the car—I seen him with the gun, I was sittin' in the back. He was holdin' it like this."

Ren gestured with the gun under the puffy down coat he wore for the interview. It looked an awful lot like what I saw *Ren* do when *he* grabbed me on the street that night. Ren straight out claimed he never used a gun on me: "I had a gun but I wasn't holdin' it on Stanley. I had it on the side."

Also, Ren didn't know where they grabbed me. "I wasn't really paying attention. . . . I don't know Ma'hatin too good."

Ren said that they got me back in the car and then "Sen is like, don't move. Lucky's askin' him questions like 'Why'd you scream like that? I'm the nicest robber you'll ever meet.' That's what he said. He asked, 'Do you have any credit cards? How much money would I be able to withdraw? Do you know the numbers?' Stanley said he only knew one number—I think that was to his Citibank or Chase card. . . . Lucky had asked, well, how much money does he gross? and he said seventeen hundred every two weeks. Lucky asked him how much money he had in his savings account, and he said a hundred thousand."

That little bomb stopped the clock. Ren practically pleaded for leniency as he explained it to the interrogators. Surely they could understand the changed circumstances. "It wasn't supposed to go as far as this . . . kidnapping. What happened was that Lucky had asked him if he has . . . how much money does he have in his savings account? He told him a hundred thousand dollars, and all of a sudden Lucky and Sen lookin' at each other and they like, 'Well, I think maybe you're gonna spend the night with me tonight.'"

And so I did.

"Lucky asked 'Is there any way that I can get into this savings account with this card?'" From the ensuing colloquy, Ren got the clear idea that the

252

white lawyer tried to keep it real—the message I had worked hard to convey. Ren recalled that "he never paid for anything over one thousand dollars or something like that. He acted like he never used that much money before. Like he just lived a common life. Lucky asked how much money can I withdraw before they tell 'em too much, and he was . . . he didn't know."

He also got the idea that I was trying to keep it cool, too. "Sen said, 'You got big eyes' . . . and asked him to take off his glasses." But Stanley kept his head down so as not to bear witness. Ren: "The rest of the time he was in the car like this"—indicating with head down—"he was like, 'I'm not lookin', I don't wanna see.'"

To Ren, I looked kinda scared but not very. Skeptically: "He was scared but he maintained . . . he looked"—pondering—"you would know that he was scared, but . . ." Ren's interview voice drifted off.

But, on the flip side, I gave them reason to be scared, too. Ren recounted my soliloquy impressively but got it only partly right: Quoting me: "You sorta picked the wrong guy. I'm an Assistant U.S. Attorney. Tomorrow's my birthday."

That had an impact. "Matter of fact, the fact that he was a U.S. Attorney kinda shook me up a little bit. Made me even more scared that I was, like, gonna get caught." As I suspected, if I'd pushed the prosecutor thing too hard, I would have been taking an awful risk.

Just as Glynn had explained that they all do, Ren tried to cover his butt by keeping his role to a minimum. First, he was only trying to scare me, akin to his brother-in-arms Lucky. "I was goin' to convince him not to run. Just scare him. But shoot him? No." Disdain at the very thought. Not only that, he lacked proper equipment. Ren: "The gun only had one bullet, the gun that I had."

Just for argument's sake, the DA piped in, "How many do you need to kill somebody?"

Ren conceded, "One."

Ren further explained that he left the apartment at ten A.M. to go to school. After school, he happened to run into Sen, and they went back to

Ren's apartment so he could take a shower. Lucky's girlfriend came by to pick them up and took them back to Lucky's place on Eastern Parkway. There, Lucky led the discussion of where they should dump the male. Central Park in Manhattan was too risky, so they decided on Prospect Park. Ren had little to say about it except to note that they were so generous as to give me money for a cab.

Generous? Just trying to scare Stanley? No big deal? All Lucky and Sen's crime? The DA switched over from good to bad cop. She asked, "Can you envision yourself in the situation, or rather, envision someone that you love, like maybe your sister, in a situation where she's snatched off the street and held by gunpoint, all her stuff taken away and blindfolded. What do you think that man thought at that moment?"

Ren conceded, "That maybe he was gonna die."

"That was a real possibility, wasn't it?"

"I don't think so."

"What was your cut gonna be?"

"I don't know."

"Didn't you discuss that?"

"No."

Following more of Ren's where did you go—"out"—what did you do—"nothing" attitude, the DA started to shout. "Where's *Ren* during all this?" she demanded.

"I was *there*"—wanting credit for his concession, but distancing himself from the crime.

"Tell me now that you didn't say to yourself, 'Jackpot'? Is that what came across your mind, 'Here's the jackpot'?"

"Well, yeah, that did come across my mind." But again, dodging with attitude.

The DA sharpened her sword. "Where is Ren? You a choirboy? Were you saying your prayers in the front seat? 'Cause you know what, I bet Stanley was saying his prayers in the backseat."

Ren continued the dodge. "Right. And I was tryin' to make Stanley as comfortable as possible."

After Lucky's confession in which *he* said his job was to make me as comfortable as possible, this was a little much for a seasoned DA to take. She burst out in a laugh. "You know what? So far everybody I've spoken to is making Stanley comfortable. Everybody's making Stanley comfortable. You know where Stanley would be comfortable? Stanley would be comfortable in his living room."

"I know. I know that."

Then sheepishly: "I did take a part in what happened, but I wasn't the one callin' all the shots. It does make a difference."

DA: "In whose eyes do you think that makes a difference?"

"Mine."

She glared at him as though he were nuts.

Ren begged for understanding. "Me and Sen had spoke about lettin' him go. But Lucky kept comin' back with this fifty-thousand-dollar thing. And we're tryin' to tell him that's never gonna work and we should let him go right now, but Lucky's like, '[gravel voice] That's the bucks, see, y'all gonna pass up fi'ty thousand dollars,' and I'm like, 'Listen, no one's gonna let you walk out the bank with fi'ty thousand dollars cash.' And Lucky's like, 'I go there and I can make it happen, too.'"

The DA pointed out that Lucky had said the same thing. That he wanted to stop it but the others insisted on pushing for the gold.

Nonsense, Ren said. It had to be Lucky, because he had the financial savvy and Ren was just a sixteen-year-old kid along for the ride. Ren implored, "But I don't have an account—I don't know about these things."

The DA decided to shift the focus in case that would help Kenyatta see the error of his ways. She inquired, "What about the women? The women were helping, as well?"

Ren wanted to protect his intimates. "They didn't help."

He sought to underscore their innocence, even though when he left at ten A.M. to go to school it was just Ramos and the girls watching Stanley. "Because I mean . . . it wasn't like they was watchin' him, torturin' him or anything like that. They was sort of like *babysittin'*, because they . . ."

She couldn't stand it anymore. Her voice now went quiet in the most fearsome form of outrage. "What's your first name? Kenyatta. Kenyatta, let me ask you a question. You're sitting blindfolded. You've got a gun to your head. You have guys threatening to kill you and your family. And that's not torture? Is that torture?"

Ren's greatest skill was not sticking to his guns.

"Okay. Yeah."

"So you think that if you don't tune somebody up and beat the crap out of them, that that's not torture?"

"I didn't think about it that way."

"Well, you should start thinkin' about it that way because that's how I'm thinkin' about it."

She paused momentarily and then decided to hit just one more time. "Did the word 'kidnapping' come into your mind? The word 'abduction'? Was there something about that view of a man terrorized with a blindfold over his eyes that clicked in your head and said, 'Gee, this is something really bad, this is not stealing a bar of candy from a candy shop'? This is the big time. This is really bad. Something that clicked in there?"

Ren: "Yes."

But "you did it anyway," finishing her closing to the jury.

As she picked up her things to leave the room, Ren, dejected, tried one last time to grab at straws. This was never supposed to be a kidnapping. "But they started talkin' about different things. And I was there. And for some reason I didn't . . . I wanted to say I'm leavin'. But it didn't come out of my mouth."

The DA: "This interview is concluded."

CHAPTER THIRTY

AN INNOCENT MAN

Ramos the landlord got stiffed by his tenants, in a big way. They gave him a visit to the slammer instead of $200 rent. Maybe that's what happens when your real estate office bears stickers from Wu-Tang Clan and Onyx on the front door. Onyx, Ramos's favorite quartet, sells pleasant tunes such as "Bacdafucup," and is a gang of rappers who take it a lot more seriously than flashy jewelry or record sales. They come straight out and say it: They want your money or your life. Ramos flashes a knowing, semi-guilty wisp of a smile while he's telling about the Onyx sticker on apartment 3D at 1430 Eastern Parkway.

With the video camera rolling, landlord Ramos sets the stage for that night's crime. He openly admits that his tenant Lucky is a "quasi-pimp" or a pimp "wannabe." He knows that the prostitutes work on Pennsylvania Avenue near White Castle. Ramos has tasted the tenant's wares, admitting to having had sex with sixteen-year-old Mercedes. But apart from the freebies, Ramos got nothing:

"They was gonna pay me the money, but they didn't pay me yet. Not even a week. They only stood there for, like, three weeks since the first or second week of January."

Soon after agreeing on lease terms, Lucky commenced expanding the tenancy by bringing his security squad and their compadres around for a taste of some sweet stuff: "First met Ren and Sen when Lucky brought them two weeks ago. Brought girls with some other guys and Ren and Sen and Sen's brother, but he's not involved, he just had sex and then leave."

The video room is occupied by the tireless DA and Detective Jack Baker. I won't forget Detective Baker. Years ago, he was shot in the line of duty. He wakes up every morning with a limp. The first time I met him, in the police station hallway, he was emphatic. "Stan, don't you ever second-guess yourself. You coulda run? You coulda fought? Bullshit. You're standing here talkin' to me. That means you did something right. Don't dare second-guess. Look what happened to me."

I need that vote of confidence after what I went through.

Ramos hangs his head as though he can feel what Baker is thinking. He has no idea why he is caught up in this. He didn't do shit other than rent out a room to some guy and his girls. In fact, the very day he was stuck watching the white guy he was supposed to be out taking pictures to apply with a friend to a Brooklyn company for security jobs. Forty-eight hours later he is incarcerated, and very, very surprised.

Before Baker took over with the DA in the video phase, interrogation samurai Detective William Glynn sat alongside Baker and squeezed the signed confession out of Ramos, just like he had with Lucky. Glynn has his own sardonic opinion of how Ramos fit in with the triumvirate:

"Lucky I kinda felt bad for. He didn't come across as a thug. There's a criminal mind, but he didn't come across that way. More like middle-class. Somebody that I wouldn't target. Ya know, most people you can read. I mean Ren and Sen, they looked street. You could tell they'd been around. I asked Lucky, 'Where'd you get that street name?' Apparently, he grew up in a financially comfortable home, and all his friends used to say, 'Man, you're lucky.' I was under the impression that he grew up right there in Brooklyn with his grandmother."

Shows you that even a pro like Glynn can be a little bit off, opining that Lucky was not the criminal mind.

Glynn continues, "Ramos was a real dope—in every way. He would be somebody I would target at some point. I mean, he's a street guy. Ya just kinda read it. I worked in Brownsville for years—my bread and butter was watchin' these guys. He was somebody that would be behind the scenes. It would be typical of him sittin' there, holdin' the gun—he won't do it but he'll back it up. He definitely had his hands dirty, I think, in the past."

The pitch to Ramos curved in toward the batter at about the same angle it had curved in on Lucky. Glynn: "I went in the room with Baker and I says, 'All right, listen. I got Lucky, I got Ren, I got Sen, I got all these girls, and they're all tryin' to make you the bad guy. And I don't believe you're the bad guy.' I says, 'I'm gonna give you one opportunity to come on my team—one opportunity—and if you decline it I'm walkin' out and we're just gonna fuck you.' So he says, 'I wanna be on your team.' So I advise him of his rights, and I say, 'You understand the rules here? You lie to me once, I'm walkin' out.' I said, 'I got everybody givin' a statement,' I said, and, 'Lucky's tryin' to make you the bad guy.'

"He tells me his story. He says he comes home and they got a white guy in his apartment. 'Now they tell me they want me to watch him.' So they give Ramos the gun. So Ramos says to Lucky, 'This is wrong—this ain't the right thing to do.' So Lucky says, 'Well, we'll give you money to do it.' And Ramos says, 'I don't want a lot of money, I just want the rent money. Just give me enough money to pay the rent and I'll be happy with that. But then they had me stay and watch this guy the whole day. I would never hurt him. I unloaded the gun because I did not want to hurt that man.' So I says, 'I want you to talk to the district attorney, and—don't forget—you gotta tell 'em the truth. As long as you tell 'em the truth, you're still on my team.'" Coach Glynn.

Convinced he was playing team ball, Ramos kept singing—wrote it all down on paper, and then with Glynn running off to catch some z's, Ramos repeated it on video with Baker and the DA in the room. He is wearing a black knit cap half over his ears. After a while, the DA gets sick of it, says it is distracting her, and asks him to take it off. He is a bit taken aback but willingly complies, and explains the hat hair issue: "My hair look funny, I wear this." He also sports a Calvin Klein T-shirt and the hint of a mustache and a tiny beard. At twenty-two, he is still young enough to have a few pimples. He has nice, big eyelashes.

Making small talk and proving no coercion, the DA chats. "How do you feel?"

He flashes a big, nervous smile. "Now I feel scared."

But a macho man can't acknowledge that, so he amends, "Not scared, *worried.*"

During the ritual second Miranda reading, his cheek rests desultorily on a big-knuckled fist. With Miranda out of the way, he clasps his hands together between his legs and explains that he was out that night visiting friends on Parkside Avenue, near Prospect Park, five blocks from where I grew up.

"I was in my friend's birthday. The twenty-first I left in the morning. I went to my friends' to see if I get a different job that pays more. I had to get a certificate. . . . Tryin' to get the job. In security. I have the address in the apartment—somewhere in Brooklyn. . . . We needed pictures, so we didn't find no place where they took the pictures so we went back home. So on Thursday I was tryin' to go get the pictures so on Friday I could get hired. He was chillin' with his girlfriend and I was chillin' with his sister Wennie. Like one-something, I left." An FBI report listed this defendant as "Luis Ramos a.k.a. 'Groovy Love.'" There was a lot of chillin' goin' on, apparently.

Ramos had no fear descending to the tunnel of the number 2 IRT subway line at one A.M. and riding it out toward the end of the line to

1430 Eastern Parkway. He didn't get mugged on the subway, but he was in for quite a shock when he crossed his own threshold.

Lucky and Ren heard Ramos throw the bolt in the doorjamb and were waiting for him anxiously when he swung the door open. It was "Thursday morning. When I went in, I got in like two somethin'—I don't remember the time. I was gonna go through to say hi to everybody, but Lucky and Ren stopped me, and Ren he had me by my finger, squeezin' me like c'mere, c'mere. I was like, 'What you doin',' 'cause I thought they was gon' do sumthin' wrong to me. Like rob me or beat me up or somethin'. I don't know, 'cause I don't trust them, 'cause they stole twenty-four dollars from me. I don't trust them.

"They wouldn't let me pass and they was talking and he was here and he was here and I thought they was gonna try something stupid. . . . First I started thinkin' they was gonna rob me so I was ready if they attack me I'ma attack them. But then nuthin' happened. There wasn't no thought of that, no looks, no nuthin'. And they was like, 'We gotta talk to you. I don't think you should be here today.' You know it was like that. I said, 'Yo, what happened? Tell me, tell me, yo, tell me, man. Tell me, I don't care what you do, I just wanna know. Just tell me.' He said, 'Ai.' He said, 'Look in the room.' Tha's when Ren holdin' me, he said, 'Hold up, hold up, hold up,' and I said, 'Yo, son, whut you doin',' and Lucky said, 'Let 'im go.' We went and I saw the guy and there was like a bed up to here and he . . . there was a man sittin' there like that blindfolded" (gesturing across his eyes). "I think it was wit his scarf, sumthing. And I looked and I got shocked and I said, 'Ho . . . what this guy's doing here?' . . . Sittin' there in a blue two-piece suit."

Ramos also noticed Sen and the girls sprawled in a variety of prone positions across the room and the adjoining living room in his railroad flat apartment. Sen had a gun: "Sen was in the room. I saw him, I think he was on the cellular phone talkin' with a four-fifth on his hand."

Ramos stammered, "I asked this guy, 'Who's that—what is he, gettin' a blow job or somethin?' I said ah . . . I told 'im, 'I don't want that kind of stuff happening here, 'cause this place is gonna get hot.'"

They responded, "'We robbin' him. He got money and shit like.' . . . They said, 'Yo, we just took him and we brought him in here.' . . . He had money and they took him and put him in the car. He was like, takin' money out the bank—that's what the guy told me. What's that guy's name again? Oh, yeah, Stanley. 'Cause I was talkin' to him over the next day."

Ramos wants to convince the DA and Detective Baker that he was repulsed by this particularly offensive new business venture: "From there I went back and I said, 'Yo, y'all niggas crazy, yo. Y'all niggas wildin' now. 'Cause first what y'all is doin', this hooka stuff, doing sellin' girls, I wasn't into it, but now y'all niggas kidnapped a guy and shit like that.' They said, 'Yo, we saw that nigga he was eating cookies.' They told me that he dropped the cookies and they put him inside the car.

"They said they was gonna hold him till the next day until he get fi'ty thousand dollis. I said, 'Oh . . . shit. Thas a lotta money.' Sen told me that."

Then Ramos noticed Lucky pulling a huge rolled-up wad of bills from his pants pocket. "Lucky had a lot of money with his money mixed in. I said, 'Oh shit.' . . . I said, 'Yo, can you bust me down with the two hundred so I can pay the rent?' Tha's the first thing I told him. 'Cause the next day on Thursday I asked him for five hundred dollars. Just two hundred for me to pay the guy the rent and three hundred for me to spend."

Pressed for culpability, lawyerless Ramos took the bait. The DA asked him why he requisitioned the extra spending money. "Because you more or less had to babysit him?"

Pregnant pause. Damning admission. "Ye-ah."

Realizing he was being trapped, Ramos parried with defense lawyer spin, insisting, "I didn't ask him yet for money. I told him, 'Yo, I don't wanna be involved with this.' He said, 'No no no, don't worry, you're not involved with this.' Ai, I said, 'Yo, what y'all niggas do is what y'all niggas do. Don't put my name on this shit, ai? Y'all niggas stay here and chill. I think you should like take his money and just leave him and, you know, just do what you gotta do.' Because if I was be, like, you know, 'Oh, now you gotta give him back his money and take him back,' they'd go like, 'Aw, son, you be a sucker, you know what I'm sayin'?' They gonna be thinking, oh, we shouldn't trust this guy, 'cause they don't trust me and I don't trust them. So when I told them that don't put my name on this, he said don't worry because tomorrow we gonna take him out of here in the morning."

Ramos wanted some bucks, but his first instinct was to stay as far away as possible. He slipped off to his own room to sleep. The next day when he awoke, he was swept into the whirlpool with the others. Sen stirred him at ten in the morning. "He told me, 'Son, you know, watch this guy for a while 'cause I have take care of bizness. I'll be back.' I go, 'Yo, what's up wit Lucky? Where he at?' He said, 'He'll be back in a half an hour.' I said, 'Yeah, 'cause I have to go. I gotta go take some pictures.' He had the caliber forty-five automatic, and the TEC-9, he gave it to me. He go, 'Watch the guy for a while. He'll be back in a half an hour.' I said, 'Yo, if you see Lucky, tell him I gotta go, ta come back quick.' I stood there, with the two girls, just watchin' the guy . . . and I took the clip off the gun and I had it in my back pocket."

Ramos admits to the DA that he held the guns and that he stood out-side on guard while I went to the bathroom. Well, queried the DA, doesn't that mean you did it to prevent him from leaving?

Not at all. "I didn't even have to worry about him—I just slept for a while there. I didn't know the guy was gonna stay the whole twenty-six hours. I thought he was gonna leave at ten o'clock. I coulda let him go free, but I was scared. . . . I was afraid if I helped him, I'd get in trouble."

There's no way he would have shot me, he says. "I was armed, but I took out the clip." And, by the way, "I cleaned the clip so that my finger-prints wouldn't be in there." Not a criminal, but the man was thinking.

Although he was holding two guns on me, there was actually nothing for me to have feared because "one wasn't loaded and the other only had one bullet." Then, gilding it, "I was thinking of letting him go. . . . Those twelve hours he was with me he wasn't gonna get shot. Even though he would have tried something, he wouldn't get shot. . . . I wasn't gonna shoot no other person—for what? So I could go to jail?"

Would he have let me walk out the door if I had only dared to try? Sure! "Yeah, I was thinking about it. You can ask Mercedes," he told the DA and detective.

Not to be outdone by Lucky or Ren, Ramos also sought penitence in the quality of relationship he and I had developed. He softened his voice to describe the relationship. "When I stood and Ren left, I was talkin' to Stanley and I said, 'I'm sorry,' and he said, 'Don't worry, it's not your fault,' and I said, 'Yes it is, I could let you go free.'"

Of course that part's a lie or I would have walked out onto Eastern Parkway.

Continuing, ". . . I talked to him, we had a long conversation. . . . Stanley didn't ask me any questions. If he did, I wouldn't have answered. I told him we was in Queens—they told me to tell him we was in Queens. . . . I was talking to Stanley that I wasn't involved with this and that I am sorry. He said it's okay. It's not your fault." Just as I had suspected when I was inside, they purposely lied about the location of the apartment to throw me off the track.

"I asked him, yo, are you hungry? He said, 'Well, I'm hungry, but I don't think I'm gonna eat, 'cause I'm worried.' A while ago I asked him again, I said, 'Yo, are you hungry, thirsty, yeah?' I said, 'You want a hero?' He said, 'Yeah, can you buy me a turkey sandwich?' I said, 'Fine, you want juice wi' that?' 'Cause I felt sorry for the guy. And Mercedes, she needed tampons, and the other girl, she was hungry, she needed cigarettes So my last twenty dollars, I gave it to her for her to get whatever."

On the day that I sat on that mattress with the glow of new afternoon sun so strong it pushed right past the velour blindfold, I had a powerful sense of Ramos's instability as he railed against his Domincan father who used to hit him for nothing and whom he fucking hated. Ramos went through the sort of hell no child deserves. He elucidates on the video that his "father was a thief, yeah. He was on drugs and he had AIDS. But he was walking, he . . . he used to go to his doctor and stuff like that." The family called on Luis to take care of this drug-addict, AIDS-afflicted father. "It was in 1995, I came home in March the second week to take care of him, 'cause he had AIDS. I stood with him and my grandfather."

They lived on Ralph Avenue in Brooklyn. Ramos didn't get to finish school. "I was gonna go to school, but, like, my father had problems so I had to work. My mother lives in Puerto Rico. She also needs help."

And then his father died while Ramos was taking care of him.

A single odd souvenir remains from his father: a handful of bullets. "I had the bullets since he died. I don't carry them—I put them away. I don't want to get caught with them—get arrested."

Since the father passed, he had held down normal jobs, working at JFK Airport since July 1997. He trained as a mechanic but worked for International Service System as a porter, cleaning.

With the background out of the way, the DA pushed Ramos for why he didn't tell me to take off the scarf or call the cops or set me free. He responded with indignation. "I didn't tell him *don't* take your blindfold off. I didn't say none of that shit. I just stood there like that"—arms crossed—"chillin', smoking my cigarette. . . . I didn't call the police. There wasn't no phone," with a sigh of resignation.

According to Ramos, he had no part in any kidnapping. "I was waiting for Lucky. That wasn't a job. That was a *favor* I did for him. I wanted five hundrid dollars. Lucky was gonna give me the money I don't know from where, 'cause he had his own money, too. . . . Every half hour he'd call and say he'd be back in a half an hour. Tha's why I'm mad at Lucky. I said fuck it yeah, this is not my bizness and I'm gonna ask him for some money.

"He told me to stay and wait for *him*. I was waiting for *him*. I wasn't even guarding, I didn't even care. If he'd'a escaped he'd'a escaped. I didn't need the two guns. You're trying to show the camera that I'm the bad guy here. I'm not the bad guy. I know, I was there. I didn't kidnap him."

The investigators are not satisfied. C'mon, Luis, you could have let him go.

The expected explosive reaction of his tenants inhibited Ramos's discretion. Emphatically: "And call me a rat, call me a rat, and then have people searching for me to kill me? Tha's why I didn't want it. I didn't want to get hurt or get shot or nuthin' like that. I was scared, too. I'm the man with the gun, but it's not loaded." But the others were well equipped. "They had firearms. They used to take out the clip and leave it on top of the radiator . . . keep the clip in they pocket. They had two of them. They had a forty-five-caliber—I think—um, automatic and a TEC-9. The TEC-9 I don't know if they stoled it, they bought it, but they got it from somebody. They *always* carrying weapons."

And the little army had reinforcements to pursue Ramos if needed. "I was planning to let him go, but I was scared. Other people know me. . . . They know where I live at and where I work at. Sen brother, he works at Sears. The other two I don't know, the other two they just be chillin'. He be a DJ. The other I ain't seen for a week."

Playing defense from as many angles as possible, Ramos also contends that his effect on my decision tree was scant. Spinning, "Even if I left, the guy wasn't gonna leave, 'cause he was scared. He don't know where he at." Because his boyfriends had already scared the shit out of me. "On Thursday they was goin' like that to him" (pointing the gun). "They were sayin', 'Yo, Stanley, you not gonna say a word to nobody about this.' They was playin' with their guns. . . . They told him, 'Yo, don't try nuthin' stupid.' I would be scared, too. . . . I'll be scared. I'd think my life was on the line."

Better still, there were socioeconomic, even racial, reasons for the white lawyer man to sit still for twenty-six hours without a peep. Ramos expounded, "I already knew from the get-go that he was afraid. 'Cause he's by himself. They got all these bunch of black people there. The majority of white people, they scared of black people. You know that."

I have a dream that someday we will live in a land where Ramos's words will have lost all hint of truth.

The DA was tired of hearing so much bullshit and she wanted to go home and get some sleep. She was about to announce once again that "this interview is concluded." But Ramos needed to make just one last point before they cut him off. He posited that he couldn't possibly be guilty of a crime when he never even ended up getting paid. "After eleven P.M., Lucky came. Tha's when I got mad and I pulled him, I said, 'Yo, give me five hundred dollars. Two hundred dollars for the rent and three hundred dollars for me to spend.' He said, 'Ai, fine,' which I knew he wasn't gonna give it to me, tha's what Honey told me. She tole me that yesterday. When they left to take that guy, I don't know where they took him and shit, so I stood sleeping. When he came back, that was, uh, six o'clock in the morning and I think he opened the door, he said, 'Yo, Luis, I'ma give you a hundred fifty dollars later.' I said, 'Ai, fine,' so I could just pay the rent. I don't have to think 'bout the rest, I just wanted to get the hell out of there."

After eight hours of allegedly gratis kidnapping service, tough guy Lucky was still paying even less than the rent. Man, did landlord Ramos get stiffed by his tenants. He could use a good lawyer.

THIRTY-ONE

GIRLS GONE WILD

Only hours before, they'd paraded scandalously young buttocks and pushed up half-exposed bosoms past a White Castle cesspool. As surprising as it was for me to end up sitting on a strange mattress in my lawyer suit, it was equally strange for three girls to end up one after the other sitting across from cops and a camera in the interrogation room. Mercedes—Diannes Santamaria—was a very pretty Puerto Rican–looking sixteen-year-old. She was born in the Bronx; her mom lived in Brooklyn, not with her. Mystic, or Shawn Landrick, eighteen, had spent good money on her poofy hairdo and tiger-print blouse and looked like the wizened older sister. She owned up to a career in "dancing." She also was born in the Bronx, and her mom lived in Queens, but she commuted between Ramos's place and a friend's apartment in Bushwick. She'd been away from home only a few months, and her mother said she could come home if she wanted to.

Berniece Warren, aka Honey or Butter, looked like a pudgy cross between sixteen and forty-five, because life had made her hard. According to Honey, her father was never there and her mother was a drug addict. Since the age of four, she had been in and out of group foster homes, sometimes living with her aunt. She claimed not to have a drug problem, though she smoked three or four weed blunts just about every day. My birthday was a normal day of marijuana consumption for this sixteen-year-old. Honey wore white pants and a blue pullover over her full body, and she fiddled with her knit hat in front of the camera, fidgeting and crying while waiting for the DA to come into the room. A legacy of abuse was etched on her face.

All three girls were originally franchised with Lucky's competition, a pimp named Leroy or Precious. They "stayed" with him. Mercedes said she'd been selling it for four or five months total on Pennsylvania Avenue in Brooklyn. Mystic said sometimes they went to Manhattan and trolled up and down Eighth, Ninth, and Tenth Avenues. Except when it was too hot.

Honey tried to dodge the prostitute label. "Sometime I go out like Mercedes and Mystic to the track. I'm not a prostitute because I don't be out there like—*be out there*. I just go when I need money." She processed her own words and then conceded, "Well, I guess I am, because I have did it before, but I don't be out there every day like that."

Lucky lured the girls away from Precious by cutting them a better deal. Rather than a "pimp," like Precious, Lucky acted as more of an agent. He managed their money, rented an apartment for them, and gave them back up to half of their gross to spend on food, nails, and hair, as required. He was new to this particular line of business. In fact, he had informed Mercedes that he was of an artistic bent. "He used to work in a studio writing songs for rappers and stuff. That's what he told me," Mercedes explained. "He also told me he had girls, but they worked in clubs and stuff. So I didn't pay no mind." A man of many, many talents. He could write songs for Hot 97.

Lucky started out as a customer, Mercedes said: "I met him by Mystic 'cause he was a trick. Mystic introduced me to Lucky." From being a trick, love grew, as I had seen with my own ears. Honey: "Lucky was Mystic's boyfriend. He has a fiancée so, like, Mystic is his mistress."

But Mystic denied it: "The only reason why I'm messin' with Lucky is 'cause he helped me get away from Leroy. I just didn't want to be with him no more." While the other girls told the DA that Mystic had sex with Lucky in the bathroom that night before Lucky went over to his fiancée's house, Mystic vehemently denied it: "Me and Lucky never had sex in the bathroom when that man was there. When that man was there, I never had sex with anybody."

It was important to these girls that Lucky not be called a pimp. He was a service provider. Mercedes explained, "Money I make, I give it to Lucky. Terrance, he holds us down—he's not a pimp, though—he's just holding us down, like we give him our money, he finds a place to stay and stuff, so like if we make a hundred bucks he'll take it and pay like the rent for the new house we 'bout to move into. We got to pay twelve hundred dollars for a house we gonna get. . . . He gives us money, like fifty dollars for food. If we made two hundred dollars, we got to keep half with Lucky. Lucky not a pimp—it's a big difference. He provide security. Ren and Sen and his brother—guy who works at Sears. Lucky had a gun in the car, I don't know if he has it now. A TEC-9."

A night's work under Lucky's umbrella was good money. The girls could "make like a hundred, a hundred and forty," Mercedes said. "He'll give you half of it if you ask him for some money, 'cause you made money. But if you don't make money, he ain't gonna give you."

Honey explained Lucky's utility as their banker. "When we was out on the track, yes, he would hold our money, because there was a number of times—well, not a number but like two times—I have got robbed and beat up out there. I do not keep money on me when I'm out there, 'cause I don't want to get hurt. . . . Lucky helped us out 'cause I ain't had nowhere to go and Mercedes didn't have nowhere to go."

Mystic confirmed the security detail, but in confession lied like hell to protect her beloved Lucky. She took any gun out of his hands. "Ren and Sen was security," she related. "Whenever we went out to work to the streets, they would watch us. They was armed. Never saw Lucky armed. Lucky would just drive his car."

For Lucky's girls, my capture was an unpleasant interruption in a working night. As January 21 changed into the twenty-second, 1998, the girls were out on the track on Pennsylvania Avenue, giving sex in between square burgers from the White Castle. Lucky explained to them that this was going to be a different kind of night once they got off. "I was at work. He called us in the car and told us there's this white guy sitting in the bed," Mercedes explained. "He said, 'I got this white guy at home. We got a plan for him. Don't say nuthin' to him, don't speak to him, be careful for what you say, and don't tell him you live in Brooklyn.'"

Honey was in the car with them and recalled the conversation with Lucky. "He was like, um, 'There's something real serious goin' on at the house,'" Honey explained. "I was like, 'Serious? Is it bad or is it good?' He was like, 'In a way it's bad, in a way it's good.' And I was like, 'What's bad about it and what's good about it?' And he was like, 'The bad thing is sumthin' that we wasn't supposed to do. But the good thing is that y'all are be gettin' your apartment. Y'all don't have to live where you're livin' anymore.' 'Cause we never liked the area. There would be money now."

When the girls arrived, there was a new addition to the furniture. "I seen a white guy sittin' on the bed with a suit on, tie, shoes, with a pretty black scarf," Honey said. "He wasn't sayin' anything, he wasn't doing anything, he was just sitting there. Ren and Sen said, 'It's his birthday, Stan's gonna be givin' us a lot of money. Stan is rich. Stan's gonna help us out. Stan's gonna help us with the money situation.'"

None of the girls had any patience for this latest wicked scheme, just as I had observed. Honey flipped. "And I said, 'What the fuck, is y'all stupid?'" she explained. "'Why are y'all doing this shit for?' Then someone knocked on the door. Diannes answered and it was Mystic. She came in the room and was like, 'What happened? What's going on?' I said, 'I'm quite sure you don't want to know. Well, um, I'm leaving, I ain't staying here.'"

Ren interjected, "You ain't goin' nowhere."

Honey said, "What, nigga, please, you can't tell me what to do."

Ren passed the ball, saying, "Yo, Sen, talk to her."

"Sen said, 'Why not? I want you to stay with me,'" Honey continued. "Then I said, 'Look, if I stay here, I will be a a part of this, too, and I refuse to go to jail with y'all, Sen.' Sen said, 'Who's going to jail?' and I said, 'You really think they not gonna find who you is?' And he said, 'Don't think negative because that's when you get caught.' And I said, 'Well, just in case you do get caught, my motherfucking ass ain't going to jail with you, fuck that.' Sen said, 'You act like you scared of jail.' Meanwhile, Ren was talking to the white man, making fun of his name, freestyle rapping what they was doing. Diannes and Luis was listening to Ren. And Luciano and Mystic was in the bathroom having sex. Then I told Sen, 'You damn real I'm scared. I ain't never been there, and I ain't trying never to go there.' Then he was like, 'So what you saying, you not gonna stay with me?' And I said, 'Not tonight.'"

Mystic said she arrived later and was no happier than the other girls. "I was talkin' to Sen on Lucky's phone," she related. "I thought they had a client for us. I went in the back room and I saw the guy. I saw him sittin' on the floor and a velour scarf tied around his face and he was in his suit. Luis said, 'Say hi to Steve,' and Steve to say hi to me." Raising her voice before the camera, Mystic intoned indignantly, "I wanted to know what the hell this man is doin' here. I was beefin'. I asked them like, 'Where'd you get him from? How'd y'all get him in the car? How'd y'all get him up the apartmint without nobody seein' y'all? Did he see your faces? How are you gonna take him home? How much money you gettin' out of him?'

"Ren would just say, 'Don't worry about that, everything is under control, we got this.' I was so surprised when I walked in the house."

Of course, what I witnessed was a short period of protesting followed by a lot of lovin'. Mercedes denied any physical relation with the gang in the apartment, owning up only to having had sex with Sen's brother. Mystic denied the entire affair with Lucky, a lover's sacrifice that she made with no mind to the fiancée who won Lucky's primary affection.

Well, perhaps her devious little mind was actually paying a lot of attention to the fiancée during her interrogation. Her memory became powerful when it came to identifying one extra little accomplice to this affair. It happened late in the day on the twenty-second, and don't think I didn't notice it at the time. Mystic: "The next day when I was leavin', his fiancée came over and asked for Steve's Social Security number. She came over to the house. When she called on the intercom, 'He said to give me his Social Security number.'" Her love for Lucky was strong enough for her to throw an elbow in the competition's face.

Mystic and Lucky weren't the only happy couple in the room. Honey cooed for her man. "I *talk* to Sen. He's not my boyfriend, but I talk to him. We gettin' to know each other better. This is how it was, you know what I'm sayin'? If Sen told me to do something—not anything, but if he told me to do something, I would do it. If he woke me up out of my sleep three o'clock in the morning and asked me to go to the store for him, I would go. I'm not afraid of him. I'm not in *love*, I'm *infatuated* with him. I have a lot of feelings, *obsessed*, you could say like that."

Love blossomed even as the white man sat across from them on another mattress. Honey went over and lay down next to Sen, with Mystic in the bathroom with Lucky and Mercedes smoking a cigarette by the window. Honey was feeling romantic. "Me and Sen were talking about us, and I told him that I wanted to have sex. And he said that he don't think that it would be a good idea for us to do that. And so I got upset and was like, 'I'm leaving.' I got dressed and I left. But I only went out to the weed spot and came back."

By then Lucky and Mystic were out of the bathroom and Lucky was about to leave. Sen told Ren to watch the white guy while he and Honey went in the bathroom. "So me and Sen went in the bathroom. He rolled a blunt and I rolled a blunt," Honey continued. "I said to Sen, 'Why did you do this? This is so stupid.'

"He was like, 'I know, but this is the last time. After this, I won't have to do this anymore. This is the last time, boo.'

"I was like 'Are you sure? Can you promise me that?' And he said, 'I promise.'"

But even true love for a dude with a TEC-9 must yield to the need to curry favor with the cops. The DA slammed Honey to admit that her boyfriend was ready to shoot me, and she promptly obliged. "Sen and Ren was pointin' guns at Stan. They was just like this, just point it, like poof," she said. "They was like, 'I wouldn't want to have to hurt you, Stan, you're a really nice guy, you're bein' a good guy. . . .' Ren said, 'You know, Stan, we wouldn't want to have to kill you . . .' And Sen cocked his gun back and pointed it at Stan's head and said, 'We can kill you,' and him and Ren started laughing. And Stan replied, 'Well, you already have made it clear to me that you know where I live, so I would just leave it alone, something would happen to me.'

"They was doin' that 'cause they knew he would be scared and they didn't want him to call the cops. They play with guns, they pull it back, click it. Stan wasn't reactin'. Stan was just sittin' there. I know he was petrified. I felt bad, I didn't want to stay, but Sen told me that I had to stay there, so I stayed. I told Stan I felt sorry for him and I wished they wouldn't do this, but I couldn't do nuthin' about it, 'cause you know what I'm sayin'? Then me and Sen would get into sumthin' and I didn't want to get into nuthin' with him. Sen said he wanted me to stay 'cause he didn't want to be there by hisself."

While they bore witness to the efforts to petrify me, Mercedes and Mystic absorbed it a little differently and were disarmed by my unshakable calm. As to whether the white guy was afraid for his life, Mercedes plain doubted it. "He wasn't scared, 'cause we—I asked him—they wasn't doin' nuthin' to him. When I got there, I seen him sittin' in the bed. He was just sittin' there. Nuthin' much happened in the house that day."

Mystic took it a step further. Stanley was having a good time. "From the looks of things, it seemed like he was *chillin'* with Luis sometimes," Mystic said. "Luis was tellin' him about some accident he had. They was talkin' and laughin' and shit."

And of course it was such a good time that the boys were nice enough to offer me head. Mercedes seemed relieved by my reaction. "He didn't want it." Mystic, on the other hand, denied any connection to the proffered blow job. "Not me, they didn't offer me that," she insisted. "They probably did that with Honey and Mercedes. I didn't talk to him."

Having waived Miranda and sung like birds, the girls did try to defend themselves by denying that they expected to get any money out of the deal. They didn't need it because they had their own, reminiscent of feminist arguments in favor of prostitution. Mercedes: "When I woke up, I saw Luis and he felt sorry for the guy and he was gettin' some money off it. We was gonna get some money, too, but he didn't promise it. Lucky said, 'You're gonna get some of the money, so y'all can comb your hair and get some clothes,' so we was like, 'All right.'" But, "Like I said, I'm not worried about the money. I would only have taken up to two hundred dollars. More, not 'cause I know it wasn't mines. Tha's how much I make a night. I didn't know they robbed the bank until I seen the packs of money they had in everybody's pocket."

She did concede that there was bad behavior going on. "I knew they was robbing the white guy's bank," Mercedes admitted. "Sen was like, 'Well, I did this for you. I wanted you to have a nice place,' and this and that. Mystic and Honey, they wanted some money so they can get their hair done and nails done and everything." However, she stuck to the version that her sole cut was from the prostitution. "But we make a lot of money, we already been had an apartment. Lucky got a lot of money. I don't know about Sen."

Honey also promoted the theme of disinterest in the white victim's money. "I wasn't gettin' no money out of that," she claimed. "I wasn't gettin' nuthin' out of that deal. I was supposed to get my hair done before Stan ever appeared. Sen was supposed to be gettin' some money this weekend. My appointment was on Tuesday. I had made an appointment and everything before all of this happened with Stan. I . . . all of us was supposed to be goin' to get our hair done."

Now of course I recalled Honey specifically saying she had better get some money out of this. Honey denied it. "I never said that [I needed to get money]," she insisted, fighting with the DA. Instead, "I said, 'All I know is I better get my shit this week, 'cause I'm flippin' straight like that. I better get my hair done and I better get my nails done, 'cause that night Sen sent me to the weed spot, to the store—whutever—and I have bought a juice for a dollar, you know whut I'm sayin'? I ain't buyin' nuthin'. I came there to talkin' about, 'I aint tellin' you to spend your money. I know you ain't actin' all shystey wi yo money and shit, you know what I'm sayin' who the fuck.' We got into an argument. I was like, 'You can go act like that now, but I know when Tuesday come, I better get my shit done straight like that. If I'm not gettin' my shit done, I'm flippin'.'"

Finishing the tirade, "I wasn't thinking about where they got it from."

In addition to the lie that they expected not a penny out of the caper, Mystic defended herself by claiming that she did nothing to assist holding the hostage. In fact, the white man just sat there on his own: "Nobody ever sat down and just sat there and watched him. Like they would go to the hallway, to the kitchen, and leave him sittin' back there by hisself. He never moved, he just sat there."

Well, the DA pointed out, isn't that because the man was afraid for his life?

"If he was scared—I couldn't tell, when he got his face covered," Mystic dodged.

Honey twisted the spin slightly by insisting that, if anything, she should be rewarded for helping me. "I felt if anything I was helpin' him from being sick. Helpin' him from not feelin' weak," she claimed. "His heart was botherin' him. He needed sumthin' to drink. I'm helpin' *you*— you said you had heart problems."

Well, now we got to the point in each interrogation where the perp is asked to admit that they could and should have walked out that door and called the police. In that context, the girls could recall with tremendous clarity just how dangerous their boyfriends were. In response to the DA asking why she didn't try to run for the door when she took Stanley to the bathroom, right near the front door, Mercedes brought the party to a screeching halt. I shivered as I heard it. "The guns are loaded. Those boys will try anything," Mercedes explained. "I don't trust none of those boys. I met them like a week ago. The first day I got to the house, they were talkin' already about guns, killin' people and stuff. I wasn't into that."

Finishing the excuse, Mercedes insisted she was compelled. "They wasn't gonna let me go out that door," she said. Oh, and one more point: "I told them more than twenty times, let him go."

Mystic echoed the same fear of the boyfriends. "It never popped in my head to go call no cops"—voice cracking—"'cause they was always stayin' there."

In response to the same suggestion that someone should have done something, Honey's voice rose to a high point of desperation. "I couldn't say nuthin'. Look, that my boyfriend, that's my peoples I'm hangin' out with them, how am I gonna go call the cops on them? How I'ma do that? Look, if I woulda called the cops, they woulda knew it was me, 'cause I was the only one goin' in and out, and I woulda had a problem. I woulda had to watch myself. I woulda had to watch my back from somebody wantin' to kill me. Do you understand that? I'm not afraid of them, but I'm afraid to die, yes."

Having failed to act when we broke bread together at 1430 Eastern Parkway, Honey shifted the focus by asking for credit for ratting on Sen now that she was in police custody. "If I didn't want to rat on Sen, I wouldn't be sittin' here tellin' y'all what I'm tellin' y'all right now," she insisted, in an effort to ingratiate.

Further supplicating, she could also see it from the victim's point of view. As to what had happened to Stan, she exclaimed, "I wouldn't want to be in that situation." Admitting how bad it felt to have guns pointed at you, she sympathized: "I been through it before. It's fucked up, excuse my language."

But the DA kept pushing and insisted that she take responsibility for the fact that she stayed and helped this thing happen. The interview ended with Honey sobbing uncontrollably into her purple knit hat. The other two girls stayed calm. The toughest one was the softest underneath.

THIRTY-TWO

IN BED WITH THE DEVIL

Later that night, after the confessions were in the bag, the master of talk William Glynn sat at a desk opposite the holding cells in the police precinct. Inside were Lucky, Sen, Ren, and Ramos, and outside the room was still a law enforcement buzz of busy FBI agents and detectives. Lucky and Sen were pacing in the cell. Glynn was dead beat by now, as he'd been going for thirty-something hours. He was getting kinda dopey and wanted to go home.

As he sat at the metal desk, pleased that all the statements were done and everybody was locked up, suddenly he heard a noise from the holding cell. "Pssst, pssst." Glynn looked up at Ramos's face pressed between the bars, saying, "Pssst" to try to get Glynn's attention.

Tired though he was, Glynn obliged and languidly approached the holding cell. When he got close, Ramos whispered to him, hoping the others would not hear, "So, am I still on your team?"

Glynn thought that was one of the funniest things he had ever heard. A deep and sustained laugh, not unlike the one at the end of Michael

Jackson's song "Thriller"—a hah hah hah, ah hah hah hah—came out of the detective and echoed off the brick walls. "I was so tired, I just started laughing so hard," explains gravel-voiced Glynn, barely containing himself. "I had tears comin' down. I had to hold on to the bars I was fuckin' laughin' so hard. I was hysterical. I almost fell through the floor."

Ramos looked very unhappy. Sen kept pacing, silently. Lucky kept pacing up and down in the cell. Glynn heard him say, "I bet they fucked us. I bet they fucked us."

Up to that point, the defendants had been separated in different interview rooms. But now that they were together, the consequences had begun to sink in. "Once they go to the cell, they realize they're fucked," Glynn says. "Ya know when the door shuts behind ya. So, up until that point, there's always that glimmer of hope. 'They're gonna cut me loose.' We all have that survival instinct. 'I think I told the truth, and Detective Glynn is a nice guy. I think he'll do the right thing.' That's what they think."

THIRTY-THREE

LIFE GOES ON

Even though six out of seven of them confessed on video, once they lawyered up every last one pleaded not guilty. I took the week off from work to get my affairs in order and to testify to the grand jury. There was not a dry eye in the house as I told them the story, except for one dude in the back who looked like he might have done the same as the perps, given the chance. I had no patience for sitting around complaining, so one week after they released me I returned to the U.S. Attorney's Office to serve subpoenas, respond to discovery, and fight those who put profits over people.

As the weeks went by, life seemingly returned to normal. I was litigating fast and furious against Mobil Oil Company, comfortable in the knowledge that *they* weren't the ones who'd kidnapped me. (Maybe they should have—they would eventually pay for that mistake.) I was managing a couple of dozen cases handled by Assistant U.S. Attorneys working under me and on my own prosecuting a diverse mix of complex environmental cases. I'd broken it off with Darcy and remained just friends with the charming Lisa P. Marantz, so I was back on the dating scene. (Worried that my dates would think I was suffering from post-traumatic stress disorder, I usually waited until at least the third or fourth date before announcing that I had been recently kidnapped, held at gunpoint for twenty-six hours, and tortured psychologically, but not physically or sexually abused. Hopefully they wouldn't think I was too badly damaged for one more date.)

Friends took steps to brighten my spirits. My friend Michael from Oregon bought me a replacement copy of *A Bright Shining Lie*. On the birthday card, he wrote, "Thank God I'm getting to send this!" And David Prosser gave me a reason to stay alive for at least one more year. He bought me two tickets to *The Lion King*, an impossible ticket to get, for January 22, 1999. I had always hated the idea of Club Med, but shortly after I was released, Dan, Scott, Matt, and I flew down to Turks and Caicos for some sun and exercise. In the photos, everything looks normal.

Back in town I was scheduled to appear in front of Judge Gleeson on a motion for reargument by Mobil Oil Company. This was the case that had failed to impress Sen. The EPA had caught Mobil red-handed on three separate days pumping hazardous levels of benzene into artificial ponds on-site with no permit. Mobil claimed that if we had gone there on other days we would have found them putting in clean rainwater, and that if we took a long-term average, they were never over the benzene limit. The analogy I made was to a mafia carting company that dumped barrels of hazardous waste in an abandoned lot, but said it couldn't go to jail because it came back on other days and dumped Poland Spring. The judge agreed, and wrote a powerful decision that the law was against Mobil's "averaging" argument.

But oil companies like to spend lawyer money and drive up the price at the pumps. They like to reargue as much as possible. We all came waltzing into Gleeson's courtroom and I could see the surprised smiles on the faces of the judge and his clerks to see the walking ghost. The judge said, "It's good to see you all, especially Mr. Alpert. You heard about his ordeal?"

The lawyer for Mobil, Paul Smith, had anticipated this. "I want to say for the record that we are so very happy to have Mr. Alpert before us safe and sound." That was the first and last time they ever had something nice to say about me.

The judge had a snappy retort. "You might want to wait until the end of the argument."

Smith continued unabated. "Your Honor, notwithstanding your decision, sir, or this case, I'm so very happy to see him safe and sound. As a former federal prosecutor, I think we have a very rich history of professionalism, of honor and integrity. Mr. Alpert's performance several weeks ago—or months ago—his grace under fire, his incredible courage, has added courage as another tradition to that long history. And, again, thank you, and we are so happy you are here safe and sound."

There was only so much the judge could take of this. He interjected, "All right. Let's stop the record of the national anthem playing in the background. Let's hear your motion."

Smith stood and read off his script for fifteen minutes or so. When I stood to argue in response, the judge looked plainly uninterested. He got up, stretched his arms over his head, sat down, got up. After listening to me drone on for a while, he finally had had enough.

"Are you finished with your argument?" he challenged me.

"Unless the court has questions," I parried.

He didn't. "All right. Thank you very much. Motion is denied." Since he'd already written twenty-five pages explaining why they were wrong, it looked to me like he had brought Mobil in to yank their chain, and he denied their reargument motion without further explanation. We turned to depositions to try to get the real story behind Mobil's spin.

A week later my office held a ceremony to thank the cops and agents who had solved the case with such speed. It was a typical government award ceremony, with plaques, speeches, photos, and a spread of free food, which always was welcome on a government salary. I had a tan from Club Med and I absolutely beamed as I thanked the brave men and women for saving me from the psychic torment and even the chance of more physical danger.

The agents and detectives congratulated me on keeping cool. A few told me they were depressed because they didn't think they would ever have a witness like me again. Special Agent Terry Mehan recalled, "You refused to go to sleep because you were determined to memorize everything you could, and you didn't want to miss anything. . . . You gave more information than any victim I ever interviewed before or since."

Right around that time, a friend sent me an article from the *Salt Lake Tribune*. There had been a series of violent robberies in the area of Brigham Young University. The article included the advice of an FBI agent about how to handle a violent "takeover" or any hostage situation. Here's the list:

- Don't be too assertive or too passive.
- Be human. Bank robbers "might be rotten people but they're still going to love their mother."
- Prepare for a long-term situation—don't lose patience.
- Don't be a nuisance.
- Don't be a hero.
- Personalize yourself.
- Stay calm.
- Remove any indication of authority. "Hostage takers are afraid of people with authority."
- Never turn your back. "It makes it easier to hurt you."
- Be natural.
- Don't be a wimp.
- Don't stare.

- Eat—whenever food is offered.
- Speak to negotiators.
- Consider using humor, but only after the first 45 minutes when the hostage taker's anger has subsided.
- Don't lie.
- Escape, only if success is assured and it doesn't put anyone else at risk.

I started making jokes too early and decided to grab a bite too late. Other than that, I had done pretty well. Wich was impressed. "You fuckin' handled them, to be honest with ya. Thank God these guys kinda liked you in a way. They fuckin' liked you."

In addition to the cops reminding me that I must have done something right, I got a call from the chief judge of the Eastern District. He wanted to know if I would speak to the judges about how to survive a kidnapping. "Sure," I said. I thought some of them might get themselves in trouble pretty fast—life tenure can make one's head swell pretty big. I kept quiet.

The fact is, I still needed to rely on my own survival instincts. The DA warned me that until trial, there was always a chance that the defendants would put out a contract on me. For several weeks, I ducked my apartment in fear, staying at Scott's and enjoying the friendship and the indoor pool. I planned to move out of my apartment to the Upper West Side, and I even looked at a few places. Then one day I went home in the middle of an afternoon, just to pick up some things, and as I looked around, I noticed that a man's apartment is a reflection of himself, a repository of things that represent his life. I sat down at my small butcher-block kitchen table, with the sun streaming through the window into my face, and finally I just broke down and cried. It was sadness at the hell I had been dragged through and joy at still living. "This is my fucking place," I screamed to myself through the sobbing. "You fucking punks are not going to keep me away from my home." I loved the East Village and the sunny, rent-stabilized one-bedroom near Astor Place that was my home. I moved back in the next day.

Yet I knew that I was a key witness and there was always the chance that the defendants would seek to have me killed before trial. Every time I came home, when the elevator stopped on my floor, instead of going straight to my apartment, I turned in the other direction and checked the stairwell to see if anyone was there waiting to kill me. Months went by and nothing happened, but I continued to check the stairwell.

In the months after the incident, I began to suffer occasional nightmares. In one I was kidnapped by a white robber. He said he wanted to kill me, no matter what I did. I ran for the door and awakened feeling the fear of bullets blasting at me from behind my back. In another one Lucky wore a beard and said he wanted to get me. Then there was a group of men with guns who had come to get me. I insisted they had the wrong guy. In still another dream, two black men asked me to help them launder money by trading my cash for their checks. Then I was warning a man I met on a UJA trip to Israel that he should not meet with the same two men, because he might be kidnapped. A black female cop criticized me for telling him that because it was so obvious. Then a black male cop told me he agreed with me, that the money they were laundering was drug money. As we walked down Albemarle Road toward the apartment building where I grew up, he told me that Lucky's girlfriend had been interviewed and was cooperative.

There were waking nightmares, too. My best friend Dan was a mob prosecutor. One night I met him for dinner at the close of the trial of two heinous mafiosos that nobody else in our office had the ability to touch. As Dan and I got into a cab, I imagined the two of us being machine-gunned down.

Some of the nightmares were real. I started getting credit card bills from stores I had not entered, such as Banana Republic and Bloomingdale's. Somebody opened a charge account in my name at Macy's. I do know that Lucky's fiancée had my Social Security number. I don't know who else had it. Any of the coconspirators' associates could have been taking advantage of being me, or they could have sold my Social Security number on the open market. Reviewing a credit card slip signed by "Stanley Alpert" with a different signature from my own was quite unnerving. Fraud alerts were placed on my credit reports, and never again will I be able to save fifteen percent on the spot by opening a new account in a store.

Stories of people victimized by crime poured in. When the federal judge I'd clerked for in Miami caught up with me, he told me how another judge in the courthouse had been robbed at gunpoint for his Rolex. He also told me his son-in-law had been held for ransom in the Bahamas briefly and then released. Upon hearing my tale, the judge decided he would go home early that day to see his wife. It seemed like just about every second person had a story about how they or someone they loved had been victimized at gun- or knifepoint.

Eventually, the anxiety openly invaded my body. I would feel spontaneous fear in my heart even when there was nothing around to cause it. It would come and go at no particular time. Sometimes I would feel it on a day when New York looked especially cold and bleak. It was suggested to me that I take medication to calm my nerves. Not a bad idea, I thought, but I had come this far on my own and I wasn't going to succumb to the pressure. I felt that the same strength that got me through those twenty-six harrowing hours could be applied to get me through the residual psychic reaction. I would get the better of this demon through the force of my own will.

Indeed, time and distance seemed to help. Telling it at so many dinner parties to rapt audiences over time, laughing about it, took some of the sting out of the experience. As the months went by, it became like other memories: real, but losing vitality with the passing days. But nobody was convicted yet. You always get hit the hardest when you let your guard down.

THIRTY-FOUR

SHANKS A LOT, JACK AND JILL

B*eep*. "I shoulda killed you."

One night in May, I got home from work to change before heading to a party at the apartment of a hipster and her Doctors Without Borders pals. I threw down my briefcase and hit the button on my answering machine.

"I shoulda killed *you*, I shoulda killed *Lucky*, I shoulda killed *everybody*."

Shit. The guy sounded very angry. Which one was it? It wasn't Lucky, since he said, "I shoulda killed Lucky." Ren was too gentle for such a message. Ramos was over the edge, so it could have been him, but most likely, from my point of view, it was Sen or somebody he'd put up to it.

That night at the party, I pondered and discussed with prosecutor Dan whether my life was at risk again. The warm air blowing through the windows and fluttering the skirts in the room was not quite enough to stop me from being preoccupied. The gang was tucked away on Rikers, but who knew if they could reach outside? The message on my machine was positively nerve-racking.

I was probably right that it was Sen, as I would learn later. This stupid, sad, scary story would take one last miserable twist and turn before the bad guys finally rested easy in a penitentiary in the verdant countryside of upstate New York, free only to terrorize or be terrorized by other criminals. Everybody had fessed up except Sen. And while I had failed to pick Lucky or Ren out of a lineup, I had correctly chosen Sen. Meanwhile, every last one of the gang members had seditiously pointed index fingers at their main man Sen—even the one who loved him, Honey. But even if Lucky would diss Sen at trial to get a few years on the outside to commit financial crimes, or Mystic would give up her love of Lucky, or Honey her love of Sen's love, and implicate the whole gang, a criminal defense lawyer could claim that the testimony of cooperating coconspirators was purely self-motivated by a desire to curry favor with the prosecutor and earn a lesser sentence. Since I had managed to positively ID Sen in the lineup, as long as I walked the face of the earth, Sen had a problem.

Nobody told me all the creepy details at the time. I would find out much later that probably Sen or some thug compatriot had also repeatedly called the U.S. Attorney's Office to issue a death threat to me. Not knowing that piece of information, I figured Sen was just one frustrated dude lashing out in anger but powerless to carry anything through. After all, if I were Sen and facing the best years of my life in prison, I'd have been pretty angry, too. Since I didn't think he had the kind of money Lucky had to hire an assassin to waste me, I just thought he was expressing his inner frustrations, nothing more. It's cheaper than therapy.

I was wrong. A jailhouse snitch tipped off Jill Contizzi, the DA, to the plot. One of the coconspirators also tattletaled to the DA about Sen's devious plan. It went something like this: Sen had managed to get hold of a shank, which he was going to sneak into the courtroom at his next appearance. First, he would stab to death his criminal defense attorney, the venerable old saw Jack Evseroff, who Sen felt was not doing enough for him. Then he might grab a hostage, possibly grabbing a gun to kidnap that hostage, and escape from the courthouse, never to be seen again. Or maybe he was going to hijack the prison bus or van once he got out of the courtroom.

Not one to skip a beat, Jill arranged to tape Sen's conversation the next time he socialized on the Rikers Island jailhouse phone. Sure enough, the tape of Sen was chilling. For one thing, the threat to have somebody on the outside kill Stanley was apparently for real. Now, too, at the next court appearance it looked like somebody was going to sneak a knife into the courtroom and pass it to Sen so he could stab his lawyer and take a hostage in order to escape.

As you can imagine, Jack Evseroff was not pleased by the news when Jill Contizzi rang him up to warn him of his impending fate. "Yeah, Jillie, how are ya?" he sang out in Brooklyn Court Street style when he heard her on the phone, thinking that maybe she had a deal to offer him. Evseroff had been wheeler-dealing with prosecutors, cutting deals for big crooks and little ones, for the better part of half a century. He was an institution. In *"What the Hell Is Justice?"* author Paul Hoffman describes his choice to write about a dean of the Brooklyn criminal bar as follows: "[Evseroff's] chief skill is not the casebook law he learned at school or jury-swinging histrionics, but 'street-smarts,' a knowledge of how the system operates and of the men who make it function."

Or women. "Jack, I've gotta see you," the prosecutor said.

"I can't. I'm on trial in federal court."

"Jack, I have some bad news. Your client, Wilbur Davis, has launched a plot to escape from the courtroom, and it involves stabbing you first and then grabbing a hostage."

"Holy shit," Evseroff exclaimed. He had defended both accused cop killers and killer cops, but none of his unseemlies had ever turned their tricks toward him.

"Well, don't worry too much, Jack. We're on top of it. It's supposed to happen at the next conference. The place will be crawling with cops, so you'll be well protected."

When he attended a meeting a day or so later at Jill's office, packed with street-tough cops to jam home the warning, Evseroff couldn't shake the thought of how little sense it made for Wilbur Davis to do this. Everybody thought Sen was the one tough guy out of the seven kidnappers. He refused to confess, refused to cooperate, and was intent on going down swinging. Unlike the others, Sen was the only one William Glynn had not been able to coax a videotaped confession out of. But unbeknownst to Lucky and Ren and Mystic and Honey and Mercedes, Sen was singing like a canary in Jill's office. He told the whole story and even fessed up to some other ATM kidnapping robberies.

According to one source, "They'd done a number of other ATM robberies. The Brooklyn case was Davis. He took sixteen hundred dollars and a cell phone." I knew that the cell phone was one of the main links that had allowed the Bureau and the cops to round up the villains in a mere forty-eight hours. "Steven" was likely a thirty- or forty-something African-American who'd gotten a ride to the bank in Brooklyn, but was released to the pavement after a short time. His savings account must not have been as fat as mine.

The Brooklyn DA had been turning up the heat on Wilbur. In March, an ADA filed an order to show cause in Brooklyn Supreme Court for Wilbur Davis to appear in a lineup. According to the DA, on January 19, 1998, at 891 Utica Avenue, Brooklyn, Wilbur Davis approached a victim in the street in front of an ATM cash machine. He was joined in the robbery by two others. Davis placed his hand in his pocket, simulating a handgun. He shoved the victim into his own car, parked in front of the bank, and the other two perpetrators joined them. Inside the car, the perpetrators shoved a gun in the victim's face and forced him to turn over his ATM card and PIN number. Davis went into the bank and withdrew $100 from the ATM. These vicious criminals then pushed the victim down to the floor of his own car and left him lying there, after stealing his car keys, glasses, and cell phone. This victim, who was not Steven, was a twenty-three-year-old African-American man from Long Island.

Two days later, the victim was shown a photo array of similar-looking individuals, and he picked out one Brian Potter. A day later, he positive-ID'd Potter in a lineup. Potter was arrested and charged with robbery. However, on the twenty-sixth of January, the victim was shown a second photo array, and this time he realized that the person who robbed him was not Potter but Wilbur Davis. Now the DA applied to the court for an order that Davis appear in a lineup, and that "if necessary, reasonable force may be used to compel Wilbur Davis to take part in said lineup." The belief was that the Brooklyn victim could pick Sen from the lineup. The pressure on Sen was growing.

Facing more than one prosecution, Davis met with Jill, cut the tough-guy routine, and dimed out himself and everybody else. He did it knowing that Lucky, Ren, and Ramos had made totally inculpatory statements about him. For Wilbur Davis's sweet song, he'd get a supper of only ten or eleven years in the pen, instead of the twenty-five to life the court could bestow upon him at the max, not to mention the Brooklyn business.

A few weeks before the threat to shank it to Jack and bust his way loose, and after he'd sung like a canary, Wilbur Sen Davis actually showed up in court ready to cop a plea, testify against his homeys, and call it a day at ten or eleven years.

Lucky put the brakes on. Evseroff: "Lucky was very cool. You could tell he was controlling. He was the boss. Wilbur Davis was a low-mentality guy. Came from a broken family with big economic problems, and I don't think he was inculcated with any values. His perception of morality was something he had garnered only from the streets. He was under the influence of people like Lucky. It's kind of mind-boggling. Somebody had to put this into him. He's very young. A Dr. Moriarty is lurking in the woodwork, an evil genius, it's got to be this guy Lucky. Lucky could very well be like a Ted Bundy type. There are some people who have blatantly insane ideations. Davis was a low-mentality kid who was under the influence of somebody—I think it was Lucky, from what I saw."

So right there in the court of law, Lucky put the lie straight out to what he'd told Detective Glynn about how *Sen had influenced him* into the plot. Who was the boss was not a matter of debate that morning in the Criminal Court of the City of New York. "When it came time to take the plea, Davis didn't want to take the plea because he didn't get the okay from Lucky. That's a fact—I saw it. I was there, in court. I saw the interaction between them in court. Right before the [later] threat in court surfaced," Evseroff explains. It looked as if Lucky said, "Wilbur, I'll put a gun to your head if you should dare to take this plea and leave me standing here."

With no plea taken, several weeks later the shank plot emerged. From Evseroff's point of view, the newly minted scheme was even weirder in the annals of criminal behavior, because Wilbur Davis's father was a lovely man, with respectable work as a low-level manager at a classy Manhattan hotel, and the grandfather was also a fine individual. "Wilbur Davis, Senior, was a very, very nice man, and Wilbur Davis's father was an even nicer man. He's from what you call the old school. Kind of guy you'd want on the jury as a prosecutor. They were *ho-ri-fied*, by (a) the nature of the crime, and then by the subsequent activities."

Sen's father actually paying for Sen to have a venerable private defense lawyer was an unusual occurrence in Evseroff's experience. In the Hoffman book, Evseroff says: "Most black defendants can't afford private counsel." Wilbur Davis the father cared enough about his son and had the resources to try to protect him from an ignominious fate. Even with Lucky cum Ted Bundy, Evseroff was shocked to hear that this gang that couldn't shoot straight was so much more defiant of the criminal justice system than even the mafiosos or Colombian drug runners he had represented over the past thirty years.

The stage was set for the next conference date. In Hoffman's 1974 book on Evseroff, he explains that a "conference" is "the courtroom euphemism for a plea-bargaining session." Sen was ready to do more than bargain, but he was in for more than he bargained for. On the fateful day, security was tighter in Manhattan Criminal Court than at the Federal Reserve. Sen's friends and relatives first had to cross through the usual metal detector at the entrance to the building. Then the cops had set up another checkpoint with a metal detector upstairs right outside the courtroom. Inside, the place was crawling with plainclothes cops, guns at the ready for the sight of the blade. Evseroff, too, was taking no chances. He sent his associate, Harry, to represent him in the courtroom and make sure the coast was clear. Evseroff sidled in through a rear entrance and waited downstairs in case he was needed.

No one knows why it never happened that day. The lawyers stood in the well of the courtroom, Jill again announcing her readiness to go to trial, and Evseroff and the other lawyers reasserting the not guilty pleas and their insistence on the constitutional right to a trial by a jury of Sen's peers. Although Sen's friends and relatives were there to wish him well, no knife ever appeared in his hands, no lawyer was stabbed, and no hostage was taken in an effort to escape. Yet again Wilbur Davis did not change his plea, and the case was continued on the trial calendar. For his stealth cooperation, Sen was about to get a gift of ten years in prison. But because of his threats to kill people and commit more mayhem, Jill pulled the plug on that deal.

"Jill called the deal off because of the threat. It was her view that the intent was there—it was just that there was no weapon," Evseroff explains. "They had him on the phone talking about it and you, too— gonna have somebody on the outside kill you. They believed the threat was real—to me and to you. They picked up on the phone threats to Stan. Gonna have somebody on the outside kill him."

Harry the associate fills in, "I called Jill and she said, 'It's not ten, it's twenty to life—take it or leave it.'"

Evseroff is mesmerized by the level of stupidity and the sheer absence of respect for the system of justice. "I've had some very dangerous clients," Evseroff says. "Gambino crime family. Ecuadorian drug dealers. But I never saw anyone over the years who was as immoral, devoid of any restraint—from the way they interact, their attitudes. I never faced this kind of nonsense in all my years. Characteristic of defendants in criminal cases, at least in my experience, on a universal plane, is the fact they submit themselves to the authority of the judicial system once they're in court, and they play the game according to the rules. This is the first time that I ever saw it. I had an Ecuadorian who by reputation was the biggest processor of cocaine in Ecuador. The guy got arrested once in Costa Rica and he was taken out in a helicopter. He escaped. He had a past life like something out of a book. Ecuadorian of Italian extraction— very charming guy—and federal Judge Goettels gave him twelve years. This was major, major trafficking. It involved a lot of cocaine. He was a soldier-of-fortune type. A businessman. He thanked the judge when he got sentenced.

"*That's* characteristic—this is not. Because these perpetrators had a complete, total disregard of the system—of the values of the system and the meaning of the system. You don't see that—very, very unusual."

When the day was done, Sen would end up doubling his time in the lockup. Dumb *and* dangerous.

THIRTY-FIVE

JUDGE DREDD

Around the courthouse they affectionately referred to the Honorable Edwin Torres as "the Time Machine." He began his career at the District Attorney's Office by putting away Sal Agron for life. Agron was the infamous Capeman who stabbed two Hell's Kitchen teenagers in the back with a bayonet-style knife, even though he knew they were not the ones his gang was actually looking for. The newspapers reported that during the trial, Agron leaned over and called Torres an *"alcahuete,"* meaning flunky, puppet, or stool pigeon. Torres shot back at the villain, "Yo mammy's an *alcahuete.*"

Growing up on 107th and Madison, Torres fought his own gang fights, and once had his jaw broken with a metal trash can handle. Later, as a judge, he wrote books and movies about crime and punishment. "A society that loses its sense of outrage is doomed to extinction," he said. He condemned any acceptance of the unacceptable. Somehow the wheel brought the case of the kidnapped fed to Judge Torres.

Not very Lucky. The boys who kidnapped me were in trouble. Torres called a defendant he sentenced in another case "the devil incarnate." In the case of a rapist who ran prison clinics for sex offenders and punched a little girl in the braces before sodomizing her, Torres announced, along with the fifty-year sentence, "A pox on the parole body that ever sees fit to unleash this demon on our society again." In another case, a career criminal robbed an electronics shop and killed Sergeant James O'Sullivan, a retired cop who was trying to stop the robbery. It happened before New York State had reinstated the death penalty. Torres, sentencing the killer to the maximum twenty-five to life, expressed his true feelings on the record. "Believe me, were it in my power, I would not hesitate to put you below ground."

Torres was the meanest judge in the courthouse. When Lucky and his lawyer appeared on October 19, Torres held an off-the-record discussion with the DA and the defense counsel. I don't know what was said that day, but one can only imagine it, given his hard-nosed record. Maybe Torres, in his heavy Hispanic accent, berated the defense lawyer something like this: "Are you kidding me? Your client kidnapped a U.S. Attorney and you think you're going to get off easy in front of me? I'll put him away for fifty years!"

The record shows defense counsel conferring with Mr. Micelli. Lucky then stood to plead guilty to kidnapping with intent to terrorize the victim, and faced a maximum of twenty-five years. In exchange for the plea, Torres proposed sentencing Lucky to twenty years to life.

Lucky's private defense lawyer had another somber request. He asked that Lucky's papers be marked confidential and that Lucky not be exposed to the other defendants, "even in this courthouse." I do not know whether Sen ever tried to make good on the threat he left on my answering machine. But I can't think of any other reason that the gang boss would suddenly need protection from his troops.

At the sentencing a few weeks later, Lucky was smooth as a stone under a stream. He was not a big guy, really, about my size, five-seven, and lighter than me at 130 pounds. He said he had no financial motive and had been led into it by the other defendants. He said Stanley was well attended to while "under my care." He also wished he had met the victim under different circumstances, borrowing a line from Sen. Detective Wich couldn't believe his ears. "It was the weirdest fuckin' thing. Here's a fuckin' guy who's gonna go away for a minimum of twenty to twenty-five years. Out comes Torres, 'Do you have anything to say?' He went into this tender spiel about he really didn't hurt anybody. It was just unbelievable. His whole fuckin' life goin' down the tube and he's cool as a fuckin' cucumber."

Lucky's beautiful speech failed to move Edwin Torres. This eighteen-year-old defendant would not see the light of day until he was at least as old as me. What a waste.

Right after Lucky pleaded on October 19, they wheeled in Ramos. Ramos was so angry and upset at what he was facing that he exploded violently right in the courtroom, kicking and screaming. It took several court officers to hold him down. The defense lawyer explained to Judge Torres that Ramos still didn't understand that he had done anything wrong. She stated on the record, "I don't think Mr. Ramos is quite understanding the rule of accessorial liability." They adjourned the appearance until the next day. After another conference with the defense attorney, Ramos finally admitted that he had kidnapped and terrorized me, and he took the plea. Twenty-two years old when he held me at gunpoint for an entire day, Ramos got off easy next to Lucky. Fifteen to life. The DA asked that the lockdown be continued. Apparently, after Sen's escape plot, nobody was taking chances with any of these defendants.

That same day they brought in Ren, and Judge Torres asked him whether he admitted to kidnapping me with an intent to terrorize. Ren asked, on the record, "What do you mean 'terrorize' him?" Still not understanding. Off the record, his Court Street defense attorney explained privately to his client what it meant. Back on the record, Ren admitted it. All done *with* a loaded pistol, for robbery and weapons possession charges they all pleaded to. In exchange for the plea, Torres went from the max of twenty-five to life to seventeen to life. Kenyatta Bandule, six-teen years old when he kidnapped me at gunpoint, had to give away more years than he had ever seen. The lockdown was continued.

Having lost the chance for a ten- or eleven-year deal because of his sub-sequent plot to terrorize still more people, Sen fessed up on October 21. Nineteen when he did it, he was sentenced to spend at least the next eighteen years of his life in a state prison. Very sad for him and his fam-ily. Much safer for the People.

After Sen's public confession, attorney Evseroff had one special re-quest. As a result of the lockdown, Sen had been unable to see his par-ents. Evseroff asked for a special arrangement that would allow for the visit. The DA was unwilling to alter the lockdown situation. Torres would offer no special favors. "Particularly with him, and specifically, I denied that petition with respect to the other defendants. So he should not get preferential treatment." Torres did, however, say that on the date of the formal sentencing, he would arrange for Sen to visit with his par-ents in the courtroom.

One party represented on the day of Sen's sentencing had strong ob-jections. The Brooklyn Assistant DA was livid. Sen pleaded guilty to the Utica Avenue ATM robbery, and the Brooklyn DA wanted another five to ten tacked onto the sentence, to run consecutively. But even the Time Machine took pity and gave Sen eighteen to life, to run concurrent with the Brooklyn sentence. They were really pissed off in Brooklyn that day.

The male defendants in this caper received substantial sentences in a case with no dead body. As Wich puts it, "I'm gonna be old and gray when these guys get out of jail. They are never gonna get fuckin' paroled on their first whack. Every one of them's gonna get denied. Unless they become a playwright or something."

As for the girls, Honey and Mercedes pleaded, too, and each got mi-nor sentences of under two years. The DA felt that Mystic was getting her life together and had played a minor role. In exchange for her coop-eration, Mystic was not prosecuted.

I was surprised by that decision. Many weeks after I was released, I struggled with a mystery. Ren or Sen gave me $20 for a cab when they dropped me off, saying to Lucky that the twenty was left over after the split of the last $1,000 of my money. But $1,000 split three ways is $333 apiece, which leaves a one-dollar remainder. Split four ways, it's $250, with no remainder. After racking my brain for weeks, I finally figured out that if you split $1,000 seven ways, you get to $980, leaving $20 over. This was strong proof that every one of the seven was getting a piece of my money and should have been prosecuted. I shared my insight with the DA, so I'm not sure why they let Mystic off.

In any event, society got its justice from a gang that couldn't seem to figure out that they had done much, if anything, wrong. They thought they were just chillin' with me.

THIRTY-SIX

GET WHAT YOU WANT

A bodega owner in the Bronx gets shot during an attempted robbery. The press shoves the mikes in the face of his wailing widow. He leaves behind two kids who may no longer get the chance to go to college. You read about it in the *Daily News* while crushed up against people on the subway to work. The story flies past you like a million others; there are far too many tragedies to absorb, and even if you tried, you could no longer function. Several days after I started living in Scott's safe house, I gawked at the police, ambulance, and television camera crews standing outside the projects next door. In the early-morning hours in the high-rise's elevator a rival had murdered somebody's boyfriend who'd had his hand, now cold and dead, in drugs. Or closer to home: A pretty Manhattan graduate student filled with promise is abducted from a SoHo bar and her duct-tape-bound body is found next to the Belt Parkway in East New York, exactly where I had imagined they were going to dump me. After the kidnapping, I suddenly felt pain for the family of the dead bodega owner, and I suddenly knew that the world in which that drug dealer got shot is only a couple of blocks from where we live. And the bound and dead graduate student could easily have been me.

Before the kidnapping I would sit in an East Village sushi place and order the Sushi Special—$17.95 for seven pieces of sushi and two rolls, one California and one tuna. No substitutions. Sometimes they would permit a single substitution if you paid an extra dollar, after an argument. Even with the substitution, there were still two or three things on the plate I really didn't want—that big pile of squishy-looking brown marbles held together by an oval dike, and that weird-looking egg pile trapped by a ribbon of seaweed that was more likely to provoke nausea than appetite. And I honestly didn't care for a California roll—I wanted a salmon and avocado roll inside out. And a spicy tuna roll. But I always bought the Sushi Special because it was cheaper that way. My father grew up in the Depression, and I had learned my lessons well.

Now I order exactly whatever I want. Spicy tuna. Salmon and avocado inside out. No longer does fish that looks scary to me sit on my plate. Even though it costs more. I will be long since dead before I spend all the money I worked so hard to save. That much was made clear to me when I sat captive on the corner of Twenty-third Street and Sixth Avenue.

For years, I kept saying how much I wanted to have a dog. Now I have a dog.

Before, I had no car. As I mentioned to Lucky, Ren, and Sen while in their Lexus, I live in Manhattan. Who needs a car in Manhattan? The price is prohibitive. By the time you add up the insurance and the monthly payments and the parking, it costs you almost as much as renting every time you get into the car. But for too long, the thirty-eight-year-old lawyer had less than the Boyz n the Hood. I now own a Volkswagen Cabrio convertible that sits downstairs in my building for whenever I feel like driving to the beach at Amagansett or to Brooklyn to visit a sick relative. On a nice day I put the top down, toss the dog in the backseat, and drive an hour to hike in nature. (Naturally the Cabrio is fuel-efficient and small. I wouldn't take an SUV if I won it in a raffle.)

All the hard work and saving that moved me for so long certainly gave me a sense of security. But I issue clear warning to those who say it is their life dream to climb Ayers Rock or hike the Appalachian Trail or kiss the Wailing Wall or boat down the Amazon sipping caipirinhas and singing "Girl from Ipanema": Do not wait until your retirement before you live your dreams. I'm talking to those twenty-eight-year-olds working at stuffy corporate law firms who wish they had done a Fulbright in Honduras or slept with several French women in Paris. Don't wait until you are thirty-eight if you want to dance the tango. Don't wait until you are forty-eight to tell your daughter you love her, and don't wait until you are fifty-eight to take your wife to a motel in Montauk and make slow love to her while Billie Holiday is coming off the CD player.

Don't wait until the kids are grown to go on a Saturday-night movie date with your wife because the babysitter charges fifteen an hour. Your wife may not wait. And if you wait till retirement for the trek in New Zealand, you may be dead of cancer or run over by a bus. If you are still alive, you may no longer be strong enough to walk it. Don't wait till your boy is grown to tell him how wonderful and talented he is and how much you love and admire him. Otherwise, your first chance to do it may be when he checks into rehab.

The anxiety eventually subsided and I managed to avoid post-traumatic stress disorder. I think it was because, even while kidnapped and desperate, I had some sense of my own power as the hunted played hunter behind the blindfold. I also think it was because my gang was bigger and stronger than theirs. I had a powerful support network of friends and detectives and FBI agents when I got out to make me feel better. I got my justice and sense of relief with lightning speed. I think if they had not been brought quickly to justice, I would have either bought a gun and gone out and killed them myself or I would have ended up in a mental institution. But getting the calls within forty-eight hours that the heroes were "bringing them in" allowed me to relax, no longer afraid for my life and confident and secure that our good work had rid the streets of a powerful pestilence.

A few weeks after I got out, I had lunch with a beloved mentor, the former chief of my division at the U.S. Attorney's, Bob Bergman. He and I sat in a Midtown lunch spot that catered to people of a higher class than myself, and I marveled at the obsequiousness of the actors cum waiters while they fetched me arugula and chicken breast that had gotten pounded. Bob told me I had now joined a small fraternity of people who had survived near-death experiences, including Vietnam War veterans and the hostages from Iran. He predicted that I would be married within the year.

He was wrong. No matter how powerful the lessons that you learn, you still are who you are and you still need a little bit of help from God. The struggle to settle down and create a family continues. I refuse to lose hope.

And the fact that I got kidnapped was not a get-out-of-jail-free card for other of life's miseries. God tossed me some nasty curveballs in the several years after his gift of the company of men. Grandma Flora died, natural enough at her age, but ripping a piece out of my side. Two years later, spending the winter months living in the tiny condo that Flora had left her, my mother fell. She was found hours later by a neighbor walking by. Although she was deathly ill and quite unmanageable, my brother and I succeeded in flying her up to New York to Sloan-Kettering for the best possible care. The surgery was stupid. Six weeks later, I sat and held her hand and told her that Josh and I would be fine, but she could no longer even respond. I hope she heard me. That night she died of ovarian cancer.

My father, suffering from Parkinson's, started to fall. He fractured his left arm. I visited him every day in the hospital and then in rehab until his arm was in pretty good shape and he went back home. Three weeks later he fell again and fractured the same arm. Things slowed to a crawl. And then the stroke hit. He clung to life for two years in a nursing home, spending hundreds of thousands of the money he had painstakingly scrimped on West Indian aides who would lift him out of bed and bathe his rigid body. When the end finally came, it was merciful.

The pain of watching my parents go downhill and leave this earth was far worse for me than any kidnapping.

So why did God decide to keep me alive? Was I kidnapped because of some horrible sin I had committed? Or, instead, was a decision made to pluck me out of the fires of hell because I *had* led a good life, giving five dollars and a smile to a beggar in the street or fixing some environmental problem or being strong and kind and reliable for an aging parent? Is there some mission I am destined to accomplish?

Several months after it happened, I pushed through the turnstile and stood on the Eighth Street platform waiting for the N train to take me to Court Street in Brooklyn. There was a commotion a few feet away. A large man, maybe 220 pounds, dressed in slacks and a sport coat, was standing on the tracks, with several New Yorkers attempting to pull him by the arms up to the platform. He looked dazed and confused and it was not clear that he hadn't purposely jumped. I could see that the pullers would never succeed with a man that size—they had no leverage. I looked to my left and saw that no train was approaching the station. I was feeling all dapper that day in my best Italian wool suit, pressed shirt, and shiny red tie. I slithered out of the jacket and dropped it unceremoniously on the dirty platform floor. I jumped onto the tracks. "C'mere," I motioned to the guy, clasping my hands together in a foothold. "Put your foot right there." He obeyed. From beneath you do have leverage—this was a street-kid trick—and I hoisted him up onto the platform. Checking once more and finding that there was still no train coming, I vaulted back up to the platform. I dusted off my jacket, slipped it on, and continued reading what the *Times* had to say about Ehud Barak's latest peace overture. The guy was so out of it he didn't even say thanks.

A year later, in the summer, I was sitting on the beach in Amagansett when I suddenly heard screams. A woman from our share house, Ellen, was being dragged out to sea by a riptide. There is no lifeguard on that beach. I can swim, but I'm a lousy swimmer. I didn't think. Another guy and I dove into the waves in pursuit. When we reached Ellen a few hundred feet from the beach, she was calm and floating, wisely awaiting rescue without burning off her energy. I grabbed one hand and the other guy grabbed the other and we held on, waiting for help. But, as I said, I'm a lousy swimmer. As much as I keep in shape, the swim out to her had left me breathless and not too far from drowning myself. I huffed and puffed and struggled to tread water with my free hand. Too many seconds ticked by. Finally, a surfer dude and his kayaking friend who had been summoned pulled close, and right after we got Ellen on the surfboard, I jumped on, too, exhausted. If it had gone on much longer, I could have died. But Ellen was saved.

Mobil Oil bit the dust. By the time the trial date arrived, I was ready to prove that to get the government off its back, mighty Mobil had faked samples and pretended its wastes were not hazardous, when in fact they were. The averaging argument was nothing more than a double reverse, designed to make us miss their deception. Now merged with Exxon, Mobil settled two days before trial for more money than I ever thought the case would bring—$11.2 million, with $3 million going to buy land on Staten Island that will be preserved forever. Nobody ever admits they were wrong in those settlements, but Mobil admitted liability under my pressure. I still make my living in private practice suing polluters, and I am not planning to retire early.

I'm doing my best. I don't know how the story of my life will turn out, but I'm sure glad that I'm getting the chance to watch it happen. It could have ended very differently. And I will never forget the brave women and men of the NYPD and the FBI who wiped up the mess so I could continue. They are the thin blue line. They are the line that divides an ordered, normal society from anarchy and violence. They are what makes it possible most of the time for somebody to go home on a cold winter's night and enjoy a hot cup of tea and chocolate chip cookies without being attacked. For that I will be forever grateful.